STILLMEADOW SAMPLER

BOOKS BY GLADYS TABER

Stillmeadow Daybook

What Cooks at Stillmeadow

Mrs. Daffodil

Stillmeadow and Sugarbridge
(WITH BARBARA WEBSTER)

Stillmeadow Sampler

BY GLADYS TABER

ILLUSTRATED BY
EDWARD SHENTON

PARNASSUS IMPRINTS
Yarmouth Port, Mass. 02675

This edition published in 1981 by
Parnassus Imprints
Rte 6A
Yarmouth Port, Mass. 02675

Published by arrangement with
Harper & Row, Publishers, Inc.
All rights reserved

Cover photograph by Chuck Dixon

"Here is a volume that will replenish the spirit, banish care and stress, not by suggesting that the eye be closed to reality, but by helping the reader to re-evaluate life and its true meaning."—*Christian Herald*

SPRING   PAGE   1

SUMMER   PAGE 63

FALL   PAGE 155

WINTER   PAGE 209

SPRING

APRIL IN NEW ENGLAND IS LIKE FIRST LOVE. THERE IS THE tender excitement of gathering the first snowdrops, the only symbol of life in the deserted garden. They are the lyric expression of music to come—as the symphony of lilacs will surely come—because I am picking the cool delicate bells of this first flower. When I brought the first tiny bouquet in and put it in an antique pill bottle, the greenish glass was the color of the center of the snowdrops. I often wonder what pills went in the bottles for they are only half an inch to an inch high and pencil-slim. My own pill bottles look gigantic in comparison! And when I swallow my vitamins, I feel as if I were choking down acorns.

Aconite and quinine, I remember, were my father's Rx for most ailments, but these tiny bottles were much earlier, they belong to the days of bloodletting. Now they minister to the winter-weary spirit by holding the snowdrops which are too small even for a demitasse cup. Possibly, I thought, as I set the miniature bouquet on the old trestle table, possibly God knows that if spring came all at once, we should die of it. So the fairy-size bells ring a chime to make it possible to bear the beauty that will come in May.

But like first love, April has bitter days. This morning, we woke to a sky as dark as the inside of a snowboot. Leftover wind from March crashed branches to the ground that had withstood all of the winter blizzards. The pond iced over in the night again, and as I made pancakes for breakfast, I had a silly fancy that winter had flung her last scarf across it because she did not need it any longer. The confused robins tipped around in a wormless world, and the winter birds made almost as much noise as a social hour after a Woman's Club meeting. The redwinged blackbirds swooped down from the sugar maples, and it seemed to me they sounded cross.

I could imagine the wives saying crossly to their mates that it was all their fault they had come north too soon. So I went out after breakfast to set up the birds' buffet. For a time we shall have both the winter birds that companioned us during the long cold, and the migratory ones coming from strange southern lands. The air is filled with the excitement of wings. However, much as I welcome the wanderers, I love most the chickadees, nuthatches and woodpeckers, for they have shared the bitter season with us, and never a blizzard too fierce for them to chatter away at the window feeder. I suspect we always love best those who share the hard things with us. Spring and summer friends are delightful, but give me winter friends for my dearest.

As I went back to the house to turn up the thermostat, I reflected that Stillmeadow has seen a lot of sharing since it was built in 1690. In the beginning, it was a world in itself, for the village was a long way off when you had to walk there, or hitch up the horse. (It takes about five minutes now.) Families, in the early days, were units. They had to be. Aside from flour, molasses, tea and salt, most of the food was grown on the farm. Hams were smoked in the small smokehouse, home-grown herbs went into spicy sausage and scrapple at butchering time. Lye and wood ashes cooked in the big iron kettle we now use for kindling. I always imagine it still smells of soft soap. The carder and spinning wheel were busy. Fuel for the great fireplace and the three lesser fireplaces came from the woodlot up the hill, and all the cooking was done over the fire. Savory stews bubbled in the iron pot hanging over the embers, potatoes baked in the ashes, "punkin" pies went in the Dutch oven and came forth spicy and rich, and made a fine end to a supper eaten by firelight and the glow from tallow dips.

The end of winter in those days was a miracle, even more than now. For in April the heated warmers for the beds upstairs could be discarded. The featherbeds were warm enough. And the three-hour sermon in the unheated church was more comfortable when you no longer wrapped hot bricks or stones or flat-irons and held them in your lap.

In April, then, as now, the men of the house went up to the woodlot to cut for next season. A countryman's life always moves steadily, with a pattern fitting the changing seasons. This week our neighbor, Joe, said he better get up to the woodlot. He does not have to chop and haul by hand. He has a small trailer to load the wood on, and he has a modern saw. But the pattern itself is the same. When the snow melt leaves a way to the woods open, the wood is cut.

The logs come down the hill to be piled near the back door against the next winter. The true countrydweller is a conservationist, and always cuts to keep the woods in good shape. In New England, we cut with an eye to taking out dying trees, lightning-blasted ones, or fallen old apple trees. Clearing out the dead apple trees, for instance, makes room for the new shoots which spring up around the old trunk. So another generation, God willing, will have a young orchard of wild apple trees on which, if they are so minded, they can graft any number of fancy apples.

Wood is still our staple for heat. A good many of our neighbors burn wood in their furnaces. Those who have gone so modern as to install coal or oil-burning units, still have the problem of four or five fireplaces in the pre-Revolutionary houses. I have yet to know of a central heating system that will prevent winter from walking right down a chimney, and indeed, in our house, it snows on the hearth unless we have a fire.

When we turn the thermostat up, it is hot as a freshly boiled egg in the kitchen, but the family room is still as cold as a polar bear. So when April walks over the countryside, we all hope we still have enough wood in the woodpile for a fire in the fireplace on cool summer evenings.

As the long lovely light of April falls on the meadow lately deep in snow, I think about the way time passes. "Time is but the stream I go fishing in," said Thoreau. "I drink at it; but while I drink, I see the sandy bottom and detect how shallow it is. Its thin current slides away, but eternity remains." I am not sure I understand this, for I am no philosopher, but it stretches my mind. The days I live now in the beginning of spring are certainly transient, dusk falls before I have sufficiently enjoyed the dew on the grass in early morning. We busy ourselves with all the things that must, we think, be done at once. "But eternity remains," said Thoreau. Days on the calendar come and go, but God is timeless. Love and faith and hope know no season, they are themselves, I think, eternity.

And, in a sense, the miracle of spring is eternal also.

"Let us spend one day as deliberately as Nature," said Thoreau. Nature never hurries, season moves gently into season, day into night. If we would all, now and then, spend one day as deliberately as nature, we would have less tensions, less anxieties. We would find, I am sure, reserves of peace in ourselves.

And be renewed, as spring renews the frozen earth.

In the early days the Yankee peddlers began their rounds as soon as the roads were cleared of snow. They drove their wagons from village to village, peddling everything from pins to pills. They sold watches that sometimes ran a brief time, and pans that lost their handles immediately. They sold spices and tea and spoons and trinkets and lengths of calico or challis. They sold nutmegs and did such a thriving business with them that Connecticut has been called the Nutmeg State ever since. There has been more than one suggestion that many of the nutmegs were wooden.

But the peddler's visit brought excitement to many a lonely farm, news and gossip and a breath of faraway places. The Yankee peddler was a sharp trader, but seasoned with humor. Along with his wares, he was a vendor of portraits. In winter, when the roads were impassable, the peddler painted oil portraits of men and women. He painted everything except the faces, which he left blank. He laid color on with a lavish brush, he garbed his subjects in velvets and silks and laces. The blank faces of the men were topped with powdered elegant wigs tied back with ribbons, the women wore jewels in their hair.

When he took to the road again, he had the portraits carefully stowed away in the back of his wagon. Many a rugged farmer was happy to wait for his face to be painted in on the canvas. Many a worn farmer's wife blushed with pleasure when her portrait was hung over the mantel, elegant in a gown such as she would never own.

Some of these peddlers had a knack for getting a likeness, and now and then one finds a portrait with the sharply weathered face and keen narrowed eyes that mark the farmer. The delicate ringed hands suit the costume, the face does not.

In return for being honored by the peddler's visit, the country women set forth their best fare. The young chicken smothered with creamy gravy, the new peas, the potatoes mashed with sweet cream and freshly churned butter, the rhubarb pie rosy with juice. Later the farmer and the peddler would sit on the stoop and drink cider, and what tall tales went round. Often the peddler bedded down in the haymow, and the sweet hay was certainly more comfortable than the cornhusk mattresses the family slept on inside the house!

Up at dawn, the peddler ate a light breakfast of cakes and sausage, and then came the big moment when he gave the woman of the house a gift. Would it be a shiny new pan or a good stirring spoon or would it be a string of blue glass beads? For the children, there was barley sugar or striped peppermint sticks. Or, if he felt especially generous, a small china doll for the littlest girl.

Then off and away, pans rattling, horse trotting briskly, peddler whistling. And the farm family sighed and went about the humdrum business of living. Never mind, the peddler would be back next spring and perhaps, if all went well, there would be money enough to buy the china teapot with roses painted on it!

With spring stirring in the edges of the brook (the skunk cabbage is up) I like to read about the past of my country. Very early spring gives one to think. Because winter is over, one looks back. The past helps interpret today. When I look back, I can see how much cruelty and persecution, how much bitterness and intolerance we have had in our own country. But there were always people who had spring, which is hope and promise, in their hearts. The dark pages of history are illumined by them. During the War Between the States, there were times when the Confederates and the Union soldiers shared rations, slipping back and forth between the lines. Over a lighted twist of tobacco, Southern drawl and clipped Vermont speech became, momentarily, one language.

Simple men were swept into this conflict with no idea of what it was all about. The Southern boys rallied to save their way of life, with its great houses with stately pillars, the Northern boys felt, in a confused way, that the Union must be saved. During the Revolution, in my valley, people were also confused. The Tories were trying to be faithful to England and the King, and for this, they were denied the privilege of getting a bagful of meal from the gristmill. They had to have faithful friends bring an extra amount. On the other hand, the soldiers in the Revolution left their fields unplanted and marched off in makeshift clothes for the long war to come.

Our valley had times like this. Brother often against brother. Child against parent. But in the battle of Ridgefield, British and

Revolutionaries were buried together. In death they were no longer divided.

I suspect this is true of men in many wars. And the day may come when one manned satellite passes another, and the pilots say, "Hello, can I whisk anything to you on the next time round?"

My favorite ancestor was the Reverend Richard Mather, who crossed the sea in 1635. He left Warrington in England and made the journey to "Bristoll" to board ship, "dispaching 119 or 120 miles in seven days," which he felt was a profitable trip. But when the passengers were assembled in "Bristoll," they had to wait a month and two days, for the ship was not ready. It was the twenty-third of May before they went on board, and on August 15 they were still at sea in a "most terrible storme of raine and easterly wind whereby wee were in as much danger as I thinke people ever were." The cables and anchors were lost, "the sayles were rent in sunder and split in pieces as if they had beene but rotten ragges."

At this point, the Reverend braced himself on the tilting deck and firmly addressed God. The storm, he says, was quelled. I can see him, short, stocky, lifting his long Mather nose, his beard drenched with spray, his voice rolling out over the crashing of timbers. I have an engraving of him at a calmer time, wearing a full robe and a white collar with tassels under his indomitable chin. His curly hair was covered by a ministerial cap (velvet, by the looks). Except for the costume, it could be a portrait of my grandfather, and the resemblance to my father is astounding. So I feel I know him well, and I can easily imagine him facing God as an equal and praying the ship to safety. The ship came to port in twelve weeks and two days. I

would give a good deal to know whether the Reverend spent the rest of his life being unbearable around the house because he had saved the ship! I pity his wife if ever the venison was not cooked to his liking!

Along with the Mather nose and imperative chin and bright eyes, the feeling of partnership with God was passed down. My father had a strong sense that God was always on his side, and that it was up to God to cooperate with Father in everything from the stock market to the national elections. When he prayed, there was not a hint of submission in Father's voice, far from it. When I was very small, I used to hope God would manage not to upset Father.

It is probably just as well Father did not live to see the invasion of Hungary, for I am sure he would have shouted at God, and then tried singlehanded to march against the Russians. He might have had difficulty getting over there, since he did not believe in passports. Mama persuaded him to get one once when they went, to South Africa, but he felt any American citizen should go anywhere at any time without signing any papers or confiding such personal details as where he was born and when. In his passport photograph he has the look of a matador in a bull ring, facing the enemy.

I note the Reverend Richard felt strongly about the "searchers" who came on board to administer the oath of allegiance before clearing the ship to sail!

A spring snow is somehow unconvincing. The old wellhouse has an extra peaked roof of pearl. The yard is drifted. The branches of the lilacs are outlined in silver and have a Japanese look. But even as we shovel out to the gate, we take a casual attitude. For it is spring, and snow cannot last. The Farmer's Almanac says "Nothing wrong here, except the last big snow of the year." The Almanac is a faithful friend and more often right than wrong. And the neighbor down the road says the peepers have to be frozen in three times, and I should not worry about them. This is only twice.

We pile the apple logs on the hearth, and say this is the last snow. I am reminded of my friends who always put on the upper left-hand corner of the envelope when they write: N.W.H., nothing wrong here. This originated with Beverly Nichols, the English writer, and is a very comforting thing. So often people only write to tell bad news. But if you see that N.W.H. before you open the envelope with the French kitchen knife, you feel happy. Nothing wrong here, I murmur.

I am frightened of the telephone, for so often it brings news of illness or trouble. A telegram numbs me. I think it would be nice if friends wired saying, "Everything is wonderful!" Or phoned long distance to say, "I have a pair of bluebirds in my yard." But usually we tend to communicate dire events, and the good times go by without comment. Perhaps we feel bad news cannot wait, but good news can be postponed.

Our telegrams now come from Waterbury, our nearest city, and this bothers me no end. I liked it better when the operator would say, "There is a wire from so and so, and I wouldn't bother with it if I were in your place. Don't worry."

In the old days when we had a very local telephone system, people talked back and forth. The operators always listened in, and made helpful remarks. Once a friend from New York tried to phone us, and we were in the village. "Never mind," said the operator, "they'll be home soon. They probably just went for the mail. Now here is how you get there." And she gave complete directions, so that when we got back, our friend met us at the door.

The eight-party line had its advantages too. If you planned a picnic, someone else would lift a receiver and happily say, "Why don't we all go and bring part of the food?" Of course, nobody had any secrets, but who wants secrets anyway?

I am no longer surprised when I go to the village store to

have someone come up and say, "I am so sorry you had that virus." I don't even try to ferret out how the news got around. I simply say I am over it and how nice to be asked about my health.

We do have a weekly newspaper, but news does not wait on it. It comes out on Friday and by then everyone knows a hit-and-run driver smashed the Kelloggs' fence, and that the Greggs' child had a successful tonsil operation, and that the Stephensons' oil burner went off again but is fixed. We also know how many black Angus calves have been born and what sex they are. And that the Langleys are expecting again and do hope for a girl this time, after four boys.

It is not that we pry, in our valley, we just share, and that is a fine way to live.

At the end of April we hope it will be dry enough to plough. In late springs, ploughing may come so late as to be almost a disaster. The ground must be dry, and friable, so the earth can be picked up in handfuls and not be sticky. Farmers go out and pick up a bit of dirt and crumble it and watch it fall back to the ground, and then they know. Ploughing is a testament to life, as planting is a testament to growth. Sputniks may come and go, but the natural occupations must go on. Ploughing, planting, hoeing, harvesting, have been the way of life here for well over two hundred years, and no matter what goes on in the world, we follow the swing of the seasons as we always have.

When that special morning comes and I hear the plough, I run out to wave at the neighbor who says he "will turn her over, and then harrow." The great blades of the plough flash, the freed earth rises in dark waves. Boulders come up too. The ploughing leaves deep furrows and great chunks of dirt, so the garden looks like a small, but rough sea. After it is sunned a day or so, the harrow goes over and levels it off. Then Jill rakes the small stones out, marks the rows with string tied to stakes at each end of the garden. The seed packages are opened and now we are on the way again. It's a good time.

Tamping the earth down firmly, Jill says, "Now we need a soaking rain." Sometimes we get it, but if we don't, she lugs pails of water from the pond to encourage the seeds to sprout. If it rains too much, seeds can rot in the ground, in which case you simply replant and hope for the best.

Down by the pond, the dogtooth violets are pale gold. Who planted them in the beginning? Nature herself, I reflect, is the best planter of all. The cockers and Irish race about, popping young frogs off the bank. Fish are beginning to jump at dusk as the water warms.

There is a great sense of life stirring in the swamp above the pond, and the upper hills are frosted with green. As the dogs fly up to the brook which feeds the pond, I wonder about the dogs the Indians had, for the Indians obviously had a camp at this spot. We were so told by an expert, but also told by all the signs we have found during the past. The stream would have been wider then, and the spot sheltered and safe. Maize would grow where our corn now stands. Fish were plentiful. There was plenty of firewood for the woods were thick, and still are, for that matter. The wigwams would be, I decide, right where our barbecue is.

And the Indian dogs would run about the same course our dogs do. I often wonder whether these dogs were native to America in the beginning or did they come from the continent

in dim ages past on some land bridge long since gone. They
were evidently small, half-wild dogs, rather tawny; suitable for
the Indians who were also hunters and wanderers.

There is considerable controversy as to the origin of the different breeds. Some authorities feel dogs are a mutation of
wolves, some disagree violently. Cockers we do know are an
ancient breed, for many very early paintings show small spaniel-
like dogs, and some of the dogs on tombs in the middle ages are
remarkably like spaniels. Shakespeare, who does not seem to
have been a very doggy person, speaks of "fawning like a
spaniel," so I gather they were loving, even in the Elizabethan
era, which certainly was not noted especially for kindness and
gentleness, whatever its virtues were! But when you compare a
cocker to a Chihuahua, it seems doubtful they both stem back to
a wolf! There must have been other small animals which preceded the smaller breeds. And there are times when we feel the
Irish is a descendant of a bird since she insists on trying to run
in the air. Whatever the truth is, the early dogs were a far cry
from the champions of today.

The first setters did not look like Holly either. The Irish
setter lineage has been traced as far as the fifteenth century. In
Gaelic they were called "Modder Rhu," which meant Red Dogs.
A sixteenth century writer called spaniels and setters "gentle
Dogges which serve for fowling."

Generations of breeding have developed the Irish of today
with dark satin coats, deep briskets, and beautiful muzzles. And
as a friend of mine says, "I feel as if I had the wind on a leash
when I go out with her."

Holly doesn't have much luck "serving for fowling" since we
do not hunt. She does her best with squirrels and bluejays and

an occasional skunk, but her retrieving is confined to bringing home the deadest fish on any beach we happen to visit. She will point anything, from an ant to a pheasant, but being a "gentle Dogge" she never catches or kills anything.

Trained hunting dogs (pointers, Irish and other setters, and cockers, springers and so on) will honor one another's point, which is to say the first dog to locate the game has the exclusive right to it. It is a beautiful sight to see four or five dogs in a field all suddenly freezing in their tracks as they honor the point.

Our cockers haven't the slightest idea of honoring anybody's point. If someone finds a mole, everyone else rushes in. Sister and Linda, the two smallest cockers, fancy themselves as mousers, and will push and shove each other around at a mousehole until any mouse not stone deaf would be long gone! They spend a long time in the barn at dusk, but Jill says they only make the mice nervous.

As planting time comes around, there is excitement in the air. The main planting comes in May, when the maples are in leaf, but lettuce and radishes and snow peas go in as soon as the ground is workable. It took us some years to learn, however, that you cannot go against the rhythm of Nature. We wasted a mort of seeds getting our whole garden in when the ground was as cold as a gangster's heart. In the damp chilly earth, the seeds simply sat. Finally we learned to wait until the ground was dry, warm, and friable. Later plantings caught up with the earlier ones, and went on to bear well.

What soil we have in Connecticut in the valley is good soil, rich enough, and not heavy. The trouble is, there is not enough

of it. Rocks and boulders take up most of the space, and no matter how carefully you clear the land, another winter brings up a whole new crop, bigger and better. No Midwest farmer would bother with our land at all, but the true New Englander gets a lot of good out of those stones. The miles of grey stone fences that mark the fields and roadsides were all built when somebody was clearing the land. The stone foundations for barns and the old houses came right to hand from the cornfield.

Our own fourteen-foot square chimney and the hand-hewn blocks of silvery stone for the fireplaces must have come from our own garden, for it is evident that the first owner of the house planted his carrots and potatoes and squash right where we do. He couldn't help it, for great ledges and the swamp wouldn't have made a garden.

The rich, black soil of the Midwest, and the dark rosy red soil of Virginia are beautiful. But there is a sense of achievement when you finally get a crowbar under a maddeningly solid boulder and move it up an inch! And the small stones that we gather are cool and polished, and shot with color. Possibly my love for stones comes from Father's being a geologist, so that I grew up with the feeling that a stone was exciting.

"Now this," he would say, "came down from Canada in the glacial age. And this was in the bottom of a riverbed, where the dinosaurs came to drink. And this one with the fossilized shell in it lay under the great inland sea." Mother used to say mildly that the house was full of rocks, and it was. They were all over, in bookcases, on mantels, on Father's desk, and in my bedroom. Every one told a story and brought the magic of time long past, as the Dead Sea Scrolls record new chapters in the life of man.

So as I poke around in the garden while Jill plants the peas, I like to pick up the small stones and wonder what journeying brought them to Stillmeadow. Now and then we find an arrowhead, a small quartz point for birds or a larger, notched one that was used for bigger game. Once the plough turned up a hollowed stone that was used for grinding corn.

Some of the Indians in our valley had wickiups, but I think the group camping this side of Jeremy swamp probably came and went and never settled down. There isn't room enough for a big village here, for one thing. Most of our forty acres is cliff and crag and swamp. In fact the State Conservationist who came to survey it during the last war advised writing it all down as a wildlife refuge!

The reasonably flat, arable land is enough for a family. But it would not have conceivably supported even the most casual of Indian villages. So I expect one or two families came, and fished, and hunted, and picked the wild sweet grapes, sent the brown children off for butternuts, and then went on with the tribe when the deep snow came.

I do hope the young lovers (and there are always young lovers in any age and in any group) found the ferny hollow where the brook bends before it flings itself down. Mint and water cress must have been there then, as now, and the brookwater run as cool and clear over the stones.

I recently met a Dane who came to this country when he was nineteen and for reasons not clear to me, lived with the Indians on a reservation. Thinking of my own imaginary Indians, I copied down the Indian farewell he gave. "Until we meet again, may the Great Spirit make sunrise in your heart, and may your moccasins make tracks on many snows yet to come." I couldn't imagine a lovelier goodbye!

I thought of this as Jill finished the last row of radishes and my basket was heavy with stones. A garden is an evidence of faith, and it links us with all the misty figures of the past who also planted and were nourished by the fruits of their planting. The truth is, none of us belongs merely to today, we are a small part of the whole progression of mankind. We have a responsibility to pass to the next generation as much good as we can, and we are also responsible for those who went before us.

It may be when you live in a house built lovingly in 1690, on land that was a dwelling place for the Indians before that, you get a special feeling of being part of time. When I lived in an apartment in the city, I never felt this. I was too busy in my rushing about to even wonder who lived in the apartment before me and whether they were happy. Time was, then, the next twenty-four hours and what I would get done in it. But now I feel my own small portion of time links me with those who walked in the garden yesterday and those who will walk there after I am gone. Therefore, it is up to us who have the loan of the land, to cherish and preserve it, so that those who come after us may sow their seeds and be assured of a good harvest.

Housework is tiresome in spring. Almost any woman gets that feeling of being simply overcome because she can never get through it. Men have a lot of troubles, but they never have a whole house in spring to cope with. Inventories, yes, but not doing over the whole plant at the same time. The light is brighter now, and lasts longer, and it shows up everything! You can't do it all at once, curtains, rugs, woodwork, attic and cellar. It is Jill's theory that things put in the cellar just grow. As for the attic, what can we do with the Bridge of Sighs, Venice, the Colosseum by Moonlight, and the High School diplomas of our children? They all add up to a firetrap and a happy haven for wasps. And if we really get in a ruthless mood, because it is spring, Jill says wistfully that she is sorry she burned up all the letters with the Pony Express stamps which were in the attic after her grandfather died.

An attic is a state of mind, I tell her. I myself have a small

chest with love letters tied in ribbon, some moth-eaten football
letters from my first beau, dance programs. (Oh what a wonderful time that was when I stayed to the very end and Father
put me on house rules for two weeks. Worth it.) Everyone has
a mental attic too. Old thoughts, faded dreams, hopes laid away
in lavender. But a mental attic is just there, and you rarely
spring-clean it. One year I crept up the ladder to our attic and
threw almost everything out of the window, and a passing
neighbor thought the house was on fire. The house wasn't, but
I was, at the moment. I regretted it later.

Both Jill and I give away anything and everything that can be
of any use to anyone who needs anything. This has caused considerable difficulty in times past when we gave away the children's things. ("I want that crib for my baby now," says Jill's
daughter.) But I know the Bridge of Sighs framed in three
inches of gilt is not going to do anyone any good.

And no child would be caught dead nowadays wearing my
daughter's first smocked dark blue silk frock (size 3). Then
there are those booties. Jill's two children are grown, married,
and her daughter has two children of her own. They do not
wear booties. Nobody does. They wave chilly little feet in the
air even in winter. But the booties do bring back the memory
of the baby feet, and somehow we can't throw them away. So
the attic upsets me no end. It has more memories than wasps,
which is saying a good deal.

The tiny white muff which Connie had as soon as she could
walk is an invitation to moths, and very dingy now. But if I
decide to CLEAR OUT and pick it up, I can see her face when
she first picked it up. She was a grave child with a delicate skin
and a fine mist of hair. When she unwrapped the muff (I am

sure it was rabbit) she suddenly sparkled, and she laughed aloud. So how can I take that muff to the dump?

It is easy to part with anything that someone else needs, but the truth is that a good many things are absolutely valueless, except for the feeling that attaches to them. The feeling can make them pretty important. I once gave away my favorite dress, which was a soft purple, because someone wanted a purple dress and had never had one. But this wasn't much of a gift, for I had bought the dress. It had no associations. The true test of my generosity would be if someone wanted my Mother's blue Staffordshire pitcher. We called it the monkey pitcher, and it is full of my childhood. Sometimes when I look at it, I am glad that it is too big to be a milk pitcher, and it would never do for coffee at a church supper because it would break.

The thing to do, I told myself yesterday, is to make a comprehensive list of all the spring jobs. I began very tidily with wasps. Rat in cellar. Clean attic. Spray. Weed out all books possible for local library. Discard any piece of clothing not worn in a year, you can get along without it.

Give away all blankets and rugs not actually in use. Check bed linen and give away all except for beds used. Take magazines to hospital and/or beauty parlor (needed).

By the time I made my list, I was worn out. So, since it was a warm April day, we went off with bread and cheese, hard-cooked eggs, a vacuum of boiling coffee. Sat by the falls at Eight Mile. I felt marvelously restored. The wild white violets were in bloom and below the falls the skunk cabbage was like the third act of a play, so dramatic and final. It always reminds me of Van Gogh, for it is a violent plant and greener than any green could ever be. The unfurling leaves look tropical.

As we sat quietly eating the crusty bread and cheese, spring was tangible. The red-winged blackbirds made a good landing in the maple trees and talked their heads off about the journey up. I was reminded of a neighbor's child who said "Mama, they have little red ribbons sewed on." The water, still sharp with snow, poured over the rocks. It was free at last. A hawk went over, riding the air. We left crumbs for the birds, and carried the rubbish to the car and drove back down the winding country road.

"Maybe it would be better to leave the attic and cellar until fall," I said dreamily, "there isn't any special hurry."

"Suits me," said Jill. "I want to work on the asparagus bed anyway. Briars are coming in."

There is a good deal to be said for the Latin Mañana, at least in spring in New England!

Spring has a special smell. As the sun dries the tree trunks and branches, bark gives off a clean odor. The pines add spicy fragrance to the air. Then there is the musty smell of leaves as we rake the yard, for no matter how carefully we rake in autumn, spring always finds leftover windrows under the sugar maples and apple trees. The earth itself has a damp sweetness. And it may be my imagination, but the snow-fed water of the pond has a fresh cool odor.

The smell of early spring lacks the heady sweetness of the flowers to come, but as we go out in the morning to sit on the terrace with our coffee we draw in deep breaths of pure enjoyment. The cockers and Irish run in dizzy circles. Often Jonquil bumps into Especially Me, her own son, and sends him spinning.

For of course my pedestrian nose misses a thousand delicious smells. A rabbit went this way, says Linda. Pheasant under the pine trees, advises Holly, the Irish. Hey, come on everybody, skunks under the kennel, barks Tiki. But Little Sister keeps her nose right by me, just in case a bacon-toast should come her way!

One reason I love dogs is that they are without pretense. When guests come that they do not take to, they all turn cool eyes on them, and retire. They do not care for people who gush or jingle keys at them or coo. They know instantly who loves them, and speaks their language, and who is just pretending to make us satisfied. When Admiral Klakring and Lois came for lunch, the whole bevy mobbed them. People might be impressed by the Admiral's war record as commander of the submarine fleet in the Pacific, his fame, his citations. The dogs didn't give a fig for this. They said, in unison, these are wonderful friends!

Lovely smiles, nice eyes, gentle voices. In fact, observed Holly throwing herself into Burt's lap, why don't you just live here? Plenty of room! Burt is fortunately a big enough man to hold an Irish setter in his lap with only that plumed tail left over. But Lois, who is small and slim, had to share three admiring cockers with the couch.

Even Little Sister, the shy one, emerged from under the bed in my bedroom and laid a gentle nose on Lois's foot. I told them they had won a Stillmeadow citation.

The fire burns comfortably in the great fireplace at night, for it may be 55 at noon but swoops down to 35 at dark. A few of the pinecones we gathered last fall make the house spicy. When a leftover wind from March howls in with a lashing rain, it is good to sit and read while the apple logs warm the family room. "The earth has its own pulse and rhythm," says Hal Borland, "and the wise and fortunate man leans with the wind." (*This Hill, This Valley*). And my way of saying it is, "Meet the storms, remembering that tomorrow the sun may shine again."

The spring rains have a purpose, although by April we are so hungry for sun and warmth that it comes hard to be patient. But the frozen earth feels the great beat of rain and the last ice

tumbles down the brook. The pond brims. The wells will be nourished. Hereabouts most of us have dug wells and in August they may go dry unless the heavy rains of spring raise the water table. The pounding of the rain means we are entering a new cycle, we shall go once more from bud to flower, from seed to harvest.

And it does mean the days of being snowed in are over! So let it rain. On such a night, we can be lavish with leisure. We can play Beethoven symphonies or recapture the magic of Caruso on the old scratchy records. Even the early records cannot dim the splendor of that voice. The orchestra sounds thin and tinkly, almost as if it were a child's toy piano playing. But Caruso rises above the mechanical limitations. We can also play folk music, if we are in a folk-music mood. "When cockle shells, turn silver bells, then will my love return to me— When roses blow in winter snow—"

Or we can read old favorites and not worry that we are not KEEPING UP with the current trends in literature. Jill browses again through Edwin Way Teale's *North With The Spring,* or turns up, a little sheepish, with Lord Peter Wimsey. I never apologize for reading Keats's letters for the thousandth time or Katherine Mansfield's *Journal* or Faith Baldwin's *Many Windows.* Or there is the *Gourmet* cookbook in two volumes. And if the rain is very heavy, I bask in James Thurber's *The Night the Bed Fell Down,* or Farley Mowat's *The Dog Who Wouldn't Be,* or that riotous *Mrs. Searwood's Secret Weapon,* by Leonard Wibberley.

Then there is television. Maybe. Rainy nights do not always coincide with "Father Knows Best" or Perry Como, but sometimes they do. Or Lawrence Welk's bouncy nostalgic rhythms. There are always Westerns but the same old plot is too much for me, and Jill says, "All they do is chase one another around and shoot." We shall be glad when this vogue is over. And how tired we get of the commercials, injected every four or five minutes at great length.

Television is a wondrous invention, but one has to know when to turn it off!

For me, April is a time of remembering. It may partly be because it is my birthday month. Or perhaps it is that the long winter is over and done with, and spring walks down the hill over the dogtooth violets. Or possibly it is just that when the air blows softly over the melting snows, and the crocus is established, and the skunk cabbage splashes the edge of the pond with emerald, one naturally has a tendency to take stock of other times, other springs.

I remember the birthday parties Mama used to give me when I was a leggy teen-ager. I don't know how she stood it. She had a one-day-a week cleaning woman who helped with the laundry also. They were devoted friends and worked together. But Mrs. Novak was shy and would never poke her nose in at a party. Mama let me ask anybody I wanted, and the house bulged. There was always a lot of breakage, but Mama said it didn't matter. The gang consumed tons of food and gallons of hot chocolate. We danced, rolling up all the rugs. Butter from the popped corn dribbled all over the floors. But in those days, nobody went out to sit in parked cars and of course nobody got intoxicated on hot chocolate.

Father retired from the scene and holed up in his study. But if the party went on too long and he wished to go to bed, he appeared and cleared his throat and asked what time it was. This was always effective.

I remember birthdays when I was away at school and I learned that birthdays weren't important at all. Classes went on, exams came, themes were due, and I was just about as unimportant as a body could be.

This was painful, but salutary. Growing up is never easy. I

still had the security of the box from home, however, with date bars and cake and fondant dipped in bitter chocolate, and a fancy nightgown. And from Father a book of Shakespeare or Byron or Keats. From my beau, a box of candy which had always melted and came out as a sticky mass.

Now I no longer look on my birthday as something special. All through the year there come days which seem to have the radiance of the early birthdays. It may be an unexpected kindness or a special letter from a dear friend. It may be the sun shining on the lilacs when they are newly budded. It may be the Irish bringing me a knuckle bone, which she cherishes and offers to me as if it were invaluable. It may be a phone call from a faraway loved one who says, "I just thought I'd say hello."

Or it may be seeing the neighbor's lights shining up the hill. I can see them now, through the green mist of young leaves. They are good neighbors, always ready to lend a hand at a moment's notice. What could be, I reflect, a nicer present than to see their supper lights on and know they are there, warm and friendly, so that we are not isolated on our forty acres.

I like to think there are neighbors all over the world, despite wars and dictatorships and oppressions. The human heart does not vary much, although we may speak in different tongues. Birth and death are common to us all, so are love and hope and a yearning for peace. We are all just folks, all over this uneasy globe, and when Jesus said "Love thy neighbor as thyself," he did not limit neighbor to just the family next door!

Yesterday Joe came to fill the furnace hopper, and poked his head in the kitchen to say in a very special tone of voice, "They went over this morning!"

I stopped stirring the eggs and said, "Oh, did they really?"

"Yes. I heard them. They went over just before six."

So the wild geese have gone over, flying in their great lovely wedge that slices the pale morning sky. We stood silent a moment, savoring the magic.

"I wish I had seen them," I said wistfully. "I was asleep."

I am seldom up early enough to enjoy the sunrise unless a cocker or the Irish is ailing. Or unless the dogs all decide to chase squirrels at five in the morning. Then as I stagger to the door to let them out, I catch the pure pearl light and see the fog simmering in the meadow. The world is shadowy, but awake. Once at such a moment, I saw a strange belled cat streaking across the silvery grass, and somehow, she seemed a part of the mystery of dawn, swift, silent, incredibly graceful.

"Oh, you should have phoned me," I said to Joe. "I would love to see the wild geese go over."

"Well, I thought of it, but it was pretty early." Then he stood silent again, and finally said, "They were beautiful."

As I looked up at the sky, I prayed it might always be open to the flight of the wild geese, and the earth full of the promise of April.

How much better to hear the wild geese crying as they go over than the sound of a Sputnik whirling in its orbit!

The hyacinths I picked today smelled sweet and cool. But they looked so tropical, I could hardly believe it was a May morning in New England. The heavy spikes of purple and pink and ivory would fit some garden on a coral isle where there are no seasons at all, but it is forever summer. As I gathered just enough for a bouquet in the milk glass swan compote, I stopped to listen to the flickers down by the pond, and to watch a towhee in the feeder. The flickers have a dramatic call, "Wick, wick, wick," and the males always look as if they were dressed for a costume party in their grey, brown, white, and bright yellow with the scarlet crescent on the neck and black crescent on the breast. As they hammer away on tree trunks, they often brace themselves with their tails, and if they feel in the mood, they can hammer right through an eaves trough too.

The towhee is a shy bird, and calls for admiration when he comes so near the house. In his black and white and cinnamon-brown suit, he is handsome and I love to hear him saying, "Drink your teeee."

We feed the birds year round and they do send the word, although how they tell all their friends and relatives just how to find the way over the wooded hills, across meadows and swamps to the free lunch counters, I do not know. But they communicate. Many people dislike crows and bluejays, for they are predatory and noisy, but when the shadow of a hawk falls anywhere within sight, they sound the warning cry, and instantly the smaller birds vanish. There is nobody there at all as the hawk wheels over.

As I went back to the house, the sound of the lawn mower drowned out the rap-rap of the flickers. Somehow the first mowings are especially lovely, for the grass smells better than any perfume and the clippings fall green and thick behind the blades.

Whenever I feel dissatisfied with my lot, I reflect on the lot of grass. It would be so discouraging if you were cut down every time you grew an inch. Possibly there is a lesson in the fact that grass will never give in. When a drought comes, it turns as brown as a vanilla bean and I am always fearful. Or when we get liverish-brown spots which are some kind of fungus, I worry. When the coal truck crunches great ruts in it during March, I give up. But grass does not admit defeat. Given a few spring rains and some May sun, there it is, green and vital and ready for the mower.

When we bought our first power mower, we felt that all of our lawn problems were over. Our lawn had always been a problem, for it is a peculiar lawn. It covers half an acre, plus stones that keep coming up, and plus a low spot that gets swampy at the slightest rain. It also has three semi-detached flagstone walks that lead nowhere but can't be dug up, for they have been there forever. Then there are patches of day lilies that spring independently on the north side and some sweet rocket beyond the driveway. And of course, around all of the immovable boulders, I planted wild violets for some years and they spread. Mowing is an obstacle course as you skirt all the various items, including the stump of the tree that died. The apple trees and maples and lilacs you may swoop around but that trunk was cut off just level to the ground and if you are not wary, the mower grinds her teeth out on it.

The power mower would be perfect, we said happily. And it was true that we could mow the whole lawn before the grass grew so high where we had mowed two days before that we never quite came out even. But before we got accustomed to it, we spent half a day getting the machine started. By the time we had the motor going, we had to cut it off and rest.

The directions were so simple. You took this thin rope and wound it around something and gave a sharp pull and off you went. It looked as easy as working a yo-yo (and I was always expert with yo-yos). But winding the rope and sharply pulling resulted in nothing at all. So you adjusted the gas. Then the rope got involved wtih another part of the mower. Then the motor gave a harried gasp and you felt triumphant. Then it died. Then you had lunch, and called the mower man who came and whirled around with it for a few swathes. I used all my feminine wiles to keep him demonstrating over the roughest part of the yard, while Jill studied the rope-winding business.

Our current mower is not so temperamental. All it does is give out of gas when you are halfway around. Modern inventions take some living up to, I reflect, and much as I appreciate them, I often get a doubtful look when I read in an advertisement that even a child can operate whatever it is. What child, I wonder.

Take the dishwasher, which is my favorite in many ways. A child could turn the knob. But would a child the age in the ads know enough not to put plastic spoons and skewers in? Would this miracle child know enough not to cover over the vent in the side with a platter, thus throwing the dishwasher into a frenzy? I can even imagine some fairly bright children capable of putting the electric frying pan right in the dishwasher too. In fact, I have heard of such a case.

Actually, living in a house built in 1690, we live in the past and the present simultaneously. The modern inventions keep us comfortable when I doubt whether we would manage just with the big fireplaces and tallow dips for light, not to mention heating all water over the fire in both summer and winter. But the old house hasn't changed much, the wide oak floorboards with handmade nails, the batten doors, the small-paned windows, these are as they always were, except with extra wax, paint and a few new panes.

May is a time to forget the demands of housework and go out to experience the delight of apple blossoms. My mother was a conscientious homemaker, but I remember especially one day when Father was away on a business trip and Mama and I left the washing undone, the kitchen unmopped and just went off on a picnic. Without Father driving, we were able to go slow enough to see the countryside, the rich greening hills, the silvery blue lakes, the comfortable cattle (black and white Holsteins), the farm women weeding the strawberry beds. We ate sandwiches and hard-boiled eggs and drank coffee (kept warm in a quart jar well-wrapped in newspapers).

We talked to each other as friends, not as mother and daughter. I told Mama my dreams and hopes and fears and she told me some of hers. It is a shining memory. Not all the housecleaning in the world would be worth losing that day. Mama was a quiet, wise woman with deep brown eyes and hair the color of a partridge wing. She led a busy life taking care of Father and me, and seldom had a chance to be herself. This day she looked different, her cheeks flushed with sun and laughter in her eyes.

I think that day in May was a special gift to us both. And it occurs to me now that it is a good thing for any parent to stop now and then and wonder what memories they are giving their children. We all try so hard to leave real property, but memories are property of the heart.

Recently a friend wrote me asking whether she should buy a cocker. In a way, she would like one, but wouldn't shedding be a problem? And wouldn't it track in dirt?

I was reminded of an aunt of mine who was a dedicated housekeeper. When my cousin and I would get the toys out in the playroom and set up an elaborate village, and fix an imaginary grocery store up with dried beans for money, we never dared go to the kitchen for a glass of milk. If we did, we would come back to find everything put away in the cupboards, and all our work in vain. After a time, my cousin said sadly, "I guess it's no use getting anything out. Let's just sit on the porch."

I also reflected that when my Connie and Jill's daughter and son were small, I often felt tired and frustrated because they cut paper dolls all over the front room sofas, spilled watercolor paint on the good rugs, and strewed toys so thickly that walking across any room was a hazard. But an immaculate house would have been lifeless, and even when I was most discouraged because every crack in the old floorboards was suddenly full of B-B shot, I still felt a house was for living.

The best way to keep a house spotless, of course, would be not to inhabit it at all, but just come in twice a week and clean and then shut it up. I have seen houses that look like that, so guests hardly dare sit down for fear they'll unfluff the sofa pillows. To me, a lived-in house is better. But it is all in what you consider important.

As I went back to my friend's letter, I thought about life with dogs. Well, Holly filches a milk carton from the trash can and tears it up in the keeping room. Jonquil pads in from a mole hunt and leaves fresh dirt on the clean floor as she wags with pride. Especially Me brings in a crop of stick-tights and Linda always manages a few briars. And Tiki can't help it if he waded in a puddle in that low spot in the yard.

For us, the love and companionship of the cockers and Irish compensate fully for any minor discomforts in housekeeping. But as far as my friend was concerned, I advised against a dog. Everyone has to set up his own standard of values, and live by them. And what is important to one person may not matter at all to another. We ourselves found that a frisky crowd of cockers and Irish kept the house from being too silent and too

solemn when the children went away to school. We couldn't be melancholy when two dogs tried to get in the television set to see where Lassie was!

Among the many gifts our dogs have given us, I might rate laughter as one of the best. They just naturally do funny things, from jumping in the air after wasps or grasshoppers to tunneling under the border after moles. The cockers never realize when they are funny, but the Irish has a gleam in her dark eyes as she knocks out a screen and leaps in. Didn't think I could do it, eh? she says.

If she decides she is tired of regular dog meals, she sits by her pan and barks until we rush out, then she moves majestically to the refrigerator and points. There's something better in there, she indicates. She gets it.

The dogs make cooking more fun. I love to cook, but I am not a lonesome-minded woman. I like to do a cheese soufflé with four helpers who snap extra bits of cheese and wag wild tails when I beat up extra eggs. Cutting up chicken or turkey leftovers is a very social occasion at Stillmeadow. I am not alone. Who could feel neglected with at least six companions bouncing about?

They also help when I am typing. They hop up and look, they lean against me, they comment. They bring toys to lure me away to happier pursuits. And the Irish often manages to rearrange all my manuscripts when I go out for a drink of water!

I have read a good deal about how to be a good hostess and how to entertain, in various publications. My theory runs counter to much of what I read. I will go so far as to say it is inadvisable to ask two guests who are on the opposite side of anything like a regional school or who have shouted at each other in the last Town Meeting. But one of the nicest buffet dinners we ever had was just an assortment of people we liked. It included dog people, interior decorators, bankers, business executives, a couple of teachers. Judging by the time they stayed, they all had a good time. In fact, I wondered whether we would get to bed before time to feed the dogs in the morning! It taught me a lesson about people. We tend to bracket them as to their profession. So how did I know the breeder of great Danes could spend two hours talking about brown Swiss cattle with a real estate man who, on the side, raised Swiss brown? The banker's wife turned out to be a wildflower expert and could not be pried away from the interior decorators who wish to have a wildflower garden too.

If the dinner is hot and easy to serve, I decided, you do not need to categorize people. You bring on the casseroles of kidney beans and ham with burgundy, the shrimp and noodles in the chafing dish, the tossed green salad with croutons in it. Put out the cheese tray and crisp crackers, and rest your feet while the guests talk their heads off.

Almost everybody has something in common with everybody. Any party is a success as long as you do not ask people who are not on speaking terms. And sometimes I wonder . . .

Even in May, the evening chill comes down. There is nothing urgent to do in the garden, for the seeds, we hope, are about their own business. We may have just soupbowls of fresh asparagus for supper, dressed with top milk and sweet butter. Then after the dishes are washed, we go out and putter around.

Jill checks the rhubarb and brings in enough for breakfast and a pie for next night's supper. I pick up a few twigs on the lawn, and toss a ball for the dogs. If I am very ambitious, I may pull a few early weeds in the Quiet Garden. Otherwise I just sit on the stone terrace and dream. My dreams range from imagining my unicorn cropping the violets on the bank beyond the pond to what would I do if I had, suddenly, a million dollars? Or I dream I am on a freighter going round the world, seeing all the strange lands I shall never see. I am on deck, sipping hot broth, and the Captain (no less) leans over me and asks tenderly if I will dance with him that night! I can smell the starch in his uniform.

However, I always have a running commentary in my dreaming. It goes like this: "Better defrost the refrigerator tomorrow. MUST clean utensil drawer in kitchen, ants any minute. Jonquil needs a bath. Mat in shower should be washed and sunned. Must answer that *Who's Who* query, and why can't they just quiet down? So difficult to read the fine print and I always write things in on the wrong line."

Then as I dance in the moonlight over a tropic sea, I begin to worry about the telephone bill. Did I pay it twice? I often do. And where is my driver's license?

Regretfully, I leave the freighter and go inside to see if my driver's license is in the kitchen basket where everything else is. Jill comes in with rhubarb and more asparagus, and at this point it seems inevitable that we freeze some of each. We set up the kettle with boiling water for blanching the asparagus. Get out the sugar for the rhubarb.

"I'd like to go round the world someday," I venture as I snip the tough ends from the asparagus stalks.

"I don't see how we'd have time for it," says Jill firmly.

Much later, as I take my shower and get ready for bed, I realize that I am definitely never going to get on that freighter, but that the asparagus and rhubarb in the freezer will be lovely next winter. You can't, I tell Holly, have everything. After all, we could hardly cruise the seven seas with five cockers and an Irish and a couple of cats. And besides, the children could not come out for weekends. We would miss that first tooth of Jill's granddaughter being swallowed. We would miss the grandson's first definite steps and the clear but unintelligible lecture he gives about the wood in the fireplace.

We all, I suppose, desire at one time or another to escape. We not only wish to escape the drudgery and routine of our lives but the frustrations and worries. We yearn, in short, to be free. Just to pack up and go. To get away from it all, as the saying goes.

But there is no place so far away that one can escape one's own self. The country of the heart is always the same.

Even in Tahiti, I am sure I would be hunting for something I had mislaid. And I should worry about every underprivileged child I saw, and every work-worn man or woman. I would, in short, be myself. I would still have my arthritis, too, and walk carefully. I would take myself with me.

Meanwhile, I know there is not time enough in my life to experience all the wonder of an acre of our forty. The life that goes on in an acre, from the burrowing moles to the red fox running over, from the bluets blooming in spring to the wild asters in autumn, every day is an adventure. It would take more than one lifetime to understand the mysteries that take place in one small bit of land, the growing things and the wild creatures that pass over and the birds that light and take off.

Underneath the surface, there are the small creatures that make the soil friable, which is to say easy to crumble in the hand. The blind-faced moles lead a secret life, the angleworms move toward the damp upper soil. Also, as gardeners know, there are grubs and larvae tucked in waiting for summer to bring them to full eating capacity in the garden.

Above ground, the violets spread their heart-shaped leaves and bloom in purple and white. I gather a bouquet for the antique pill bottle and set it on the trestle table, for neighbors are coming for a pick-up supper. It is ham slices and pineapple done in the electric skillet, with asparagus on the side. Spoon bread goes well with it, and coffee, Wisconsin cheese and crackers for dessert. And also a fire blazing on the hearth, sparked with pine cones and good conversation.

Nice to have folks drop in, says Holly, as she accepts final tidbits. Jonquil has already had hers from affectionate guests, not to mention Especially Me. In fact, the plates are empty and quite ready for a rinsing and a stacking in the dishwasher!

When I occasionally go to the city to visit my daughter, I am stunned by the noise. When I lived in New York, I grew accustomed to the endless roar of a world of noise. But now that I have been in the country so long, I find the voice of the city appalling. I can hardly hear what people say for I am always conscious of brakes squealing, trucks grinding gears, sirens screaming. Trucks grinding gears all over again.

There is nothing wrong with my ears. It is a psychic affair. At home I can hear the squirrel leaping on the bird feeder, the distant bark of a fox in the upper orchard, the sound of an axe in my neighbor's woods. I hear a drip in the cellar when the tank begins to leak, and the sweet melancholy of a mourning dove in the swamp. And from the first floor, I easily hear mice skipping in the attic. But country sounds are individual against a backdrop of quiet. City noise is an ocean assailing me. In a group of chattering people, I sit glassy-eyed after an hour or so trying to count the number of times that same bus has roared past outside.

And then I notice when weekend guests come to Stillmeadow, they are often tired in the morning because the birds got them up at dawn. And if the cockers and Irish see strange things at night and bark lustily, nobody visiting gets a good night's rest at all! In the days when our neighbor kept horses on his completely unmechanized farm, the thudding of hooves in the barn at night unstrung guests who could sleep through a five-alarm fire in the city.

It all goes to show, Jill remarks. And always adds that her feet hurt walking on those awful pavements. This is not strange, for we have not even one sidewalk in the village. We walk on grass or country roads or on garden earth. And even in a drought, these give to the footsteps.

In the country too, when an occasional car goes by, we know by the sound whether it is Lovdale's car going up the hill, or the postman. And now and then we stop whatever we are doing and say, "That's a strange car. Must be on the wrong road."

The dogs know too. They are mouse-quiet when Joe drives over to tend the furnace in winter, check the kennel heaters, burn the inevitable rubbish. But just let someone drive by looking for Hull's Hill road, and they give tongue. They instantly recognize the sound of our own car as soon as we get to the top of the hill when we have been away, getting our hair done in the next town.

But the only approximation to city racket is when four horseback riders clop past. Then, I admit, our cockers and one Irish could almost do justice to Times Square. This is why everyone in the area who has a timid horse trains it by riding back and forth in front of Stillmeadow. They figure if a horse can stand that, he will stand anything.

I do not understand how dogs recognize automobiles. A good many cars make the same sound, I would think. For while we know the difference between a few cars, I could never tell one Plymouth from another. But they can. At one time our neighbors in the charcoal house had a small station wagon the exact duplicate of ours. But the dogs knew when Phil and Bebe drove up in theirs and when ours came in. From this I deduce every car has a special tone of voice.

Sound itself is a mystery to me. The right sound evokes such quick happiness. The wrong sound makes me melancholy. A shrill harsh sound tightens the nerves, and a slow easy one rests the spirit. In music, which is the soul of sound, I find that Bach is like looking at immortality. Folk music, whether gay or sorrowful, has to be nostalgic. It makes me feel a longing for all I have not known, even if I cannot define what it is I have missed! And if I have a fever and a diet of pills and tea, I am marvelously restored by "Maple Leaf Rag" as rendered on an old-fashioned tinny piano by Tiny Little Jim.

Tiny Little weighs well over two hundred pounds, unless a stringent diet gets him down to one hundred and ninety. He has no traffic with the modern be-bop or whatever is the newest at the moment. He plays an old-fashioned piano with something done to the felts so it hardly sounds like a piano, but a plucked instrument.

What it really sounds like is my childhood. Big Tiny began playing at the age of five in Worthington, Minnesota, and I wasn't probably even born. But he grew up and did his stint in the service and decided he liked what he called "the barrelhouse piano." My record includes "Hindustan," "Maple Leaf Rag," "Spaghetti Rag" and some others.

Modern rhythms have made no impression on him. He just bangs out "The Sheik of Araby" and I feel marvelously restored, no matter what kind of a day I have had. I begin tapping my foot, and if nobody but the dogs are around, I even take a few dancing steps, jiggling my shoulders.

I try to understand the newest music, the most modern art, but I think there is a place in life for simple, old-fashioned things. All of us grow in understanding and appreciation, and as we progress, we repudiate much. But many of us still like candlelight instead of neon glow, and hand-hooked rugs instead of fancy synthetic carpets. We love pressure cookers but still, if time permits, get out the old black iron kettle for simmering. In the same way, I like to put on Tiny Little's record, and pick up Jonquil, the smallest cocker, and waltz around! Old-fashioned music and old-fashioned dancing suit my taste, and Jonnie agrees with me.

Faith is a strange and wondrous thing. All winter we see the lilacs leaning against the blizzards, grey, lifeless. Nothing could look more dead than a lilac bush in January. It is only a bunch of sticks. The only thing alive about it is the chickadee swinging on a doughnut hung on a branch. Quite casually the miracle begins. There is never a moment when we can say, now the buds have begun to swell. As love ripens in a good marriage, the lilacs turn the tight glassy buds into small spikes, and then into visible purple. And then, in May, a flowering time comes. The air is filled with deep, rich fragrance—and who can describe the odor of lilacs? It is a romantic scent, heavier than roses, but never cloying.

Lilacs, I think, are the theme song of New England, even more than apple blossoms or the ramblers which will follow. Yet they are not peculiar to New England, for I remember in northern Wisconsin in Door County, we used to drive out to gather great bouquets of them growing around deserted cabins. Or where a house once stood, around the blackened chimney, the lilacs gave a sweet kind of immortality to the home that had gone.

The previous owners of Stillmeadow did not like lilacs, but they were queer. Eventually the husband shot his wife and then himself. But I would have known that anyone who would cut down lilacs was capable of anything. In time, with lime and care, they came back, for lilacs are hardy. We added a Persian lilac, that red-purple, and a French lilac in the stone-blue color, and encouraged the white ones to spread. We now have practically a lilac farm.

I would not, I think, care for a yellow lilac. I like plants and people to be what they are and have been. I notice the seedsmen keep offering prizes for new colors in everything from sweet peas to marigolds. When I want yellow, I prefer a naturally yellow flower. When I want shell pink, I don't want it in a nasturtium. I'll take it in a Dawn rose or a hyacinth. I don't

know why people are so restless. Nature is fine just the way
she is!

Now Jill comes in, smudged with garden dirt. She has been
planting more beans. From now until the black frost, the garden
will be a constant excitement. The pink crisp rhubarb, the
asparagus, the first snow peas, the lettuce and scallions usher
in the season. How delicious is a sandwich of freshly baked
bread and young scallions well salted and peppered! (We always remember with pleasure the day Jill's daughter, age ten,
said she was just simply tired of being the family scallion!)

We can now carry our trays to the Quiet Garden where the
Lincoln lilacs overhang the picket fence and the flowering crab
gives a rosy glow. The lilies of the valley are spreading out of
bounds, we note, and the lemon thyme planted between the
flagstones half covers them. When we step on it, a sweet odor
fills the air. The iris is beginning to bloom as the late tulips
go by.

Some years ago, we put in white pansies as a border in the
Quiet Garden. They have re-seeded themselves ever since but
they skip from one spot to another so they are now all over the
place. Also, as time goes on, they are reverting to their natural
color so some of them are moonstone blue and some flecked
with darker blue. The blooms themselves grow smaller each
year, but on the whole, I like them better than the giant size. I
prefer flowers that are modest.

The small garden is the one place off-limits to the dogs, because of the bulbs and lilies. So as we carry our trays out, they
line up by the picket gate and watch. Jill says some day Holly

will appear with a placard (lettered by Little Sister, the neat one) saying "UNFAIR TO COCKERS AND IRISH."

The Quiet Garden is not actually a true garden at all. When we moved to Stillmeadow, a half-demolished corncrib stood there, furnished with corncobs and field mice. The crib itself was too far gone to be remodeled into anything, even a puppy house, so we chopped it up and used the wood for the fireplace all one winter. Then we put a low picket fence around the spot and laid flagstones in the center, leaving a border for flowers around the edges. One side we reserved for herbs, tarragon, chives, lavender, sage, borage (the blue flowers are lovely in a May bowl). Applemint and savory were planted. We had sense enough to plant the dill in the vegetable garden where it can be restrained, although with difficulty.

We put in the spring bulbs and a few roses and some nicotiana. Nicotiana has leaves like a tobacco plant (it is a variety of tobacco). It grows so vigorously that Jill has to keep grubbing it out, and the plant itself is leggy and ungainly. But on hot summer nights, it fills the air with an almost tropical fragrance. The flowers vary in color from a bluish white to a garnet red, but the rank growth of the leaves obscures their beauty. Never mind, the scent is worth everything.

Next to music, I find scent is most evocative. An odor can recreate a whole memory. For instance, the smell of dried lavender takes me back to my childhood. My mother had a friend whose whole house always smelled of lavender. She was a retired French professor and lived just down the block from us. She always treated me as if I were grown up, pigtails and all, and she often asked me to lunch when Mama was busy.

She gave me China tea in a fragile flowered cup, and black

walnut croquettes and a green salad with her special dressing. She wore soft silk dresses with lace around the neck, and she was always cool and unflustered. I minded my manners and politely refused a fifth croquette, although it was hard. She talked to me about poetry. Those were enchanted times and I hope she knew how much they meant to me. And they come back, completely realized, when I smell dried lavender. I think she must have tucked tiny silk bags of it in her dress.

The scent of sun-warmed pines takes me right back to the great forests in northern Wisconsin. We used to summer in Ephraim, and hemlocks, spruce, fir, red pine and white pine covered most of the peninsula then, for farmers were just beginning to clear the land for cherry trees. We walked on pine needles. We gathered balsam needles to make pillows (I pine for you, for you I balsam, was my favored motto). We burned pine branches in the fireplace, for Father stacked them by the back door as he hacked a path to the water. Around the curve of Green Bay, pointed cedars and junipers grew, and from our front porch, we could see the white village with the green of the pines like a tide breaking against it.

Unsavory odors can also evoke past times. The smell of a scorched rag takes me back to the night the barn burned down, for Jill had put a couple of dog blankets on the workbench that day. There was also a mattress in the haymow (which was my studio) and for days we smelled burnt mattress and blankets from the ruins.

But now, on a sunny day, I can smell the pines we set out on the site of the barn, and most comforting it is!

In our particular part of New England, pine woods are not too common. But there is a stand of hemlocks not far from us, and we often drive there to see the delicate, feathery branches, almost the color of old jade. It is always shadowy and cool under the hemlocks, and quiet. We have one solitary hemlock on our own forty acres, on the hill above the old orchard. Occasionally we cut a little green from it for Christmas. It is very old, and I wonder whether it was a seedling when the house was built, and just how it happened to grow there.

This is not really a piny-woods countryside, although both red and white pines grow well. Maples and elms, wild cherry, hickory and a few butternut and black walnut trees strike the dominant notes. The chestnuts went in the great chestnut blight, and only a few white birch trees have resisted the wild winter storms we have. There is some oak, but I suspect it has always been rare, for a section near us has always been called White Oak, as if it were very special.

Our postman, whom we call "Mr. Conservation," is determined to bring back chestnuts. He keeps a small sack of Chinese chestnuts in his car as he goes his rounds, and entices everyone possible to plant Chinese chestnuts. The tree resists the chestnut blight, grows sturdily and relatively fast and bears big glossy nuts. Korean nut pine is another planting project of Mr. Conservation, and most of us have planted Korean nut pines.

Ever since I have known him, I have found our postman a rare and wonderful man. He doesn't know what a stumbling block is, and I doubt whether the word obstacle is in his vocabulary. He noticed, as he went hunting with his sons, that the face of the land was changing. Good soil was being eroded into rivers and streams. Cut-over land developed great gullies and the good soil washed away. Bird cover was scarcer every season and wildlife diminished. Sewage poured into the Pomperaug and the smaller streams. Forest land was being razed for housing developments for factory workers in the nearest cities. And as the trees came down, so did the water table. Wells began to go dry, brooks diminished to a trickle.

It would have seemed to most men a hopeless proposition. This particular man had never had an opportunity for training as a naturalist, horticulturist or forester. He was already working for a living when he would have liked more education. Now he worked hard as a rural postman, a quiet, pleasant man who minded his own business, and never even got involved in local politics.

But he began to read everything he could lay hands on about conservation. Government bulletins, fish and game reports, reforestation articles, books by such naturalists as Edwin Way Teale. He read late at night on weekdays and on Saturday afternoon and Sunday, he walked the land and studied it.

"We have to do something about conservation," he said mildly.

And so began a one-man crusade which resulted, in time, in a program that is now being copied in many states, and in fact, he even has letters from Australia asking for advice on conservation there. Meanwhile he has farm-folk, week-enders, retired people, young business executives who work in the nearby city, all planting, setting up feeding stations for the birds, fighting water pollution. He set up a training program for Boy Scouts because he said if they learned about the value of natural resources, they would grow up to conserve instead of destroy. And constantly he experiments with plants and trees which he calls just trying things out.

His method was simple. He pulled up and honked his horn,

and when the householder came out, he always began by handing out a few seedlings with the mail. "Noticed you have a place on your upper hill where erosion is setting in," he would say. And once the householder took the first handout, he was hooked. Now it is not unusual to see a bevy of young housewives out early on a Saturday morning planting multiflora roses along a devastated area where the power company has slashed through, or the pipelines for gas have left areas that look as if they had been bombed.

We ourselves, in the midst of the heaviest work in the vegetable garden, have rubbed our aching muscles and gone off to put in a hundred red pine seedlings where he felt they were needed! And I think his only failure was when he tried to teach us how to graft apple trees, for we never made fine apples grow on wildlings, but that wasn't his fault. We lacked the skill.

His energy never flags, although one might think that a man who had lost one leg would tire of tramping around the land. If I ever complain about my arthritis, he grins and says gently, "Ever try exercise?" His post office work involves a thirty-five-mile route, summer and winter, and what with the time in the village post office, he often works more than a twelve-hour day; and then when he gets home, the dining room table may be piled high with his own mail, from conservation groups all over the country. Then a couple of State Conservation men drop in for dinner. His wife, who is a superb cook, and used to people coming in any time for meals or to stay for the weekend so they can, as she says "tramp around all day," can whip up a gourmet meal while the men go over reports and pleas to mail to the legislature for some important bill.

His horizon is unlimited. Possibly this is true of all dedicated men. During our worst floods, he spent his spare time (and what spare time he could have is always a mystery) photographing flooded areas. The next thing we knew, everybody was planting autumn olive on the banks of brooks and streams, for autumn olive checks flooding. Then he discovered the turtle menace. Nobody had paid any attention to turtles until he revealed that snappers were decimating the fish population. He had the valley turned into a vast turtle trap in no time.

The other day he pulled up and honked and I went out, wondering what he wanted us to plant this time. Jill was already in bed with a bad back from too much work in the garden. I walked with a decided hobbling step. But this time he handed out a magazine from Russia and said, "Can you translate this for me?"

"Oh my goodness," I said, "who can read Russian?"

It was a story I wrote about his work, which the State Department had used in the magazine we send to Russia to give a picture of how Americans live. It even had the picture of Mr. Conservation, against a stand of pines ten feet high, that the conservation groups had planted not too long ago.

"Well, you'll have Russia planting autumn olives along the Volga I expect," I said, "and feeding the birds and trapping turtles."

"I don't know whether they have turtles," he said, "but most countries do have fish. And fish is—"

I went back into the house and got out Thoreau. From his hut on Walden Pond, I thought, he influenced the thinking of more people than anyone could estimate. He didn't particularly work to preserve Nature, except by writing about it. But somehow I felt our postman and Thoreau had a lot in common.

The children were here for the weekend, my daughter and Jill's son and daughter. I suppose parents never really get used to the idea that their children grow up, but they do. There is one way they do not change, however, and this is in appetite. Over Saturday and Sunday, the biggest roast beef from the freezer was consumed to the last sliver, along with quarts of vegetables, a large pie, a dozen cupcakes, a pound of Cheddar, and a vast amount of green salad. It is a joy to see them eat. We get so tired of counting calories and eating cottage cheese and canned pears. And those slim size nines and fourteens can latch onto all the mushroom gravy and Yorkshire pudding and top off with a second helping of dessert and never gain an ounce!

Watching them, I do not give a fig for the diet experts. I am glad the children all took after the thin side of their parents. I couldn't, for there wasn't any thin side for me to take after. All my people for generations back on both sides were plump as ripe apples. Along with a nose quite like Cotton Mather's, I inherited a frame about like his. But my daughter often finds size nine is a bit big for her! She is a wonderful cook and a little in the French school of sauces and things simmered in wine, but she stays pencil-slim. Whereas I can gain on a peanut.

Jill's children, too, were so thin always that we kept stuffing them with vitamins, and felt sure they were anemic. They weren't. They were just born to be thin. I used to think that being a good cook was a handicap, although I never felt any appeal in a small dry broiled chop. But lately, I have changed my mind and think a good dinner, savory and well-sauced, may be better than a diminishing waistline. Cooking is not only an art, but it makes for gracious living, and the year I lost fifty pounds, there was nothing gracious about the living at Still-meadow. My svelte figure got me nowhere. I felt awful. I was dull when we had company, and cross the rest of the time. I did not agree with all the articles that say dieting can be fun. It was a pleasure to have people worry about me because I seemed to be in one of those Victorian declines, fading right away. But it was no joy to discover a lovely new recipe that would figure out at two hundred calories a sniff.

At the year's end, the family sighed with relief when my

plate had exactly what was on their plates, instead of the lonely bit of broiled meat and the green salad with lemon juice. We were all suddenly very merry.

At this season of the year, I think often of Thoreau living his solitary life in the hut by Walden Pond. I too, in spring, feel impatient with the busyness of life. Thoreau knew what he was about. "I went to the woods because I wished to live deliberately, to front only the essential facts of life, and see if I could not learn what it had to teach, and not, when I came to die, discover that I had not lived."

Sometimes, I think, we rush so, we finish a schedule only to make a newer and busier one. We do not, ever, live deliberately and fully, for we haven't time. I know few people who go outdoors now and sit quietly for a couple of hours just looking at the miracle of spring. Sometimes as we drive along the country roads, I see occasional figures stretched out in lawn chairs. But they aren't observing May, they are reading the newspaper or a magazine. They are like the people I have seen on the great beach at Nauset on Cape Cod who never hear the music of the tide because they have portable radios playing hot music!

I hate to think what Thoreau would have said to that!

Perhaps the color of May is pink and violet. The apple-blossom buds are pink, and some of our trees bear true pink bloom. The violets cover the ground and invade the lawn so that it is hard not to step on them. In the meadow, the tiny wild dark purple and the white make a rich carpet. The Confederate violets have taken over the border and advanced to the terrace where their pearl blooms with blue centers are lovely against grey stone.

When I let Holly out, she seems winged, barely putting a paw to the ground but rather skimming through the air. She almost goes over the picket fence. Our first Irish, Maeve (named for the Irish queen with a high heart and lucky eyes), could top a ten-foot fence any time. But Holly pauses at the top rail and stays *so far* safely inside. That old song, "Don't Fence Me In," has a theme most of us respond to. The world actually is a series of fences, some of which we build, some which we would like to tear down. We are fenced in by convention, by habits, by laws, and also by fears and anxieties. But there are fences we would not be without. Love can be a fence, safeguarding those we love. Faith in God is a protection without which life would hold no promise.

The picket fence which we built at Stillmeadow to protect the yard and keep it safe is a symbol of the fence I try to build in my heart, one to keep bitterness, unkind thoughts, and hatred out. Love thy neighbor as thyself sums it up.

It was only last winter that the barn burned down. Hal Borland says in the country a barn is not a building, but a way of life, and so indeed it is. Our barn was around two hundred years old, and with the grace and dignity of hand-hewn chestnut beams, hand-forged hinges and latches, and a lovely slope to the ancient roof. Wrought-iron railings marked the horse stalls. Some of the windowpanes still had the greenish glass from the early days.

When we came to Stillmeadow, the old carriage house had fallen to pieces, a crumbling sleigh still under the mossy fallen roof. But the main barn was staunch, and it did become a way of life.

We took out the small pen that still smelled faintly of pigs and built a good workbench for Jill, for when you buy an old house, you buy a lot of minor carpentry and general repairing. The iron railings we used on stairs to the haymow as guard rails. We cleared the hay-dust from the mow, and moved in a desk and chair, a Boston rocker, a maple settee and a coffee table which was really a butchering block. I loved to work there and in the course of time a number of books emerged from the old haymow, as well as countless short stories. The stillness, the drowsy air, and the smell of newly cut hay from the meadow made a rather special world for me. In May I could look out through the open door almost as if I were a mariner looking from a ship's deck. How green and deep the meadows looked from that height as the new grasses invaded the earth. Apricots, peaches, nectarines and seckel pears made a flowering lane this side of the fields.

Often in summer, we took tea there for it was cool and shadowy even in August. Water cress or cucumber sandwiches and iced tea with fresh mint leaves made a pleasant break in the day's jobs.

Downstairs there was room for four kennel units, each opening on a grassy run. There was room enough for a car, but we used that space for the ping-pong table for the children to use on rainy days. There was space for croquet and archery sets, fishing tackle, lawn mowers, snow shovels, rakes and hoes, bags of cement and peat moss. In fact, whenever we looked for anything, someone would say, "Oh, it's in the barn." Usually there was a piece of furniture there, half refinished, such as the old butternut chest, the maple highboy, or the spinning wheel bought at an auction. It was a way of life.

The night the barn burned down was the coldest of the winter. We sat by the applewood fire eating popcorn and reading. Jill was, I think, re-reading *The Nine Tailors* by Dorothy Sayers. (She reads it every year.) I was re-reading *Romeo and Juliet*. This was partly because in the novel I was working on, the secondary character kept taking over and I wanted to consider Shakespeare's problem with Mercutio. Nowadays one cannot kill off a man in a duel just because he is more interesting than the hero, but I felt I might get some help, duel or no.

Suddenly an explosion shook the house. "A jet plane in the swamp," I cried. For some reason I am always expecting one to crash in the swamp. Jill shot up and looked out of the window. "The barn's burning!" She flew to the door, flinging back the words, "Call the fire department!" The whole building was already a wall of flame. The roof wore a fringe of fire. Jill was racing across the yard with a fire extinguisher, in what was probably the greatest peak of optimism ever recorded. The yard lights lasted until she got to the kennel gate, then they went out. But when she called, miraculously the cockers poured out, Hildegarde coming last, being elderly and somewhat stunned from being flung from her bed by the blast. Jill's problems were added to by a dogfight for we had two jealous females who fell on each other with fury.

I had my problems too. Even normally, I am no good at all on the telephone, and in a crisis, I cannot even dial. I dropped the phone four times, and finally got it braced against a shelf. Naturally I dialed incorrectly four times. I have not much idea of who answered except once it must have been a nightwatchman in the Medical Center in Waterbury. Finally I dialed Long Distance and screamed, "We are burning up!" I managed to tell where we lived, and she rang back to the fire department in Southbury. So the report about our fire was relayed via Waterbury which is fourteen or fifteen miles away!

The local volunteer fire department was attending a Lions Club dinner, and the speaker of the evening had just begun a talk on first aid for ambulance cases, when the siren shrieked. To a man, the audience jumped and ran. Five minutes later, the first truck rolled up and men in their best clothes, topped by helmets, began hauling the hoses out. Fortunately, because of Mr. Conservation, we had a farm pond not too far away, and as our young neighbor dashed across the yard, he said, "Get the hoses down this way." Without the pond, the house would have gone too.

Fortunately for us, Phil, the neighbor, had stayed home from the Lions dinner because he was coming down with something. He had on slacks, a sweat shirt, and moccasins. When he heard the siren, he grabbed a jacket and said to his wife, "I don't know where it is, but I'm off." By the time he backed his car out, he could see half the sky flaming. No doubt where this fire was. By this time, Jill had stuffed the separated cockers in separate rooms, put the rest in the back kitchen. And as the hose snaked out, Phil paused to say to me, "Now just don't worry. Everything will be all right."

Three hours later the fire was dying down. The firemen came in, sheeted with ice, their best suits ruined. They had climbed to the inferno of the haymow to play extra streams of water down on that tank of kerosene stored below. They saved it. They had chopped at burning timbers, and one of them had rescued a single lawn chair which stood on the ice in the yard. Meanwhile about thirty neighbors came to stand in the dreadful cold, waiting. They offered to take some of the dogs home, to put us up overnight and so on if the house caught. To do anything at all.

My contribution to the disaster was limited. It took me two hours to figure out that since the kitchen current had gone, I could plug the coffeemaker in on the radio plug in the front room and have hot coffee. I also took my purse out in the yard, for I had a dim idea that we would need money, and I had just cashed a check. Jill was busy telling the fire chief about that oil tank and the gas in the power mower and running about. I stood clutching my purse in the yard, supported by the warm arm of a neighbor.

Around midnight Phil's wife turned up with a bottle of rum and as the ice crackled down on the hearth, the firemen drank some with the coffee. "Not as bad as that night on George's Hill," said one. "Fifteen below then and four o'clock in the morning before we got it licked." He added, "Only one thirty now."

The fire inspector came in and said gently, "I am sorry. It is a total loss. There is nothing left." We thanked him. Then he put away his notes and remarked, "I would say there must have been a fault in the kennel heater."

Then they all went home. The men would be up and at work in the morning, farmers, storekeepers, young executives commuting to the city. The women would be up fixing lunches, getting children off to school. And around two thirty when I began to cry, and I really cried, it was only partly over the loss of that cherished barn, but chiefly because I was overwhelmed at the goodness of people. Our volunteer firemen get no pay. They raise money by an annual clambake and such projects as selling brooms or whatever. Rural distances are far, yet they are on call day and night. Whatever they are doing, they hear that siren and run. And then I cried about the neighbor women who stood those hours in that killing cold, some of them shivering until they positively rattled. They were just there, in case.

We lost our barn, but we saved the dogs, and we also experienced all over again the infinite helpfulness of people. The house got very hot on the roof, but it did not catch because a merciful wind blew the other way. And then I finished off my crying by remembering that everyone, even those who do not give a fig for dogs asked first, "Did you save the dogs?" for they knew that, to us, they were priceless.

I have never learned whether that lecture to the Lions Club was finished to an empty room or given all over again. And I have worried about the suits that were drenched with water and then iced like a cake. All our fire department asks is money enough from the clambake to get new hoselines that will go farther, or to replace a fifth-hand truck that breaks down when they are on their way to a fire. They would like a small fire station to house the equipment, and possibly they may get it. We hope so.

The morning after the barn burned down, we discovered that we had plenty of trouble left. Charred chestnut timbers lay in a tangle. Bits of twisted metal strewed the ground. One unburned door sprawled over the still-smoking floor. And as we inspected the desolate scene, the Irish came to look and suddenly bounded through a burned-out window frame and was off into the wild white world. Then we realized, as three plump cockers followed her, that the barn itself had been a fence!

Now, in May, as I walk around the yard, I can see the roses

we planted where the barn once stood are going to live. The pine trees that had one side scorched are beginning to show signs of life. Nature herself has great possibilities for recovery. In time, the site of the barn will not prick my eyelids with tears. The barn will be a memory, a precious bit of life past. We were fortunate to have had it during the years when the children were little.

But every now and then, Jill hunts for a level or a scuffle hoe. And suddenly stops and says, in disbelief, "Why, it must have been in the barn!"

Now the shad roe man comes down the road with his treasure from the icy river. He is a cheerful, rosy man, and he always gives us two or three extra roes when he lifts them onto our pan. He drives a small truck with the back section bedded well with ice. The big shad for baking look clean and silvery.

Shad roe and crisp bacon for Sunday morning breakfast is perfect. We serve it on the Canton platter, garnished with lemon wedges dipped in chopped parsley. And we eat in the Quiet Garden where the iris is coming out and the white pansies are in bloom. It is a good way to begin a busy day. I am not of the school which leaps at the day after a hasty cup of coffee. Breakfast should fortify one for the busy hours. A sandwich at lunch eaten on the double may be all right, but breakfast should be leisurely and varied as to menu. I don't know where the idea came from that cereal, eggs, bacon are inevitable for breakfast. There are dozens of things which are fine, creamed chipped dried beef for instance. Broiled mushrooms on crisp toast. Sautéed kidneys garnished with fresh water cress. One does not, of course, want mashed potatoes and pork chops and gravy, but a potato pancake flanked with baby sausages is heartening in January. If one is counting calories, they can be subtracted from lunch or dinner.

And shad roe goes with a morning in May the best of all.

After freezing asparagus, hoeing the garden, doing the chores, getting blankets out to sun, and back in again, we take a breather again at suppertime. When the sun goes down over the green hills, there is an afterglow the color of a fire opal. The valley below is already blue with evening. The stars are always a mystery. I never really see them come out, one moment the sky is empty and the next, there are the stars.

As the swallows swoop by, Holly chases them, leaping high in the air. Often they stop to perch on the electric wires and talk back to her. She will never be able to fly, but it is not for want of trying! Teddy follows her as fast as his cocker legs can go. When the birds have gone, Holly finds her faithful bone and tosses it in the air a while. Then she drags Teddy along by one golden ear until he protests at summit level. The rest of the cockers busy themselves around the yard. I notice that dogs never go to sleep gradually. They can be in full chase and suddenly they flop down and are off to sleep in a wink. When we go in the house, they get up and follow us in, and then collapse again. When I have trouble getting to sleep, I often wish I could be like the cockers or Holly.

Moonrise silvers the sky as we put the house to bed. And May, like Byron's love, "walks in beauty, like the night of cloudless climes and starry skies."

SUMMER

Summer

IN JUNE THE WILD HONEYSUCKLE OVER THE BACK FENCE SENDS forth such sweetness that I feel as if I could gather it up in handfuls. Honeybees and wasps and hummingbirds make themselves welcome. The whole air seems busy. The individual florets are fragile and small, but the strength of a wild honeysuckle is more than the strength of ten men. It took us some years to notice the small patch in the corner was spreading all over the far end of the garden where the soil was too poor for Jill's pedigreed peas. She cut it back before it reached the Blue Mexican corn rows. "Seems to be spreading," she remarked.

Shortly it flowed over into the grapes, and the wire fence for the Concords began to fall over with the weight. When we went to save the grapes, we saw that tendrils of the vine had wrapped around every bit of wire in the fence. By the time this crisis was met, the honeysuckle had made a flank attack on the flower border. And then it reached eager fingers toward my wahoo tree that Mr. Conservation planted. This tree bears beautiful scarlet berries which the birds enjoy. By then, Jill was chopping and uprooting madly. Now we manage to keep it at bay as long as we don't turn our back on it.

We have learned that it is wise, in the country, to understand the habits of growth of everything, not only the wildlings but what we plant ourselves. The French pussy willow rapidly turned into a tree just where we did not want a tree. The neat shrubs around the terrace developed into giants. The iris and day lilies have a policy of expansion suitable for General Electric. And the small pines we set at the back of the yard now suggest the forest primeval.

It may be that growth itself is unbelievable to the mind. The concept of a pencil seedling becoming a monster is hard to figure out. When we first put in our garden, we read all the directions for the seeds. Sow thinly, we read, and the vegetables came up thicker than grass. The same thing happened to the flowers. We had a jungle the first few years. Even now Jill looks with a wary eye at a marigold.

This is the season for roses, when the ramblers burst into splendor, deep red, ivory and candy pink. They grow on old stone fences, on picket fences, on trellises in gardens and on tumble-down sheds. Clouds of color seem to settle all over the valley. The reds are dramatic but I like the pink gingham Dorothy Perkins better. And the Silver Moon is such a pure white. We bought the Silver Moon many years ago for ten cents, in the days when we seldom had a penny left over from our collapsed budget. The children always needed orthopedic shoes, or Indian costumes or braces for their teeth. But we planted the ten-cent rose by the picket gate, and I find it as lovely as any costly rose could be. In fact, I like it the better for its simple background.

The fancy roses with specimen blooms take a great deal of care. They now come in almost every color, from salmon to a red almost black. There is even a rose called Gray Pearl. And the snowy Glacier. Then there is Peace which changes from a golden bud frosted with pink to a pale gold as it opens. But it is the ramblers that make June in New England.

Down by the pond, Mr. Clark's rose blooms early. This is an old-fashioned yellow rose, very prickery on the stem, and bearing small lemon-colored blooms. We call it Mr. Clark's rose, for Mr. Clark brought it over from his garden one day when he came to repair the wellhouse.

Will Shakespeare said a rose by any other name would smell as sweet. But actually a name can add to a flower, or detract from it. If we called roses stinkweeds, I don't think they would seem to smell as sweet! If I could, I would like to name a few roses myself. White Summer Night, for instance, Lady-in-Ermine. Embers for a coppery red. Summer Sunrise for a clear yellow. And Young Love for that delicate pink. I do not think New Yorker is a suitable name for a rose, nor Frau Von Druschke.

Wallace Nutting used to live in our village, in the house now owned by Victor Borge. His colored prints hung on nearly every wall when I was a child. In my bedroom, I had one of an old white house, with pink roses climbing the trellises by the door, and a girl in colonial costume on the front steps. Roses never bloomed so pink as those, although I now think Wallace

Nutting was not so far off. For some kodachrome shots Jill has taken are unbelievable too.

In the little town where I grew up, art was limited to oil paintings of cows knee-deep in clover, of Rebecca at the Well, and Rosa Bonheur's horses. If my father had ever seen a modern painting, such as a Picasso, he would have fainted. He even thought Maxfield Parrish a bit extreme.

In these times, security is an outmoded word. True, we hear about National Security, Social Security, security in investments and so on. But just plain security, in the old-fashioned sense could well have *Obs.* after it in the dictionary. Obsolete it is.

Into the vocabulary have come instead, "fallout," "long-range missiles" and, alas, Sputnik. No amount of hard work, moral responsibility, or spiritual strength can provide security for our children. We can do our best, and pray while much of the world busies itself with destruction. Even our own nation goes right on polluting the air we breathe.

But I do not believe in letting fear take over life. I believe in using the twenty-four hours of this day to our best advantage, to live fully, and when the day is over, to say in our prayers, "God, we are in your hands." I find that any sense of anxiety the day has brought vanishes, and I feel assured that the forces of good in the world will defeat the forces of destruction. I wish we could leave the sky to the stars, moon, and sun, but I still have faith in ultimate sanity.

The sound of the lawn mower on late summer afternoons is pleasant. It has a family sound to me, and reminds me of Father racing around with his shirt tails flying and the mower blades whirring. In the little town, fathers always mowed the lawns. Home from the office, or the college, or the mills, they doffed their coats and vests and went to work. By suppertime the lawns were finished. After supper, families sat on their porches watching the fireflies flicker. On warm nights, pitchers of lemonade stood on the porch tables.

In the moonlight, when I walked out with my beau, the dew would be falling, and the smell of the new-cut grass was the smell of summer. June bugs bumbled against the arc lights, moths went blindly to their ends. A good many people had gas lights, which sent a yellow glow through the lace curtains.

In time, the gas lights with flickering jets were replaced by the white light of electric bulbs. Recently when the new light bulbs tinted pale yellow came on the market, I felt as if time had turned backward.

On Saturday nights in summer when I was growing up, you heard the clop-clopping of horses' hooves as the farm wagons pulled away from the day in town. The farmers traded, the womenfolk shopped in the dry goods "emporium," the children bought jellybeans or candy corn or licorice. The farmers brought eggs, new peas, lettuce and strawberries in June. It began the cycle that ended with the loads of blue Hubbard squash, pumpkins, winter cabbages. A good deal of the trading went on from house to house. "The vegetable wagon is here!" I would call. Mama would hurry out, and ask how the children were and whether "the wife" was over the grippe. She carried a basket to put the purchases in.

Life had a leisurely tempo then, except for Father, who went at everything with breakneck speed. Nowadays I often hear women say they never have time enough for anything. All of the modern conveniences do not seem to give people more time. What happens to the time saved, for instance, with a washer and dryer, with a button to turn on the heat instead of carrying in wood and starting the old range? I do not know.

For mowing the lawn, we now have a power mower instead of the narrow hand one. But the neighbor who runs it is a man after Father's own heart, for he guns the motor, races after the machine, whirling around and around the house until I get dizzy if I watch him. The grass is not going to get the best of him, not for one instant. He ignores the half-buried Connecticut rocks and consequently I often look out in time to see the mower leap in the air as it hits a boulder. He rises briefly in the air too, clings to the handle and they rock merrily on. We have to replace the mower blades when they are too serrated, but I like the idea of never giving in to an obstacle, and certainly Father would approve. No use wasting time, as he always said.

June brings hot days, and cold. As the Farmer's Almanac says, "Fair curious sweet air, then whirlwinds the trees in pieces tear." And "Quick get back, the horizon's black." Thunderstorms usually begin with still air and intense heat. Then the black clouds crest on the horizon. They move over the sky in a curving motion, and if they have streamers hanging down, we cover up the chaise longue in the garden, get the dogs in, and close the upstairs windows. Suddenly a kind of night comes over the countryside, laced with lightning. Thunder almost cracks our eardrums. Then the rain comes almost like shrapnel. Water seeps in under the ancient sills and we mop. The telephone makes small cheeps.

As suddenly as it began, it ends. We go out and the air feels as if it had been dipped in crushed ice. A few branches have fallen. The delphiniums are flat. Rose petals carpet the Quiet Garden. But every grass blade shines, every tree leaf is lustrous, and the garden earth smells damp and cool. It is as if the world were made new in some way, and it makes me wonder if in our own lives we should accept the storms and sit them out, the way we sit out the thunderstorms Nature visits us with. In the country, we do accept storms, droughts, blizzards, floods. "Why should it have to happen to me?" is a phrase I have never heard hereabouts. If a giant maple crushes a roof in one of these storms when lightning ripples down the trunk, the owner never feels his house has been singled out for persecution. It just happened, and now to rebuild. When an early freeze ruins the crops, most farmers shrug and sigh and start over.

"Well, we ought to get a spell of good weather after this," a neighbor remarks during a period of impossible weather. And the year all the tomatoes were blighted, someone said, "Comes now and then." I think this attitude is due to a realization of the balance of Nature. We have lived through three severe hurricanes, floods which made our region a disaster area, bad forest fires in a dry season, and yet bridges are rebuilt, rivers and streams are cleared, forest lands begin new growth, and crops are planted again no matter what happens.

For next season may be a good one!

Our electric company sends out a bulletin with the bill, probably to cushion the shock. A recent one advised that if we put our candles in the refrigerator for twenty-four hours before using, they would not drip. I found it touching that the light and power company would be concerned with our candles. Candlelight does not make that meter whirl around a jot. But supper eaten by candlelight has a special charm, and I think the company did a better job in public relations than if they had said, Don't use candles, they drip. They melt. They drop wax on the table. All of which is true.

How strange it is, I reflect, as I scrape the wax from the milk glass candleholders, that man still needs candlelight. Is it some bond with the past? For with 25-, 40-, 60-, 75- and 100-watt bulbs, not to mention the elegance of concealed lighting which some people have, there is something about the flickering candle which adds charm and comfort to the supper table. I would expect that I would feel this, for candles evoke a memory of times I never knew, a nostalgia for Colonial times. The Wythe House in Williamsburg lighted with candles is like a remembered love story.

But I would not have expected the electric company to give me a recipe for preserving my candles!

And for their benefit, I will admit that during the times when "the electric" goes off in a blizzard, I am not very happy trying to read by candlelight. In fact, I can't read. Candles waver so. And the romantic glow is less than one 25-watt bulb, and who reads by 25 watts?

Nowadays there is a company that makes Colonial candles, and bayberry candles. They come in pastel shades, in fat shapes or tall willowy shapes and they are all lovely. I don't care so much for the decorated candles with roses and silver and gilt. The candle should be a holder for the flame, I think, shaped well, and preferably dripless (although they all drip some). On our trestle table, we use plain, plump, ivory or sage green candles. At Christmas we use red ones and the traditional big one that burns seven years, for the window. We once had candles shaped like angels and when the angels' faces began to burn, I was through with that kind of thing.

Father did not want candles ever. He said he liked to see what he was doing. Mama's silver candelabra rested most of the time, unless he was in a jocund mood. The battle of the candles went on all during my childhood, and I was staunchly on Mama's side. She said they were pretty. He said he wanted light.

And now when we light the candles for a supper in June, I often think that Father would come in and turn on all the lights in the room before asking the blessing.

"No use living in the dark," he would say.

Even now, in June, my African violets are blooming. I almost feel they want to rival the outdoor flowers. Evening Star, the color of moonstone, has put forth a bevy of blossoms all at once, after a rest period when I got discouraged. I felt she was ailing. Pink Cheer has a trio of buds about to bloom. African violets, I thought today while watering them, know no season, like love. Some people have trouble with them, and some experts write books about them, but I know the reason mine do so well is because I talk to them. Mine never have the right exposure because in a 1690 house, you have the modern radiators steaming under almost every window. The windows themselves are small, twelve panes over eight, and draughty. The temperature in the house bounds from a neat 40 to 80 as the furnace acts up or it gets very hot in summer. About all we can do is pin newspapers up across the panes when the sun is blistering, and hope for the best. In winter, Jill puts up cardboard to cut off the cold air.

I do give them a fertilizer but have trouble figuring how much to add to a pitcher of lukewarm water when the directions call for so much to a gallon. Nevertheless, my violets bloom so hard that they thrust the leaves aside to get up. Jill repots them when there are more than three crowns in a pot. Otherwise, I just visit with them. I water from the bottom if I have time to set them in the dog dishes filled with water. I water from the top when the dog dishes are full of dog food. My conversation with them goes on every day.

"Now you brace up," I say to Pink Lady when she begins to turn yellowish. "Don't you dare get crown rot for you know you have the loveliest flowers." "My, you are going to have a wonderful new extra bloom," I say to Red Girl.

And when the Irish knocks Tinted Lady from the shelf, I give a pep talk much as a coach does to a team. "Now this was a shock. The pot is gone. She didn't mean it. You try."

I used to feel I was peculiar on this account until Hal Borland laid the success of his vegetable garden to the fact that his wife talked to the plants. It might be that those who are said to have a "green thumb" have a communication with the plants. Who knows? Nobody really knows much about plants. But it is certainly true that a plant that is cherished does better, just as a cherished child does better.

"Summertime, an' the livin' is easy," goes one of George Gershwin's songs. And so it is. Not late summer when the vegetables come in, but June. There is work enough, but the pressures of ripening crops is not yet upon us. Days are hot but nights cool, with the moon tossed into the sky like a silver ball. It is a time between the excitement of spring and the fulfillment of harvest. A time to picnic and to drive over the hills to look at June in the next valley. A time in the evening to read, or play Beethoven's Ninth, or to work on a jigsaw puzzle. In a curious way, June is like January. You let Nature take her course and relax the pressures of your life.

Jigsaw puzzles are easier to do in June than in midwinter, for the cockers and Irish are out chasing things. In winter, they gather around the card table and hop off hopefully with the one piece I need the most. They are very fond of games, and when the children were little, often snipped off a jackstraw at a crucial moment.

Or just when someone poised the lifter and everyone was barely breathing, a round mahogany paw patted the table edge. "Oh Mama," was the constant cry during a game of jackstraws.

Also in June, after a mowing, the croquet set can go out, and the game seems especially designed for cockers. They can't get their small mouths wholly around the wooden ball, but they can almost manage it. In any case, the shot is ruined. We have had a fine time, however, leaning on our mallets and watching a small cocker work at a big ball. A good many of the celluloid ping-pong balls have tooth marks too but we feel games would be lonely without a flurry of wagging tails and eager noses around.

When I read all the personality-analysis articles with those charts that you check off about how you treat your husband when he gets home at night and so on, I am amused. You can tell almost everything about a man or woman by how they be-have when playing a game. Possibly in games we go back to

childhood and our basic selves, I do not know. But I have a
good idea of what anyone is like after half an hour playing
anything from Scrabble to pingpong. There are players who
must win. They are pleasantly expansive explaining how they
won. If they lose, they are, I will say candidly, sullen. Defeat
has a bitter taste. They never vicariously urge on an opponent,
or help with a difficult word in a word game. They are set for
the kill. These are people who must always be on top, hold the
winning hand in any field. They are, I think, jealous of others'
success. They are people also who are preoccupied with themselves.

Then there are the indifferent players who really do not like
to play games at all. They are polite, but their heart is not in it.
It seems childish. Most of those I have known that fall into this
category had a childhood without much gaiety. Family life was
not jolly. Father never went out and batted tennis balls to them

and Mother never played Rook with them because she was too busy. Life was real, life was earnest as they grew up, and games were "a waste of time." There must be always an overhanging sense of guilt at wasting time on a game.

Then there are those who pay no heed to the rules of any game. They play for fun, they say merrily. These people pay little heed to any rules, I think. And responsibility is something to be tossed off lightly.

In all the arguments about education, I find much good. We do need, so far as I can see, more solid educational training all along the line. Mental discipline and training have been on the sidelines while we broadened the horizons with courses in radio and television, stagecraft and how to teach whatever you taught. And a great deal has been said about the home and just how parents should deal with this age and that age. When children are in the independent period, and when not and so on.

But I believe that parents should play games with their children and have fun, and forget what the books say. And I believe a really good coach can teach High School boys a lot off the cuff as they have inter-class contests. Play can be very important, for it is a capsule representation of living. And for adults, play can do more than any amount of the new drugs to ease the anxious mind and heart. Instead of a pill, a good bout with a crossword puzzle accomplishes more.

I have little patience with women who complain so bitterly that they are fishing widows or hunting widows or golf widows. If they are wise, they will know the tensions ease when a man plays a game and he will face the problems of his job and the family support with more courage after he has made a hole in one or landed a trout or shot a partridge.

Women should have their own games, if they do not like hunting, fishing, golf. There are so many games that do not involve shooting innocent wild animals or birds, getting damp worms all over one, or chasing balls that inevitably land in a pond.

In the early days, women had quilting bees and as the needles flew back and forth on the fine muslin, what gossiping, what good talk. Nowadays women go to club meetings and serve church suppers and so on. But whoever heard of a woman getting up at 3:30 A.M. when the fishing season began and picking up two or three friends and just going off for the day?

I am no feminist, and I think the battle of the sexes has been greatly over-talked about. But I do note that if a woman goes off to a Garden Club convention in the nearest city, she has to turn the house upside down first, and cook enough for three weeks. Then if she comes home a little late, clutching her bouquets and pin holders, she is not warmly welcomed. The family has felt deserted. The air is chilly.

But when trout season begins, the man has a hearty breakfast of bacon and eggs and a good lunch of ham sandwiches and deviled eggs and woe to the little woman who feels lonesome if he does not get home until late. He was fishing!

On the other hand, what is better than a fresh-caught brook trout sautéed gently in butter and served with lemon wedges and sprigs of water cress from that same trout brook? I notice the most resentful fishing widow does not hesitate to enjoy it.

As I was hanging out the washing this morning, I thought about homesickness. Hanging out the washing is not a quiet occupation at Stillmeadow, for a golden nose keeps poking in the wash basket to retrieve a sock or the Irish plays catch as catch can with a hand towel. But I still had time to think.

I began by wondering how I should feel if I had to pull up the deep roots of twenty-nine years and leave Stillmeadow. A house and the land are so much more than a building and meadows and old orchards and woods. I felt quite faint, suddenly, and sat down on the old butcher's block we use as a bench. I remembered the courage with which Faith Baldwin faced selling the big house in which her four children had grown up, and moving to a smaller, more practical one.

I had a feeling that I would be a complete coward and probably have to be dragged screaming to the picket gate. For there isn't a spot in the house, or on the land, without memories. Upstairs is the bedroom floor we painted the weekend we moved in. We painted ourselves into the farthest corner while busily discussing modern poetry. When we tried to leap out lightly, we took large amounts of paint with us and that meant painting the upper hall. This was the paint that was supposed to dry "overnight." As day after day and night after night passed, we told ourselves it just had to dry eventually. Finally we laid a catwalk of planks across it so we could get into the middle bathroom. The plumbing had given out in the front bathroom.

Upstairs, too, is the maple highboy I did over as a surprise for Jill's birthday. It had seven coats of paint, including one of the ox-blood paint Connecticut pioneers were addicted to. I didn't know anything about paint removers at that time, so I did it all by hand with pieces of broken glass (which took bits out of my hands too). I finished with steel wool and pumice and countless coats of wax. Since I scraped mostly with my right hand, I acquired a list to the right that took some time to get over.

Downstairs is the great fireplace in which Jill's son used to sit on a milk stool right by the embers. Eventually, when the legs of the stool began to char, we made him move out.

Even the telephone, which is just like any other telephone reminds me of the time during one of our worst storms when I was answering it and a ball of fire came hurtling down the ruffled curtains a handbreadth away. Pale and shaken, the furnace man (working in the cellar) appeared in the door saying, "Don't move. Don't move." I couldn't have moved if the house had fallen in.

The cellar has its own memories. I never peer down the ladder stairs without wondering whether there is another black snake down there and should I carry a rake? I am the family snake-killer, but I prefer a battle outdoors and not in a small dark cellar.

The Franklin stove in my bedroom brings back a day of scarlet maples, drifting smoke from burning leaves, and country roads bright with goldenrod. We drove to a town some miles away and poked around in a junk shop and found half of the stove. And at the last minute, under a pile of dirty rags, found the top. Coming home in triumph, we stopped to eat a picnic lunch at the top of a ridge and saw the whole valley spread below us, smoky blue and pricked with the red fires of the maples.

And so it is.

Then I decided sensibly that there was no use being homesick for Stillmeadow when I was right there, pinning up the sheets on the line. But homesickness is a strange affair, for as I leaned over to pick up the last clothespins, I suddenly got homesick for a clothesline strung between two stunted pines on the seacoast, where I also have spent some golden days. It was the clothespins that did it. By the ocean, they turn greyish from the salt air. If they are the clip kind, the metal rusts. When you take the clothes in the sea wind and the sun are in them, the smell of scrub pines and bayberry. The clothesline has a view of sailboats and a tanker standing out to sea. Gulls go over crying their lost lonely cry.

Yes, I thought, pinning up the last of the socks (they never come out even), it may be I am the one person in the world who can be homesick for the place I am in and a place I am not in!

My first attack of homesickness came when I left home for the first time. I immediately took to my camp cot with a fever. The camp was on a green island surrounded by a bottomless lake in greens and blues. I was an earnest camper. I wanted to take swimming tests, weave things, collect bugs and do all the rest of it. I loved the campers and the staff that supervised in a harried way. But at night, when the moon rose, I just got sick. Since I did not break out with anything, the camp Doctor merely prescribed a weekend visit with my father and mother. They came up, bearing extra blankets, cookies, a layer cake, and a few sundries. By Monday morning, I was marvelously restored and, the fever gone, turned out for canoeing.

And when I got back home, I was homesick for camp!

Such a temperament is discouraging to those who must deal with it. Mama got tired of hearing about the better way everything was done in camp, for one thing. Father did not see why I spent so much time writing letters to every single camper, not to mention all the counselors. I was at home, I had passed everything except beadwork (I never could count well), and why did I mope around?

When I went East to college, it was worse. For my Junior and Senior years at High School, I hardly saw my parents at all. I was so busy. I drifted in to eat and to sleep, unless I spent the night out with my best friend. I wanted to be free of all restrictions and be on my own. I was as full of yearnings for independence as the American Colonists before the Revolution.

But once I got unpacked in the dormitory room with livid roses crawling over the wall and mock-oak furniture around me, what did I do? I met the great release, the great adventure, by getting sick with a high fever. And since I did not break out with anything, the college Doctor left a few pills (probably sugar-coated with nothing inside) and said I would feel better soon. When I got tired of milk toast, I got better.

But all the four years as I bicycled around campus, sat drinking pink cocoa at night in the dormitory, formed lifelong friendships and had what the children call "a ball," I always had a feeling around suppertime that I wished I were at home with Father rocketing around the house and Mama quietly dishing up fried chicken, and the phone ringing for me.

It may be homesickness is a nostalgia for everything you have ever had. But I doubt whether I could be cured of it. I can get homesick at the drop of a cap for any place I have ever been and anybody I have ever known. Because every place and every person seems so special. I can even get homesick for a very dark awful city apartment in which I spent some years when I was at Columbia. The elevator man was an ancient gentle Negro and he helped me with my crossword puzzles. And a lot of neighbors whose names I did not even know rushed out to help find my black cocker who had skipped out when the apartment door was momentarily left open. With the help of Albert, the elevator man, and all the neighbors, Star was located in an alley chasing a cat.

In that apartment, I wrote my first story and sold it. At that point, I hardly needed the lights on (ordinarily they had to be on all day). And in that apartment, our first cocker had a beautiful litter of puppies, which she kept carrying into the one closet because she liked the closet. I can see her now, worried, and lugging puppy after puppy from her pen to that closet. And I remember when she came down with eclampsia from too many babies and a scarcity of calcium, that Albert just left the elevator and flew out to grab a cab for me so I could get her to the vet in time, and anybody who wanted to climb to the sixth floor could just climb by themselves, he was busy helping with that little dog.

And it was, of course, during a taxi strike, but the cabman we finally located sat outside the hospital on his own time until I came out. "I just wanted to know the little dog was all right," he said. The dog was fine, but his taxi barely made it back to the apartment. I think it ran on bolts and screws.

I do not believe in letting homesickness take over, when we have to make radical changes in our lives. There is no use crying over spilt milk, Mama used to say firmly. And when she said it, it was not a cliché but a pronouncement. Raised in New England, she managed to rush all over the country and live in Mexico besides while Father whipped about on his mining-engineering jobs. I never heard her utter one word of complaint. If we holed up in a shack or in an adobe hut, she set packing boxes around and somehow made a home. Nobody ever had to feel sorry for her. But now, looking back, I can see that there were times when she read and re-read letters from home. But she always made any place seem gay. If we had to live out of suitcases, she made little chests of them, covered with cretonne or frills of leftover material from dresses she stitched up.

Even during the desperate days when Father vanished into Mexico and we were stranded in Texas in a boardinghouse and no letters or money came in, she made a good life for me. I have the happiest memories of that time when the landlady began to think Mama had no husband at all and was about to turn us out! It was a respectable boardinghouse, she said, and I had no idea what that meant. Mama took me on walks and we looked at everything. We ate sandwiches and had a picnic. She was too proud to write back to New England to the family for help, for this would diminish Father's stature. She simply kept me happy, and waited.

When he finally turned up, having been held up in the mountains of Mexico, I thought it strange that Mama cried. But all I heard her say was "Rufus, I am so thankful you are back, and safe."

I guess Father was pretty lucky.

He was weathered and wore a sombrero and swept me up in his arms and laughed. Paid the bill, charmed the landlady. I ate myself sick on the meals we had then. It was a special Christmas out of season with presents and Father singing funny Spanish songs while Mama mended his clothes and packed for a return to what was called "home."

Very often, I think, people are homesick for the past instead of for a place. Or simply for a different way of life than the one they are currently leading. No matter where childhood is spent or how much difficulty growing up has involved, it is easy later on to think of it as an eternal meadow filled with flowers. Surely birds sang daylong and air was always honeysuckle-sweet. In the same way when people move from East to West or West to East or South to North or North to South, the country left behind glows in the memory with a light never seen on any land.

I was reminded of this when a friend, reft away from her home in California because her husband was moved East, wrote miserably listing everything wrong with the East. There was plenty. She mourned for her house with a mountain view, her garden with the oranges ripening. Snow and sleet horrified her. Frozen pipes bedeviled her. Even her cocker moped about (naturally he would, since his mistress was unhappy). "But," she added, "I keep reading over what you have written about winter and I am going to like it if it kills me!"

It is my guess that if, after some years, her husband is sent West again, she will have acquired some memories of trees flaming in autumn, of tulips and narcissus blooming after the snow has gone, of crystal winter nights when the snow itself seems to give forth a glow. She will remember brooks running sweetly over stony beds, ponds fringed with willows, lakes dropped like blue stones in hidden valleys.

The truth is, I reflected, having done so much thinking by the clothesline, that if you look for the best in any place, it is there. If you look for the worst, you can find it easily. And a swift piercing pang of homesickness is really what the Sunday school teachers would call "a challenge." A challenge to experience every bit of beauty that is afforded by wherever you may be. A city, for example, is like a great drama. The surging sense of life quickens the blood. Skyscrapers at night are as dazzling as any wonder of the world. Young lovers drift along dark canyoned streets hand in hand, and stop to buy roasted chestnuts from the old man at the corner. In the park, men play chess in the afternoon, putting the board on their knees. Starched children stand in awe in front of the seals in the Zoo. Chauffeurs and housemen walk fluffy poodles who wear inlaid collars. And a shabby old woman creaks along with a happy mongrel. "Now, Irene," she says, "you stay right on the walk."

If the city happens to be New York, the river is there. Sometimes destroyers come to a shadowy anchorage in the dusk. The ferryboats look like dollhouses with candles in them as they pull from the Jersey shore. Small boats skim about as aimless as waterbugs. Ragged boys fish endlessly from the banks for fish that never bite. And a firm on the Jersey shore tells you the time to the minute in neon, if you care what the time is.

The open-air markets are in the city, glistening fish, cheeses, vegetables brought in at dawn, spareribs and chops. Uptown one may buy love herbs and peppercorns and saffron and a pinch of graveyard dust from under a stall. In the Italian section, whole shops have nothing but pasta. Macaroni, noodles, spaghetti, sea shells—lasagne pasta with scalloped edges—long tube forms for stuffing, and a dozen others. Some sell ravioli "to take out." And always next door is a bakery where long wooden paddles bring crisp crusty loaves from the brick ovens. Usually you can hear opera or folk songs at the same time as the workers sing.

And all of these delights are quite aside from the theatre, the concerts, the museums, the ballet. A city offers a rich feast.

However, I am thankful as June dusk draws in, to walk across the grass without benefit of street lights. Instead of the excitement of the city, I look forward to a concert on the hi-fi. Or to Peter Pan on television. Or to reading. I am now at the age when I am glad not to dash for a cab, wait in the rain after the theatre for one, wait for an elevator when I get back to the apartment. I like to be comfortable. I understand very well my Aunt Minnie who says she is a comfortable hunter. She sits on a log and waits for the deer to come by. I sit cosily in the house and wait for something good to come by on television, and if it does not (often the case) I have a wall of books waiting. Or I can play Caruso records, or Elizabeth Schumann or listen to a symphony directed by Toscanini.

And after the evening program, whatever it is, a homemade corned beef sandwich with Bavarian mustard tastes as good as one in a crowded city restaurant. If I sometimes wish for the German potato salad such as you only get in the city in places like Luchow's, I reflect that freshly dug potatoes, blushing with youth, garden scallions, and a bit of young green lettuce for garnish still make a very edible salad.

When Jill comes in after a day in the garden, nobody could hire her to go anywhere. She wants a steaming bath, a good supper, and a relaxing time solving some murder in the new mystery book. Then she is ready to plan tomorrow's jobs. She always lines up a week's work to be done in one day and is let down when it doesn't all get done. But it helps to make a list and cross things off. Nothing is better than a list with half of it crossed off!

June is the lyric part of summer, and it is what we need after the epic of winter and the rich sonnets of spring. There is plenty of time to arrange roses in a milk glass compote, time in the evening to watch the fireflies over the meadow. It is a season of ease. As soon as the water in the pond accepts the warmth of the sun, we can go down and swim while the small polished green frogs jump in and out along the bank. Butterflies drift in the air on the bank and an occasional dragonfly "hangs like a blue thread loosened from the sky," as Rossetti says. As dark deepens, bats wing over the pond, mysterious and shadowy. Their flight is graceful and they are silent. When the bat utters its cry, it is a mouse-squeak, rather pitiful. Many people are terrified of bats, and I suppose it dates back to some early era when they were vampires—or thought to be. But I have never felt fear of them.

I do not figure what Japanese beetles contribute, except a lot of work on the part of a gardener who has enough already. For even the birds will not eat Japanese beetles. They are not food, they do not pollinate anything, they do not make the earth friable as the humble earthworm does. They just eat up the roses, the grapevines, the delphinium and everything else. I am sure they must have a reason for being, but I do not know what it is.

Consequently my conscience is clear when Jill goes with a can of kerosene to hand-pick the beetles. It is a battle of survival between our garden produce and flowers and the shiny predatory pests. They are like subversive elements in a nation, eating away until nothing is left but the skeletons of living plants. And when I go out to pick the first rosebud and find it a cluster of metallic beetles, I am tempted to scream. It is too much like evil attacking good for my taste.

But like evil, they come, devour, and eventually pass. Such plants as have had a helping hand, survive. Some even put forth tentative new leaves to catch the sun and air. Half-eaten roses bloom, and to me it is a testament to the will to live and grow.

This is a time of anxieties, scary headlines, turmoil. Many people have resorted to tranquilizing pills to get them through the days and nights. A good many parents worry about the fallout and its effect on their children and children's children. All of us, I think, like to feel our family will go on and a probable generation ahead of leukemia and other diseases for children from the atomic explosions is not easy to contemplate.

I am very glad that it is not up to me to decide whether the tests shall go on or not. It is not up to me, being a plain countrywoman, to settle world policies or create new satellites. I think if every nation begins whirling things around in space, there will be repercussions from space which may be lethal. But I have decided that it is my business to live my life as best I can. In season we plant. In season we harvest the crops. In season we pile the apple logs on the fire. And here at Stillmeadow we try to live every day as if it were a fresh gift from God. The sun shines, the rain falls, the snow blots out the windows still. Birds come as usual. They nest at the same time. And in so far as we are able, we help our neighbors whether they live down the road or in Hungary. We share what we have whether it is money or blankets or seeds for planting in some foreign soil.

Now that we live in such an anxious age, it is quite natural that we turn to tranquilizing drugs. I have heard of a man who takes tranquilizers to quiet himself down and then takes pep-up pills "to level it off," as he says. I doubt whether tranquility is something one can swallow in a pellet. I was subjected to them at one time when my blood pressure skyrocketed. They helped the blood pressure but they didn't improve my disposition at all. Whenever I wasn't groggy, I was cross.

Tranquility is something we must reach for in ourselves. Prayer can help. Often when we are heavy-laden, prayer brings a sense of quietness. It also helps to stop whatever we are doing and take a breather. Even going to the window and looking out at the sky a few minutes may help ease tension. Or taking five or ten minutes to dip into a book that has nothing to do with business or our jobs. If we are fortunate enough to be able to go outdoors and pull weeds in the garden for half an hour, we may feel bitter about how vigorous the weeds are, but we come in relaxed.

I have a friend who says when she is too keyed-up, she irons. Ironing would never make me feel tranquil, but she says it is very calming. She even gets up at night if she can't sleep and irons up a few shirts.

Most of us have, I think, some refuge from this exceedingly disturbed era in history, but it is an individual matter. I find, for myself, washing the milk glass is good medicine!

I was greatly relieved when the United States Post Office admitted that economizing on glue for stamps had not worked out. I have seldom been more frustrated than during the period when I would affix a stamp to an envelope and have it come right back off with my thumb. I finally took to weighting down envelopes with dictionaries, bookends, the portable radio, paperweights. My room resembles the "I get letters, letters" on the Perry Como show, except mine were all outgoing. Once our dear postmistress sent on a stampless letter because she said she could see I had worked on it.

Before this battle ended, I bought a tube of glue, and just glued the stamps on. It seemed to me I should have had a discount of a cent or so on the stamps. Or bill the Postal Department for my glue and my time!

As a plain citizen, I can't see why the Postal Department is always in the red, with ferocious deficits. With the price of a penny post card 3 cents, and letters four cents, air mail seven, and a probable raise again any minute, somehow it should balance out. It seems to me, from what I observe in rural and town post offices hereabout, that some streamlining in the offices themselves would help. Who could cook efficiently if it were necessary to run across a big room for a pinch of salt, run back for pepper to the opposite corner, and go downstairs for a pan?

Edible-podded peas are our favorites. They are sometimes called snow peas or Chinese peas. They come in early, and you pick the tender green pods and wash and string them and cook them whole. Jill says I barely cook them at all, I pass the pan over the stove, but that is not really true. I cook them briefly in a small amount of salted boiling water, add butter, milk or light cream (if not dieting). We often make them our main supper dish, served in warm bowls and dusted with freshly ground pepper.

The pod is the most delicious part, crisp, and sweet. I do not know why so many gardeners are unacquainted with them.

When we cook them, we have to save a dish for Jonquil, who is our vegetable addict. She not only adores peas, but tomatoes, carrots, parsnips, turnips, cabbage (raw or cooked), lettuce, even onions. While she snaps up string beans, the rest stand around, like Joseph in the Cherry Tree carol, and wonder what she is wagging so about. She is fond of fruit and Jello too but vegetables are really her dish.

I am always amazed at the variations in taste that dogs have. A litter of puppies properly raised on Pablum and scraped beef and egg yolk and evaporated milk will stagger forth from the nursery with individual opinions about what is good and what isn't. There was the cocker who loved melon and apples. And dill pickles, of all things. Holly has a passion for walnuts and pecans (cracked and served on a saucer). One blond cocker we had insisted on tomato juice once a day. Teddy will stand up on his back toes to get a leaf of fresh cabbage. Star used to like fresh beans better than meat.

After twenty-five years of raising completely healthy cockers and Irish setters, we have stopped worrying about their eating something not on the regular diet. If they really yearn for a radish or a slice of peach, we find it does no harm.

With children, the case is a bit different, for usually snacks seem to result in a lack of interest in any regular meal. I know a couple of very young children who seem to subsist chiefly on graham crackers, bananas, and cookies. They look perfectly well, but I can't feel this diet is very well balanced! I grew up having to eat something of whatever was on my plate, but this was no hardship as I liked almost everything anyway. I even liked spinach!

The customary hatred of spinach comes, I think, from bad cooking. Jessie Conrad, the wife of the great romantic novelist Joseph Conrad, boiled spinach for three hours. In my childhood, it wasn't as bad as that, but often a kettle of greens of any sort would simmer along on the back of the range for an hour or so. Mama was an individualist, and the spinach we ate still had some shape to the leaves, but this was not common. When I was raising my own daughter, Connie, spinach was still cooked to death, pushed through a sieve and served as a green soapy mass.

Spinach can be delicious. A spinach soufflé pleases almost everyone, and is easy to make. Chopped crisp bacon added to steamed spinach gives a better texture and flavor. Adding a bit of horse-radish is worth while too.

Creamed spinach as served in France is delicious, and at Still-meadow we make our version by adding half a can of cream of mushroom soup to a package of frozen chopped spinach.

Raw spinach, tender young and green, makes a green salad special.

As far as diet itself goes, there are other things which will do in place of spinach. So there is no reason to make a cause of it. About the only table rule we believe in is that, when a child is present, no adult should make a face at any item on the menu and say heartily, "I'd as soon eat hay." Food patterns are fatally easy to pick up.

With the cockers, we have found that if we set the bowl down with a flourish and say, oh how good THIS is, they wag up and devour it. It may have yeast or vitamins or any additive advised for special reasons by the Doctor, but they eat it happily. Often if we are worried about the illness of a friend and simply put down the bowls, the cockers look up and walk away, non-wagging. The Irish unhooks the screen door and goes outside. The basic food may be sparked with steak fat, bits of leftover roast or chicken broth. No matter, it is uninspired because we are so indifferent.

People are much the same. Faith Baldwin professes a great antipathy to vegetables. "This is my day to have scurvy," she says firmly. But I have known her to eat three helpings of spinach soufflé or French green beans cooked with diced onion and broiled bacon bits. The next day she will say, "Don't bother to cook any vegetables for me, you know I don't eat them." And I go right on basting the carrots with lemon butter and a touch of brown sugar.

In June, the house is cool and quiet. The dogs play their games in the new-cut grass. When the day is hot, the old house never gives in to it. Roses in a milk glass bowl look cool too. We change to soft green candles for the dragon candlesticks on the mantel. But this is as far as we go for summer. I don't like to tear the house to pieces just because it is hot in summer. Rolling up the good rugs, putting on pale slip covers, and putting away my cherished antique bottles and the milk glass to save cleaning and dusting is not for me. We get more dust in winter anyway from the furnace.

Putting the house away for the summer used to be traditional. And during the years I lived in the South, I often hardly recognized a house when the dust covers went on, the bric-a-brac vanished. I might do this myself if we lived in a very hot climate, but in New England it is not really necessary. I do concede spraying and packing away the knitted hoods, mittens, woolen scarves and the afghans. That is as far as I go. We do not have a revolution in blankets. If I want a blanket when a cold wind comes up in the night, I want my own regular blanket. I don't want a gossamer thing that I cannot even feel.

Before it gets too hot, we face the problem of the attic again.

I am very emotional about attics. I feel an attic should be full of treasures which some day someone will come upon and love. An attic should contain sea chests packed with satin slippers, wedding gowns, old love letters. There should be a good cobbler's bench where children can crack butternuts on autumn days. An attic should be a love letter from the past which we give to our children. When we bought Stillmeadow, our attic did have old books, old maps, a First World War canteen, some broken-down early pine furniture.

We added a trunk full of diplomas, ours and the children's. Boxes of old photographs and a chest of old quilts partly worn. A few spinning wheels left over from downstairs (we were awash with spinning wheels and carders). Then we put remnants of wallpaper there and two cradles, and a carton of dolls.

But mice chewed up everything chewable, moths ate everything suitable for moth dinners. Wasps built their long cylinder nests under the beams. An attic in a house built in 1690, we found, is not a romantic haven. Even insulating did not help. So this June, we decided to TAKE STEPS. And with us the steps usually turn into a marathon. When I saw the mouse-nibbled contents of the attic, I said we should just throw everything out of the window and burn it all.

"Well, you can't burn Connie's old ice skates," said Jill. "You remember she was after us last winter to find them. They were behind the oil painting of David when he was a baby. And what are you going to do about those cartons of letters?"

"Oh, I'll save those," I said hastily, "to re-read in my old age."

"You can't burn up diplomas either," Jill pointed out. "I mean a diploma is a diploma."

The truth is, life has a way of accumulating treasures which you cannot part with and yet have no place for. This is also true of memories, I think. There are some you cannot part with but that have no place in your present life.

Anything that anyone else can use should always be given away, but there are some things we naturally collect as we go along that justify an attic. In the days when I lived in a city apartment, I kept sending cartons to Mama, and after she died, I found her own attic was jammed with my accumulations.

As far as the rest of the house goes, Stillmeadow is too full of a number of things, like Stevenson's world. Jill manages to keep her room uncluttered and the children's rooms are relatively ordered now that they are away so much of the time. But my room would give a decorator a nightmare. It is a small room, and it is not only my bedroom, but my workroom. It is also the television room, since there isn't an inch for the set anywhere else. It also has a Franklin stove, an antique maple daybed (comfortable for the dogs), a Pennsylvania Dutch chest (I have to have some storage space somewhere). Between the office-size desk and the maple four-poster is a low bureau which just squeezes in. It holds the radio, clock, a pile of books, magazines, and the crossword puzzle I am working on.

My desk does not resemble any I have seen in the lovely colored pictures in the magazines. How elegant they are with a single bouquet, a neat telephone, and one desk pen. How uncluttered indeed must be the life of the owners of those desks. Just an expanse to preside over! If there is a typewriter, it lurks underneath somewhere and springs out when needed.

On my desk I have thirteen objects, not counting the pile of unanswered mail and the two piles of manuscripts. It looks like a rummage sale. But it can't be helped. The wide window sill back of it takes an overflow of dictionary, World Atlas, Treasury of Great Poems, and my best white African violet.

I have only ten books on the desk itself, chiefly poetry. The pictures take up some room, although I also have the wall at the left covered with family pictures. My cocker Honey, who companioned me for fourteen short years, is in a silver frame next to the Severn portrait of Keats. A dreamy picture of Connie is at the right. She looks as if she might write a sonnet any minute, but actually the picture was taken of her when she was perched on the top of a stepladder. The ladder does NOT show. At the left is a portrait of Faith Baldwin taken at the time we first met. She gave it to me the first time I went to visit her, and this was quite an occasion in many ways. As I turned into the driveway in front of her house, I ran into a fairly good-sized shrub and mowed it right down. (It was an imported something or other, valuable.) I then went to the front door. There was a storm door on it, and the bell inside. I hauled on the door and broke it open with a splitting of boards and the sound of the knob being torn out. (The door was nailed shut for the winter.) I ended my visit by getting myself locked in the powder room where I wept miserably as the members of the family wrestled with the jammed lock.

This was the beginning of our friendship, and I may say I think Faith was remarkably brave to risk it! In this particular portrait, she has a grave gentle expression but with the half-smile so characteristic of her.

On the whole, I expect my desk will always be just the way it is, even to my two favorite milk glass mugs full of pens that won't write.

Picnics are easy. Sometimes I pack a basket with a loaf of fresh bread, a small jar of sweet butter, a wedge of Wisconsin cheese, a sharp knife for cutting, and a thermos of coffee. Then we stop work around noon and drive half a mile or so to the trout brook or the piny woods stretch and eat in the warm sun. We seldom talk much. Jill is never a talker, sometimes I ask her a question and never do get an answer. I talk in spurts, sometimes spilling over like water over a dam, sometimes with just a trickle. But it is good to sit silent, drinking the hot coffee and looking at the stream flowing by. Silence can be a communication too. There is peace in the stream, in the green of the woods, in the cloudless June sky. And in the fact that we do not have to do anything about anything at the moment.

When we drive home, the garden needs attention, the cockers all need baths, dust has gathered on the trestle table, and the wellhouse definitely must be repainted. But we have had a piece of time without pressing responsibilities and we are ready again to go to work.

Leisure is a rare commodity in this time, and we need it. Ladies no longer dress up in flowered frocks and rock on porches in the summer afternoons. They are in blue jeans weeding madly. Men no longer sit with their feet up talking, without rancour, about the fact that the world is in a bad way. Men are fixing things or changing their clothes to go somewhere for something. There are always meetings. Church, School Board, Community Chest, Red Cross, Cancer Committee, Heart Fund. Nobody fritters away any time, and of course time is too valuable to fritter.

But the spirit needs renewing and what a renewal a little quiet time can be! One needs to look at the sky, at the countryside. Or in the city, one needs to sit on a park bench half an hour or an hour and just not be doing anything. A good many problems solve themselves if one is quietly looking as the stars come out. Fatigue blows away on the stir of evening air. Even grief is lessened when one sits quietly in the dusk as the fireflies light the meadow.

We busy ourselves too much. Now and then the well of our spirit needs time to fill up so that we can draw from it again. And when someone says to me that he or she cannot bear to be alone, I always feel sad for it means the level in the well is so low that no bucket can reach it. Also the people who skim like waterbugs over the surface of life are in a bad way when they need spiritual depths to sustain them. But those who are able to have a quiet time for a small piece of day always find an armor against trouble.

In June, I find it easy to drop everything and sit in the garden and watch the butterflies and admire the opening roses. Suddenly I feel the wideness of the universe and gain a new sense of well-being. My thoughts are not profound. I think about how much the lemon thyme has spread over the flagstones. I think, without anxiety, that we ought to do something about the rose canes next fall. I think the wasps should not gather right under the arm of my chair. But chiefly I am absorbed in just being.

Then, restored, I am ready to shell peas again!

On a June night, the moon steers her silver sail over a quiet sea of sky. Lights are on all along the valley. Children, freed from the imaginary horror of homework, skim about in every yard. They are drunk with the vacation ahead which will bore them in a couple of weeks. The leaves are so thick that we only see a faint gleam from our nearest neighbor's house. All winter, when the blizzards are raging, we peer out and say, "Well, they are all right, their lights are on so the electric has not gone off yet."

Now we are isolated by the heavy growth of the trees so that we might be islanded in green. The telephone is our only link with our neighbors and that is chancy for if I lift the receiver, there is often only a loud buzz. But the road is open and no drifts pen us in, so we know we can drive out any minute if we need to. We miss saying that the Thomsons must be out at a meeting, or that they have come home and are safely tucked in. But living in a green world has compensations too. I am reminded of Hudson's *Green Mansions*, a very special favorite of mine. For we are able to watch birds flying, see rabbits hopping after our carrots, hear every note of the cicadas. The chunk of the frogs down by the pond is clear, not obsured by any traffic or any sound of radios or hi-fi's.

Our country ears and eyes are attuned to the crackling of a twig as some wild neighbor goes by, maybe a 'coon or woodchuck. I sometimes think I can hear things growing on a still night.

I like to open the door just before I go to bed, and lean out and listen to the world breathing. June fills the air with sweetness, and the meadow brims with moonlight. And I have a quick sense of the loveliness of summer.

June light is gold as afternoon lengthens. It is queer that light is never the same in any two seasons. June sun is like a Chinese lantern, warm and richly glowing, but not yet too intense. It is lifegiving, and it is dreamy. The hot dry spell is ahead. The trees have a liquid look about their leaves, from thundershowers. The lawn grass is almost too green to be believable. The garden grows overnight. Some of the early lettuce begins to bolt. The rosy chard and spinach have lustrous leaves.

The Japanese beetles have not yet come, so we do not have to spray incessantly. Everything is quite perfect. Nights are cool enough for a small fire on the hearth. Days are full of poetry from the first silvery webs on the grass to the fireflies carrying their lanterns in the dark.

The leaves of the spring bulbs begin to turn brown and lie down. But it is a world of blossoming with the roses and the late, late lilacs. It is good shampooing weather for the dogs, for they can roll in clean grass and dry in the sun. The Irish lies flat, paws upheld, and lets the sun bake her.

Neighbors drop in, easing aching backs as they sit down. The talk is of gardens, naturally, and whether we shall get the tomato blight again this year. Everyone has a theory and a remedy. The sweet rocket is spreading, someone says, and so it is. It has taken over half of the side yard. Someone else says he will plant potatoes this year, trying for a succession crop. His first planting is up and those will be pearl nuggets, but he wants enough to "put down" because potatoes have been so poor the past few years.

In the pale green light of dusk, the neighbors go home to finish the chores, let the cat out, let the dog out, let the cat in, let the dog in. And after supper, to reach for a bottle of linament for those garden-weary muscles.

Jill gets out the garden encyclopedia and announces the Mimosa tree should eventually be eight feet tall!

The Fourth of July is really hot. Heat simmers on the corn rows, and the Firemen's Clambake finds everyone almost on the boil along with the clams, chicken, fish fillets and sweet corn. The men drink quantities of cool draught beer, children consume bottle after bottle of orange pop, the women reach for iced cucumber sticks. I used to play at horseshoes while the clams were steaming but I decided men can stand heat better than women, and gave it up. Nowadays I sit in the shade of an elm tree and watch the men rush about.

I am an addict of clambakes, but I have reservations. I have attended a good many, here and on the seashore in Massachusetts, and I find my natural cooking sense disturbed, although I never admit it. I do NOT think sweet corn should cook as long as lobsters or chicken. If you pile everything up in layers on the steaming seaweed and cover it all with a tarpaulin, you will get overdone steamers, done chicken, sweet corn that is mushy and tastes like clams, and potatoes that just have to be soggy. At clambakes I therefore eat the clams and lobsters and/ or fish. Skip the corn and potatoes. Corn is delicate and should be popped in boiling salted water very briefly and then fished out, slathered with melted butter, salt, freshly ground pepper and eaten at once. It should not taste of anything else either. The clam is a queen of shellfish, but corn should not taste like clams!

Potatoes are best cooked in the jacket—buried in coals or baked and then split open. An indefinite steaming period makes them acquire the consistency of wet sponges. But never mind, the clambake is fun, no matter what indignity the vegetables suffer!

In July, the grass has a singed look, lilac leaves droop, roses are full-blown. The pond level lowers. We open the well-cover and shine a flashlight down to be sure we have water enough for the next washing. At night, fireflies lantern the meadow. The air is sultry and it seldom cools off before late evening.

This is our hottest month. Often when it rains, it is hotter than ever, a steamy tropical heat. My Virginia friend says you never really know the South unless you live through summer there, and possibly this is also true of New England. Perhaps we need to experience the heat before the apple-crispness of fall comes.

In any case, July has its rewards. In early morning there is a

pearly freshness about the world and the birdsongs are cool
and liquid. The air smells sweet, of roses and ripening tomatoes
and honeysuckle. Breakfast is pleasant on the terrace on the
cool side of the house, and we linger over it, fortifying ourselves for the day of climbing temperature. And although my
English friend tells me hot tea is the best antidote for hot
weather, I often have my coffee iced.

When we go for a swim in the pond, the water has a reedy
smell and looks like dark glass. There are enough springs to
keep it reasonably cool but it is not exactly brisk. In the upper
reaches, where the brook comes in, the blue heron stands on
one leg as motionless as if he were painted there. Barn swallows
swoop over.

Sometimes a plump woodchuck ambles along on the way to
eat our hybrid corn. Deer come down infrequently and
cautiously for too much woodland has been cut down in recent
years. We used often to stop and wait while they crossed the
road, the fawn's delicate hooves twinkling along beside his
mother. Now and then a weasel streaks along the old stone
fence beyond the pond, or a red fox looks down at us. At dusk-
dark the bats come out.

Last spring an owl lived in the stone fence, and his melancholy cry sounded all night long. I don't know why he decided
to live in the fence, but the grey boulders have plenty of comfortable nooks between them. Chipmunks and squirrels poke
inquisitive noses from dark holes as we go by. Pheasants tiptoe
along the edges where bittersweet and barberry grow. The
swamp back of the pond is home to a good many small people.
The mourning doves retreat to it, the mother pheasants nest

along the edges, the hylas and snakes and turtles live there. Where the brook flows in and gets lost, muskrats (which we call mushrats hereabouts) raise their young.

There is no way for a human being to get into the swamp itself. It is full of huckleberries and blueberries and we used to try putting down planks and teetering in far enough to pull down the branches and pick the smoke-blue berries. We gave it up when I fell in one day and was hauled out with difficulty. Swamp mud and water and treacherous hummocks that slide away from under you, do not make safe terrain. I am glad of it. When the hunting season begins and the fatal guns pop in the upper woods, I know the swamp people are safe.

I hope that after we are gone, nobody will drain that swamp and put a development there. As wildlife refuges diminish, mankind also suffers. A dust bowl is easy to come by, but hard to reclaim. And as we drive about the countryside and see new raw stretches where a good stand of trees grew, we know the water table is lower. The bird population will diminish, and no amount of spraying can replace the birds, valuable not only for their beauty and their music, but because many of them eat almost their own weight in insects daily.

And we should have an impossible problem trying to pollinate by hand, whereas the bees manage with no fuss and bother. We should, I feel, be very careful about upsetting the balance of Nature.

It is amazing how fast an Irish setter grows. At seven weeks, Holly was easy to tuck under my arm as I went around the house. At four months, she tipped the scales at thirty-six pounds. Weighing her was difficult as our scales are upstairs, in the bathroom at the top of the steepest stairs in the world. We enlisted the help of our neighbor, Joe, to weigh her. First she had to be carried up, dangling legs and tail and looking over her shoulder in great surprise at this new game. (We had not encouraged her to climb the stairs because the upstairs is reserved for company.) Joe got weighed, then lifted her up again and weighed them both, Holly licking him effusively all the time. Then we subtracted Joe's weight, all of us getting a different result. And then we decided her weight was according to the books, and gave her a nice snack as a reward.

The cockers weigh in all the way from Linda's petite eighteen pounds to Especially Me's twenty-seven. I prefer cockers that are compact and easy to gather up, practical to travel with. And I do not see why breeders can never let any breed be the way it should be. They invariably try to change it. They bred out the noble Collie head to a sharp wedge. They bred some other breeds until the powerful rear turned into something resembling a pair of stilts. They bred the good hunting cocker into a mass of coat under which the dog is invisible. And of late, alas, they are breeding a new type of cocker with a head that looks as if a potato topped it. The high dome and extra-long ears tend to draw the eyelids down and give the cocker a warped look, melancholy instead of merry. Anybody, I reflect, would look depressed at carrying a feather bed around. Our cockers are definitely not in the mode, with their smooth short body coats and sensible muzzles. And not a drooping eyelid in the place.

So far they haven't gotten around to re-modeling the Irish. The flowing grace, dark mahogany coat, well-shaped head and triumphant plume of a tail are still untouched. And probably will be until the Irish gets too popular, at which point someone will begin to breed something "curioser and curioser."

I suppose the answer to all this is that people are never content. How many marriages have been ruined because the wife tries to make her husband into something different? Or a man who chose a wife because she was good, gentle, and gay suddenly wants her to be a glamour girl seal-sleek and sharply sophisticated? Parents, too, keep trying to make their children into something other than they naturally are. Few business men care about their sons writing poetry or painting pictures. Few executive clubwomen want daughters that are "different."

A good idea, I thought, picking the beans for supper, to let well enough alone.

Coming out of church Sunday, I looked up at the spire. Esther Forbes, in her delightful book, *Rainbow on the Road,* calls the New England church spires "icicles in the sky." This is a happy description. For the spires look so slender lifting above the green valleys. And they have a pure clean silhouette. A church without a spire is not a church to me. I have seen some modern churches, low, flat, shed-like in shape. Or looking like a collapsed balloon. Now a lifting line is an inspiration to me, a flat line is not. My eyes can follow our steeple up into the infinite blue and my thoughts are lifted nearer to God.

Our church, re-roofed in 1732, has not been changed much. When we worship there, we go in automobiles and park them where the old carriage shed stood, but the church itself has the traditional architecture, simple, dignified. Sun slants through the small-paned windows. The furnace is a concession to our modern weakness and the dark pews now have pads on them. The lighting works by switches instead of tapers being carried about. But the church itself is still the kind of sanctuary that Lafayette and Washington visited when they came through our valley, and I like to think they would still feel quite at home in it.

Families now sit together, instead of the men on one side and the women on the other. And this is, I think, an improvement. It is just as well to have Father's help when Junior decides to make paper airplanes and launch them during the Gloria Patri when Mother is busy keeping the baby from climbing over the back of the pew to pick roses from a tempting hat.

I believe it is a fine thing to go to church regularly. Our village news sheet says "Attend the church of your choice."

There are many reasons to go to church, aside from the inspiration of the sermon and the music. First of all, it gives one a chance to step aside from the problems of life for an hour and sit quietly, and reassess values. Daily worries and anxieties suddenly reduce themselves to a fair proportion. And then it is good to gather people together who believe in the power of God —or good—and all bent on a serious hour of worship. People gather incessantly for political rallies, club meetings, committees, all full of controversy. How blessed to spend an hour thinking about the meaning of life.

Not all communities are as fortunate as ours. We have a federated church, which means that as long as you seriously believe in God and intend to lead a Christian life, you are eligible to be a member no matter what sect you belong to. I think the church would be a greater force in this age if it were a single united congregation. Minor theological differences should not separate men of good faith.

On this particular Sunday, our young minister had preached about the brief period when the carpenter's Son called the fishermen on the shore of Galilee to pick up their nets and follow Him. I fell to thinking that the greatest miracle in the history of man is that all over the world even now, people are still trying to "pick up their nets and follow Him." In spite of wars, oppressions, dictatorships, nobody has ever been able to permanently get rid of God. This is a comforting thought in this atomic and satellite age.

The farmers are haying now, and in late afternoon great loads of hay come down the country roads. The smell of hay is heady and sweet in the air, and a fine choking dust rises.

Heat simmers in the fields, and the farmers burn to a deep copper. Small boys reach the height of glory riding on top of the hayloads. The barns are filled almost to the rafters and there is a great scurrying of mice and the swallows are agitated. The barn cats have good hunting.

Haying goes on most of the hot summer days. Much of the year, the farmers do extra jobs stringing fences along boundary lines, repairing machinery, cultivating gardens for weak cityfolk. But nothing calls them from the hayfields except the fire siren, which probably means some barn is burning. Hay seems to generate so much heat that even a small thunderstorm may set an explosive fire. I wonder at the eternal patience and persistence of a farmer when he has just put in the biggest load of hay of the summer and loses the crop and the barn too.

Jill spends the dry hot days in the garden hoeing and spraying and picking potato bugs and Japanese beetles. She carries pails of water from the pond to encourage the succession planting of lettuce. When the squash leaves fold up, she carries more pails. She comes in with her hair a damp cap on her head, her sweatshirt justifying its name.

"Those colored pictures in the catalogues," she remarks, "never mention how much work is involved!"

But when we have stuffed baby pattypan squash for supper, she allows it is well worth the labor. Or zucchini in a casserole with tomatoes and onion and Parmesan cheese. People who do not care for squash are usually those who rely on store vegetables. A crook-necked squash should be picked when it is not much thicker than two thumbs. The skin is pale and waxy, not knobby and mustard yellow. It should slice with a table knife. The slices, dusted with seasoned flour, can be sautéed in butter with a suggestion of diced onion in it. This is squash as it should be. By the time a squash must be peeled, I am losing interest in it.

Cucumbers, on the other hand, are delicious when they are ripe. They turn to the color of a new-minted penny and are large and plump. Then we split them lengthwise, scrape out the seeds and stuff them with anything from poultry dressing to creamed chicken. And bake in seasoned milk, not quite covering them.

Baked stuffed cucumbers and a tossed green salad make a gardener's supper. For dessert a bowl of everbearing raspberries with sweet cream, and plenty of coffee. Afterward Jill decides she will plant another row of cucumbers next year.

Beans are the bumper crop. Once they begin to bear, beans do not give up until the killing frost. Even while we pick basketfuls, we can see new bean blossoms opening on the vines. We learned the hard way that there can be too many beans in a garden. The first few years we put down in the freezer enough beans to supply the Army, Navy and Air Force. We ate beans day after day. Still they kept coming. We gave basketfuls away —but this was not easy, for everybody else was trying to give us beans too. Now we are cautious about how many beans we plant.

Beans will stand almost anything once they are established. They will even bear if we have to go away for a few days and the beetles make lacework of all the leaves. It is a little discouraging to come home exhausted from a dog show and shed our store clothes and have to go right out and PICK BEANS. But the true gardener will never let anything be wasted.

So beans it is!

It is a fine thing that America has moved outdoors. I can remember when a barbecue was an uncommon sight. Now every back yard has a cooking setup. They may tower like fortresses and have dozens of subsidiary gadgets as well as chopping blocks, serving shelves and rotary spits. Or they may be a few bricks with a broiler unit from an old stove set on top. The portable grills that can be wheeled around are inexpensive and give a good bed of coals for cooking. And one of the best outdoor cooking units I ever saw was one Smiley Burnette made from an old oil drum.

The yearning to cook outdoors is rather strange when you consider how inconvenient it is. Indoors, you have push-button heat control. You set timers. It is just a step from the herb shelf to the range. The modern kitchens make cooking so easy. So what do we do? We lug everything out the back door, utensils, dishes, seasonings, salads, meats, French bread, butter, dessert. Then we build a charcoal fire in the barbecue unit. (There are a hundred ways to do this, and all of them require time.) Then we wait until the fire is right, for you cannot turn a charcoal fire to high with a button. It takes its own time. Finally you cook. Then you eat. Then you gather everything up and lug it back to the house again.

You always make extra trips too. Somebody goes back for the coffee. Somebody goes for the salad set which you forgot. Somebody whips back to get the ice cream resting in the good old reliable electric refrigerator. And then some guest wants sugar in his coffee!

Why do we do it? It doesn't make sense. But it is true a charred hamburger eaten outdoors tastes delicious. Possibly we have a deep racial heritage from the days when the coffeepot always boiled at the edge of the campfire.

Possibly it gives us a sense of freedom from routine. Or possibly we like the tent of the sky overhead as we unwrap the ears of corn that have been roasting. Whatever the reason, eating outdoors has become a national pastime. I even know city people who set up a portable grill on a balcony outside an apartment and crawl out to cook their steaks in the smoky air of the city.

My own emotions about this subject are deep. I would rather sit wrapped to the teeth in sweaters and scarves while a chill wind blows, and have a burned frankfurter, than eat a fine dinner inside. I would rather simmer in the summer sun and baste the chicken on the grill than cook it inside in an insulated oven. Jill says I begin suggesting outdoor meals before the snow is off the ground and that I am always persuading her in October that it is not really cold by the pond.

Actually with a little practice, outdoor cooking can be elegant. The first rule is to start the fire AHEAD of time. Usually it is just right for cooking as you serve the dessert. The second rule is to load everything you will need on trays or in baskets and get everyone who expects to be fed to do some of the lugging. Before I learned this, I used to be so tired I did not want to eat, for our pond is quite a stretch from the house and after twenty trips back and forth, I was tired out.

The third rule is to have self-service, for it is hard for the cook-hostess to keep running about with platters of barbecued chicken or garlic bread wrapped in foil. If the food is there, guests can jolly well help themselves and not simply lie down in the nearest chaise and brightly accept chair service.

And after the fire dies down and supper is over, the wise

hostess will intercept any guest who tries to sneak back to the house without carrying anything. If every guest takes a trayful, the clean-up is easy.

I learned this after one nearly fatal shore dinner we gave in the summerhouse down by the pond. The pond is about a block from the kitchen door through a gate and across the vegetable garden and past the raspberries. We had asked twenty or more guests, and a few extras dropped in. It took us all day to get everything lugged down to the pond, and then we had pails and pails of clams to wash and put in kettles (we ran out of kettles) and nothing to cook the lobsters in but a washboiler which was too big to go over the barbecue anyway.

Everyone said it was a lovely party. The clams were delicious, so was the lobster. We rushed the corn from the garden while the lobster cooked and filled the clothesbasket with husks. The corn was delicious too, they all said. Everyone ate three or four ears, some ate five. The melted butter was served in a quart bowl with a new paintbrush for spreading. The salad was crisp and dressed with a light garlic dressing. The melon balls with mint made a fine ending.

It took a day and a half to clean up after this affair. Pails of clamshells, pails of lobster shells, dozens of limp paper plates, wet paper cups, drifts of paper napkins, and then all those corncobs! And melted butter over everything.

"I hope you're satisfied," said Jill as she made her second trip to the dump.

Now when we entertain down by the pond, we have one main dish and a salad and a dessert that can be eaten from our hands, not in separate dishes. And we never, never serve anything that has a shell. We learned the hard way. "Use your

head to save your heels," Mama used to say, and how right she
was!

This week we took Holly back to Boston to spend an afternoon with her celebrated parents and her breeder. It was the
first time since she was seven weeks old that she had seen them.
It was quite an experience. Mother Holly skipped around getting in people's laps and paying little attention to her daughter.
Father sat in his wing chair looking like a banker. Being an
international champion, he feels important. When Jill took out
the camera, he crossed his paws, lifted his head and posed. We
wanted a royal family portrait. But big Holly (Champion Red-
Log's Strawberry Blonde) wandered to the kitchen where something good was simmering on the range. By the time we got her
back, young Holly was upstairs changing the furniture around
in the bedrooms. Meanwhile, Father, bored with posing, slipped
out the front door and got into our car, which had one open
door. He wanted a ride, he indicated. No amount of coaxing
and hauling on our part budged him an inch. Paula, the breeder,
was brushing big Holly and posing her for the portrait. Finally
she came out and got Int. Ch. Red Star of Hollywood Hills to
abandon the hope of an immediate ride and go inside again.
We got them arranged, and my Holly, tired from her upstairs
work, hung her tongue out half a yard. I kept tucking it back
in, and it slipped. We were finally ready for the important picture of three Irish, and at that point Cricket, Holly's younger
sister, bounced in from the back porch and jumped around.
Paula hauled her away, protesting, and I pushed Holly's tongue
back in. By this time, Father was ready to go back to clipping

coupons and he left the wing chair and took his briefcase to the kitchen. Big Holly got in my lap.

When things were organized again there was a breathless moment as Jill snapped the shutter. It would have been better if the flash bulb had gone off, but it didn't. It was defective.

"Animal photography," murmured Jill, gritting her teeth.

We began all over, while Paula squeaked a toy poodle to keep the banker interested. It kept him interested all right, but drove my Holly into fits, for she had never seen a squeak toy such as this in her life.

In the end, as the sun was setting, the royal family portrait was taken. Then while Jill put away all the trappings which seem inevitable with a camera, Red Star slipped out and got back in the car and clung firmly to the seat when we told him he could not have a ride NOW. He was quite fretful, in a gentlemanly way, as he was hauled out.

Like most family reunions, it was wearing. But rewarding. All afternoon, I kept noticing how like Holly is to her mother, and yet how like her father too. Every once in a while, Holly feels noble and she acts noble. (This is from Father.) She will be noble five or ten minutes, grave as a judge. The next ten she leaps from sofa to sofa and skims through the air. (Mother.) I mentioned, with hesitation, the trouble we had keeping her inside the fence.

"Oh," said Paula airily, "big Holly can take a ten-foot one with no trouble. No trouble at all. She climbs."

On the three-hour drive home, I told Jill that Holly was the best of both sides of her family. She had, I said, her father's sound sense and stability and yet her mother's elfin spirit and grace and charm. I said she was noble but not stuffy. And I said she had her father's head and elegant chest but her mother's lively candid eyes. And her charm. After I had worked this out for fifty miles, Jill said, "so all right. Holly is perfect. You are completely besotted over this Irish."

I retired into a hurt silence. We got home and Holly indicated she wanted her supper fast.

After she had eaten and had fresh water, Holly let herself out by jumping on the doorlatch and thumbing it with a firm paw. We warmed up our own supper.

"You know," said Jill thoughtfully, "I do think our Holly sort of combines the best qualities of her father and mother."

I held my tongue.

When my daughter came for the weekend, she took one look at the pond and said, "Oh, Mama." I suspect parents need to be nudged frequently about various things. Connie said there was so much algae in the pond that it was dreadful. We should take a broom and SWEEP it, she said. I never believe in taking a negative attitude with the younger generation. So I said yes, we should sweep it. Well, the pond is nine feet deep in the center and swimming with a broom in one hand turns out to be quite a proposition! It is practically impossible to swim and sweep simultaneously. In the end, the algae took its own course.

The truth is that you may have a Hollywood sort of pool with a painted bottom, tile sides, water pumped in and out, or you have just a plain farm pond, plus frogs, turtles, waterbugs, and algae in season. Also a watersnake now and then gliding along the edge. A natural pond is edged with wild iris, forget-me-nots, and the water is far from sterile. Minnows swish by,

frogs jump in and out, birds skim over looking for insects. In autumn leaves spread over the surface and my last swim is usually quite leafy. The brook purls in cool and ferny from the upper reaches. I like it. If we dumped something in to kill the algae, we would have just another swimming pool.

It is a law of Nature that a natural pond fosters wildlife, and a Hollywood swimming pool is just for swimming. As I happily poke across the pond, I am glad that ours is just a farm pond and I don't mind pushing the algae aside for I know it is food for many creatures.

As I climb out and sit on the bank, I reflect that one cannot conceivably have everything. There is always a choice. I myself prefer to put up with algae, and I might feel uneasy in a cerulean fancy swimming pool without so much as one small minnow in it. I like the sense of living that belongs in my pond. And when I sit on the bank sipping a glass of lemonade with fresh mint in it, I like to see the frogs go back to their accustomed places and sit eying the water. They consider me an intrusion but not a menace.

And we are satisfied, all of us, because we do not encroach on one another. We peaceably mind our own business. Which is a very good idea, I think. It might be a good idea for nations to pursue.

What a great gift water is, I think, as I climb on the bank feeling cooled and refreshed. Actually, I understand, man can live longer without food than without water. How casually we turn the faucets in our houses and let the water run. We simply assume that there must be all the water we want. But without water, mankind is helpless. The rains are lifegiving to the crops, so also are the winter snows which melt and sink into the ground in the end. The rivers which flow through our countryside provide the electric power which keeps us furnished with light and heat and electric appliances. The tumbling brooks not only make a home for the shining trout but carry water on down the watershed to the lakes without which we soon might be a desert area. Even the dew which sparkles in the sunrise on the grass gives support to plant life when the drought is over the valley.

Those of us who are countrydwellers know the value of water. We watch the streams and rivers during a dry season, and mark the lack of flowing water. When lakes and ponds diminish we are careful of our own water, even if we have artesian wells. Most of us have surface, dug wells, but even artesian wells can give out. When we have weekend guests from the city, I note with horror that they turn on the faucets and let the water run indefinitely. Even in the last terrible shortage of water, all the pleas of the officials in the cities could not make people stop letting the faucets run.

In the country, we have Nature to discipline us. A few weeks of carrying pails of water from a never-failing spring up the hill made us realize how precious water is. I discovered water is very heavy to lug, and a pailful does not go very far after you get it in the house. You just go back for another before you know it! In July, water is an important subject of conversation at the village store. In fact, it takes priority.

"How's your well doing?"

"Figure she's kind of low."

"Need a good soaking rain."

"Yeah. Do."

Then we carry our groceries home and figure out ways of saving water. We can hand-wash dishes instead of using those gallons in the dishwasher. We can hand-wash lingerie instead of running the clothes washer. We can, and do, take showers instead of tub baths. We save the sudsy dish water to do the dog pans in.

And we get through the worst of the dry spell very well unless we have a houseful of city guests for the weekend. Then we spend three days resting the well and "letting it come back" as the saying goes.

A day is a unit. It begins, flows like a small rivulet toward eternity, ends as we fall asleep. No day can ever be like any other day, for no two experiences are exactly alike. Often we spend a lot of energy trying to recapture some delight, but nothing repeats itself. We can store precious moments away in memory but never relive them. Life is a process of growth and is no more static than the seasons. And the roses I gather today are not the same as those of yesterday. Some are more fully open, some as the season progresses, are smaller. There is a slight color variation too.

This one unit of a day lies ahead as I wake up on a still July morning, and I must consider what I shall make of it. My day will not be sensational, but filled with small delights.

First the cockers and Irish go out and the lawn is criss-crossed with bounding paws as they investigate who has been there in the night. Ears fly out, tails wag, noses are quite drunk with sniffing. Coolness is a fine gauze over the earth then, and we savor it fully, for later it will be hotter than boiling maple syrup. The giant sugar maples cast wide shadows and squirrels seem to fly in the upper branches. Swallows swoop from the barn across the road.

Jill makes coffee. "I wish it could taste as good as it smells," she remarks, sniffing the fragrance. I cook the eggs in the covered coddlers we found in a junk shop once. A fresh country egg cooked in an English coddler with an acorn-size piece of butter melting on top and seasoned salt and freshly ground pepper is a fine start for a day's work. Since we gave up hens after the war, we get our eggs from a neighbor, big brown ones, often double-yolked.

There is a great difference in the flavor of eggs. I am not over-particular about food, I like it. But the egg is either perfect or you can have it, as far as I am concerned. When you break it, the yolk should not lie flat and hopeless in the middle of a watery white. The yolk must be upstanding, butter-yellow and independent enough so it doesn't break and run all over the minute you put knife to the shell. The white should not be cloudy or runny.

And the flavor—ah, the flavor. When I go to the city I give up eggs for the duration. The pale tasteless blobs are not for me. I want an egg worth its salt. Seasoned salt.

After breakfast, we do the maintainance chores. When I was involved with Mrs. Gilbreth's book on Management in the Home, I had a bad time. Motion study is fascinating but when I tried to chart ours, I had to give up. No matter how you chart and plan and figure, motion at Stillmeadow cannot be tabulated. My first attempt ran like this: do dishes. (Holly wants to come in.) Sweep kitchen floor. (Jonquil brings in a mole.) Sweep kitchen again. Dispose of mole. Make beds. (Holly and Teddy remake them while playing with a ball.) Make them. Dust. (As if that did any good.) Answer phone (A marathon, as phone is in far corner of front living room and I am in back kitchen by now washing dog pans.) Phone goes dead before I get there. Rings again just as Jill is out in the kennels and I am in the back yard picking something. Mad race. Phone dead again. Empty ash trays. (Holly has emptied them on the floor.)

Manage finally to make it to phone on last ring. "Is this Gertie?" Hang up and go back to wherever I was, which am not sure of.

I am a great admirer of Mrs. Gilbreth and I think most home-keepers do run around a lot unnecessarily. System is the thing, if you can have it.

But it just isn't possible for us. We fly around on those maintenance chores for a good hour and a half, not speaking to each other unless we bump in the narrow doorways. We can't even regulate the dog-feeding for somebody always needs a pill added, somebody else needs yeast, and somebody whose calories we count has to be fed alone.

And then, when we are reasonably in order, there is the middle kitchen. Elswyth Thane once pointed out that if we had a middle kitchen, we must have *three* kitchens. This shows how the research mind of a historical novelist works. It is no problem to us, it is just the middle kitchen. Then there is the back kitchen. We have no front kitchen at all.

The back kitchen is the worst. I clean it up after supper and by morning it looks like a junk shop. Formerly it was, I suppose, a summer kitchen. Now there are times I wish I had a machete to hack through it. It has the washing machine, so there is always laundry on the counters. It has the dog's medicine cabinet, grooming counter, food shelves. It also has all the cleaning supplies, including the snaky vacuum cleaner. It has a trash basket always brimming. It has a mahogany side chair for me to sit in when I give up. It has Holly's daybed. It has all the African violets not yet in bloom. It also has grass seed, a bag of salt for the asparagus bed, and that old banjo clock which won't run. In winter it is garlanded with jackets, hoods, mittens, boots. In summer it wears bathing suits on a hook by the woodshed.

This is its normal condition, but of course it is never normal. A fine silt of book wrappers, cartons, clothes to go to the cleaner, empty mason jars, bags of sunflower seeds, seems to settle over the room. And no matter how I work at it, getting everything put away or disposed of, by the next morning a whole new crop of oddments is there. I often sing, as I lug things from one counter to the other, "Oh, bury me not on the lone prairie," with the idea that I should be buried right in the back kitchen so that my spirit can rise up and dematerialize the piles of Sunday papers and the old *Kennel Gazettes* ("Don't throw them away YET").

As we drive along the country roads, after the day's work is over, the unit of the day seems to have been a very small one. Where did the hours go? Now there is time for a ride in the sunset, for the evening chores, supper and a night dip in the pond. The villages hereabouts have no street lights, fortunately, so the gleam of lamps shines from the windows of the old houses. The white church spires catch the last flare of the ebbing sun. The villages still keep the look of New England, but the countryside is changing. The old stone fences diminish as people quietly drive out to take the best stones for terraces, paths, fireplaces, or barbecues. A good many stone foundations have the best of old stone fences in them. Farmers sometimes string a few strands of rusty wire along the top of denuded walls to keep the cattle in.

Meadows are still rich with hay, and occasional herds of black Angus raise their furry heads to look at us as we go by. The calves look like overgrown teddy bears. A few sheep and some Holsteins and Guernseys are pastured in the good grass. But all too often a good farm has been sold and bulldozers are at work. Candy-box houses spring up and Pleasant Valley development is on the way. It was a pleasant valley once. The houses have yards just big enough for a clothesline. The picture windows have a good view of the house across the street. Shocking pink, mustard yellow, lime green and sky blue are the favored colors.

I do not blame the people who want inexpensive homes outside the industrial centers. I do heartily blame the real estate men who would sell twelve-foot lots if someone devised a house that could be built in ten. There is naturally more money to be made if you have more lots. It is easier to level a stand of pines, flatten an old orchard than to tuck the houses here and there with a piece of the green world for every one.

But when I see a two-hundred-year-old white oak go down, I hope the development men have an uneasy sleep that night. True, they may gain space for a garage, but that oak could cast grateful shade on children for many years to come.

I blame the villages even more. Many of them now have zoning boards, but some of them believe man's freedom is jeopardized by any kind of regulation. Most zoning boards lack power to enforce their own rules. Some of them spend so much time bickering as to whether Mr. Jones can have a cement mixer in his yard when Mr. Smith doesn't like to have it outside his picture window, that they never get on to the consideration of the whole area. It is always possible to kill the goose that lays those golden eggs, and I foresee the time to come when nobody will bother visiting New England to savor the natural beauty. In one village I know of, the Main street was bordered by arching ancient elms, and if there is a tree lovelier than the elm, I do not know it. So last summer the town selectmen cut down every single elm in order to widen Main street and speed up the traffic. Autos can skim by pretty fast now over the hard pavement blazing with sun.

We take our sunset drives on yet-untroubled roads, where the brooks run clear close to the edge. Wildflowers grow on either side in spring, bouncing-bet comes later, and soon goldenrod and chicory will be in bloom. Bittersweet and black alder mark summer's end. The farmhouses are set snugly against the slope of the hills with whole meadows for dooryards. The barns and silos have a gracious look, settled as if for generations to come.

When we come home after such a drive, Stillmeadow is shadowy, waiting for the lights to be turned on. The dogs rush about as excited as if we had just come back from Arabia. They check the yard to be sure no enemy has come by. Then they settle with long satisfied sighs.

What has my day been worth, this unit of time given to me? Possibly I said a comforting word where it was needed, or offered practical help to someone in trouble. Nothing worldshaking, to be sure. I cannot influence the world. I can only live every day as well as I can, keeping my home, cherishing my neighbors, helping in the community in a small way.

But perhaps I have grown a little in understanding, patience, and lovingkindness. And perhaps I shall do better tomorrow, another precious unit of time.

A cool air stirs the ruffled curtains as I sit down with Katherine Mansfield's Journal, which I am re-reading. The moon is so bright that it gleams on the wide oak floorboards beyond the circle of lamplight. A hunting owl hoots in the swamp, and a hound halloos in the upper orchard. Otherwise it is a serene night, except for what we call the tree frogs beating their drums. I think they should be called cicadas, but whatever they are they sing the song of summer.

And tomorrow, I think drowsily, we must freeze more beans!

The turning wheel of the seasons rolls slowly now, in August. People walk without hurry. Cows seek the shade of oak or sugar maples in the pastures and chew their cud dreamily. The wild country cats tiptoe along the stone walls at dusk, instead of racing with tails flat out. The hounds bark in a halfhearted fashion when they tree something. Even the haying lacks the feverish haste of early summer, for most of the barns are full. Pumpkins and squash are ripe, corn silk darkens in the corn patches.

There is a hiatus between the hard work of midsummer and the brisk days of woodcutting, filling woodsheds, chopping kindling, to come. Weeding in the garden is about over. From now on, the vegetables can hold their own, weeds or no. High time too, says Jill, after all the tending they have had all summer. Nature and man both seem to me to move on a light rein for a short time, a restoring time.

I wonder whether the fact that so many vacations come in August is because of the heat itself or because it is a natural time for man and Nature to relax. I have read that energy is highest in October, and it may be so. If this is true, then August is the time for dreaming, for taking a thoughtful look at life, and for letting some chores go by the board.

However, if we have a litter of eight cocker puppies, there is not too much time for relaxing. Last week we had to be away over the weekend and my daughter, Connie, came to baby-sit.

Her condensed report was not very restful!

DEAR MAMA:

Arrived safely. And spent first two hours cleaning puppy pen, and occupants. Ate an egg. Went to bed. Got up. Fed puppies. Went to bed. Let Sister out. Went to bed. Let Sister in. Went to bed. Got up, played chase-the-mouse with that Siamese cat. (She was darling, tossing it.) Went to bed. Got up at one A.M., screamed at dogs, all yelling. Barked until three A.M. (lonesome for you). Read a fine book.

Friday, up at 6 to feed puppies. Let out dogs, put in dogs. Cleaned puppy pen. Chased strange terrier through hole in fence. Closed hole. Removed Jonquil's collar which stuck in her teeth. Caught Holly who escaped by opening gate. Lured her. Let dogs out and in. Fed puppies. One fell in Pablum. Gave him warm bath. Went to bed. Worried he might be cold. He was. Rubbed with warm towel an hour. Went back to bed. Up to let Jonquil in. Brought large very dead thing with her. Now understood why she didn't come in earlier. Caught her. Removed THING. Turned green.

Saturday. Mice in bedroom wall so not much sleep. Cleaned puppy pen and puppies, fed them. Holly had eaten through pen. Chased to excited cheering of cockers. Got her back. Propped shovel against hole, wheelbarrow against shovel. Dropped both on toe, am limping. Callers dropped in. Defrosted chocolate cake, made coffee. Nice time they had. Noticed a headache, remembered no time for lunch and only coffee for breakfast as Lilibet was eating Sister's breakfast at the time.

Leaving for train in fifteen minutes—no, Holly is out again. If you get in in time, phone Steve and Gustl.

And thank you for the MOST exciting weekend I've ever had, and why don't you come to the nice peaceful city for a REST?

Connie

In August, we turn toward autumn, here in New England. We have just grown accustomed to summer, it seems, when suddenly nights begin to cool off, and the light slants a little differently across the lawn in the afternoon as the sun changes its glare to a milder glow.

Colors change in the garden as russets and yellows replace the summer pinks and reds of roses. There is little white, except for the clematis and the mums. Nature is rubbing out the hues of summer's palette and splashing on the sharp tones of fall. Pumpkins begin to turn orange and eggplant brightens into deep purple. The roadside stands are a rendezvous for city folk, who buy everything from zinnias to pattypan squash.

Even in our rural countryside, roadside stands have become more and more like open-air grocery stores. You can buy fresh eggs (not raised by the man who runs the stand), oatmeal bread (not made by his wife) frozen Rock Cornish game hens (definitely raised by Mr. Victor Borge). You may buy plants or shrubs, jellies and pickles, fertilizer and birdhouses. It is a tribute to the ingenuity of the owner of the roadside stand, and it certainly adds interest to a drive in the country.

One does not have to be a flower-arranging expert to make lovely bouquets at this time of year. Wild grasses are feathering out in brown and mauve. Goldenrod is lovely when it is still in bud. Zinnias and marigolds are gay. Gladioli last until the first frost. It does help, however, to know just a few rules about making bouquets. Flowers need an understanding hand when they go into the container, and not to be simply jammed in a vase.

Now I have learned that not only is any home lovelier with the grace note of flowers but that a few rules can help make the bouquets charming. You can study flower-arranging for a long time and read many books but my expert friend Ruth Kistner boils it down. For a mass arrangement which is suitable for most of our houses, you choose a container that suits the type of bloom. Roses take to pewter, milk glass, silver or glass. Marigolds and zinnias like copper or brass or wood. Gladioli, being dramatic, are fine in fancy Chinese bowls or very heavy glass.

Anything will do as a container. In fact, once when Jill's son was small, he watched me doing a bouquet and said thoughtfully, "Why don't you ever use the vases? You always seem to use bread pans and sugar bowls and teapots and things."

I was then doing a very nice bouquet of fall flowers in a wooden bread tray. And I had a salt and pepper set ready for tiny bouquets. I had finished what I felt was a handsome arrangement of berries and greens in a glass pie pan.

Boiled down, and I do mean boiled down, the rules for a bouquet are simple. Delicate flowers take a delicate container. Heavy rough-textured ones need strong solid containers. Then you gather your flowers and if you have no garden, you pick weeds or grasses, or you buy a quarter's worth of daisies at a flower cart. Then you set up your container full of water and look balefully at it while you take off the lower leaves of your flowers. (They get gangrene under water and smell.)

Then you put in one flower which is two and a half times the height of the container. If you are using a basin or bowl, you will have to have a needle holder or a wad of chickenwire or some sand or else you will have to glue it to the bottom, for it won't stand still a minute.

Then you cut a flower stem two-thirds the length of the first and put it in slanting to the right. (It will slant right to the counter if you don't catch it.) And another, one-third the length of the first, goes to the left. This is easier as it is a shorter distance. Then you fill in the interstices (a good sound word) with blooms of various lengths. No two should be just the same and your scissors will fix that. Meanwhile you put the heavier blooms and darker colors toward the bottom and make a focal point of one special one at the lip of the container, but not leaning on it. (Never let anything lean.) The lighter tones go to the top. Finally you have to be sure each flower has a breathing space and does not cross stems with any other. And there you are, with a simple bouquet. If it falls over, you have made a mistake. Very well. If the Siamese cat eats off half of it, that is not your fault.

I am not, by any means, making fun of the art of flower-arranging for I think it is a creative art and a home beautiful with perfect arrangements is a joy. I have known men who do not know a rose from a cabbage to relax and feel easy because the room they walked into had two lovely bouquets. And a bare city apartment acquires charm with a few daisies in a small copper teapot. Flowers can really furnish a house. You don't sit on them or eat them, but they make you feel serene.

I am not deft, except with a French whisk or an egg beater, but two experiences in my life were so exciting that I shall never forget them. One was when I finally mastered the art of putting soggy clay on a potter's wheel and making a rather dizzy soup-bowl. The other was when I made a good bouquet.

Seven or eight of us in the valley took lessons in flower arrangement once a month when Ruth Kistner could stop off in New Haven and be driven over. We met at the house of a member, who provided lunch, and when I simply could not make my dried arrangement stand up, I was much comforted by lobster thermidor for lunch. When I finally achieved a handsome one, I carried it home in a carton and bore it proudly in. It had, I remember, everything in it from milkweed pods to bittersweet. It had a focal point of strawberry corn. And then it had oats and dried goldenrod and veronica. It was lovely. I set it proudly on the trestle table and sank down, exhausted. I dozed off while Jill broiled the chops and was roused by a chewing sound. Esmé, the Siamese, was polishing off the best of the arrangement!

Esmé also loved roses. She would lift her paw and knock off the biggest petals and then play games with them. Sometimes she took small nibbles. She ate violets too. And any time I had a perfect spring arrangement, I could walk in and see her leaning with interest over the best tulips.

But now when nobody disturbs my bouquets, I would give a good deal to have that dark wedge-shaped face leaning over them and that long velvet arm reaching out. I sometimes think nobody ever really appreciated my efforts as much as Esmé. She knew what I had on the table and the cobbler's bench. She was not only interested but helpful, in her own way.

There is one thing about a cat, especially a Siamese. Whatever you do is interesting!

I have never been able to understand the cat versus dog controversy. Cats are themselves, dogs are themselves. That is all there is to it. A well-furnished home has both. From a dog you get the passionate dependence, from a cat you get a sense that you must be worthy or the cat would simply move away. A cat is loyal, and has plenty of affection but it is on the basis that she or he grants it to you as a favor, and you must be grateful. A dog is wholly dependent, a cat wholly independent.

An example of the difference is that when I used to have to go away briefly, the dogs met me with wags and wild barks and carryings on. The cats spoke to me only in cold tones, implying that I was not worth bothering with. I went away. The Siamese went further, and cursed roundly in Siamese. The warm welcome of the cockers and Irish was fine, but the bitter remarks of the cats was fine too. In the end, they always forgave me for deserting them for a night and with great condescension acquired the warmest spot on my bed. After a few hours, the Siamese would give me a few licks with a sandpapery tongue. There was no mistake, she was forgiving me.

The Manx, Tigger, simply gave me a chilly look and vanished for the rest of the day. Let me worry where HE was, he had worried as to where I was. Around suppertime, he would mellow, and come in with a mouse. And when I screamed and took it away and put it outside, he sat down on the hearth and washed himself elaborately, saying plainly, Well, there it is, a man does his best, and what thanks does he get?

Esmé, the Siamese, had a fine sense of humor. She enjoyed sitting at the top of the stairs behind the stair rail. When an unwary cocker would come up, she shot out a sudden arm and slapped him soundly, her expression like that of the legendary Cheshire cat. She also liked to get inside a paper bag and suddenly an animated paper bag would fly around the room, most disconcerting to both cockers and Irish. She would pounce on me suddenly from the bookshelves and loved it when I dropped an armload of clean clothes.

The love affair between Esmé and Tigger was touching. He was by nature a sober, industrious cat who worked hard at his mouse business. Esmé was a femme fatale and also flighty. They would sleep with their paws around each other's neck, Tigger having done a hard night's work in the cellar. Suddenly Esmé, bored with peace, would turn on him and growl fiercely, pulling bitefuls of black fur from his neck. If he ignored this (just wanting to rest his feet and look at TV, as it were) she would pounce, attack, retreat, roll on the floor, address him plaintively. You don't give a fig for me, she would say in her firm Siamese voice. Was it for this I became your companion? The best years of my life, etc., etc. He would shrug and eye her with his big topaz eyes. I bring home the mice, he would indicate.

Mice never meant anything in her life. He would lug in a good one and lay it tenderly at her paws, and she would flip it over idly and then turn her back. She never even thanked him.

But when he died, she never recovered. She sat upstairs in the bathroom for a week. She ate almost nothing. She took her widow's weeds seriously. In time, she came back downstairs for chicken or spinach, but she was never gay again.

She did, however, condescend to catch one very small mouse in the barn and carry it delicately to the house and into my bedroom. She laid it on my bed and switched away, as if to assure me she could also be a mouser, but her heart was not in it.

We felt she needed another companion, and this proved to be disastrous. We brought home a blue-point Siamese named Moonlight, a nice conventional cat (the only Siamese I ever

knew with this temperament). Esmé nearly killed him. We introduced them gently, with a screen door between them, we followed all the rules. But the first time she could reach him, the whole air was full of silvery fur and Moonlight fled screaming. We spent some weeks shutting doors and finally shutting Moonlight in a dog carrying-crate for protection. But Esmé would utter such jungle sounds as would do credit to a tiger at the kill and would fling herself at the crate. If we had any idea she would cotton to an interloper, we were put in our place. So when Moonlight developed an inferiority complex and shook most of the time, we had to give it up. He wasn't Tigger, and we had to realize that she would have none of him.

Whenever friends say they don't care for cats, because cats have no feeling and no personality, I think of Esmé. She had both to give away.

Our next venture was with Aladdin, an Abyssinian, who came from California in a compartment with Dallas Burnette, and was a small, pipe-cleaner of a kitten with an apricot undercoat and a ticked uppercoat. He had mostly ears. His eyes were blue and innocent. Being introduced to a houseful of dogs did not bother him, although he had never seen a dog before. When they flew at him, he just eyed them and sat still.

He had no cat competition for Esmé had gone on to be with Tigger. But he had a lot of cockers and an Irish to adjust to. So he decided to be a dog. He imitated them in so far as possible, and in the end, got to be one of the gang. But he did two things they could not do. He got in the bathtub whenever possible and played with the water dripping from the faucet. He would, if feasible, get in the shower when anyone was taking one, and only get back out when the water was scalding. And he climbed trees.

He climbed expertly but he could not climb back down. We always had a ladder handy, but the time he got a hundred feet up in the sugar maple, we had to call for help. He clung, mewing pitifully, and he looked no bigger than a thimble up there in the branches. It made me dizzy to look at him. A neighbor came over and climbed up after him, and at the risk of his neck, brought him down.

I understood his predicament, for I can always climb up a

firetower or a ladder or go up on the Empire State Building, but I too can never feel comfortable about the descent. The ground just looks too far away after you get to a height. It not only sinks down, but it seems to sway.

"There's Aladdin up in the McIntosh again," Jill would say. "I don't know whether the ladder will reach, but I'll try." I would go in my room and shut the door. Eventually, covered with leaves and twigs, both would come in.

"If he only wouldn't just stick," Jill said. "I have to pry."

When the gladioli are at their best, summer is in full bloom. They will bloom until the first frost, and they are lovely in the house, for they keep so long. They have more variety in color than most flowers, too, from the ice-white with a touch of violet in the center to the dusky copper tones. If you strip off the green sheaths on the upper buds, they will open in the house. Glads make handsome bouquets in pewter or silver bowls. They do not look well just stuck in a tall vase. The stems should be cut in varying lengths and the blooms arranged in the container with the deeper colors at the base. I use a Sheffield silver oval server with an extra bottom container which originally kept creamed kidneys hot on an English breakfast table. If the day is very hot, I put a few ice cubes in the warmer part.

I also like an all-white bouquet of gladioli in a thumbprint glass compote. And if I have a few buds left over, they look happy in a milk glass mug.

Although I am so fond of gladioli, I will admit the foliage is homely. The plants stand up like fenceposts. The leaves are stiff and ungracious, so it is better to plant the bulbs in a cutting garden or at the edge of the vegetable garden. We plant ours at the end of the plot where the peas are.

When I gathered the glads this morning, I stopped to watch a load of hay lumber down the country road. The farmer was deep copper and his blue shirt dark with sweat. But he rode like a conqueror. He waved and grinned at me. Golden drifts of hay fell on the road behind him.

The air was golden too from the dust. I wondered when man first discovered that if he cut and dried meadow grass it would feed stock all winter. And who, for that matter, discovered the value of silage? So many things we take for granted were amazing at first. The early women who sun-dried preserves, the ones who found out that a pan of milk set at the side of the hearth would result in pot cheese, those who froze pies in winter in their pie cupboards—these were benefactors. And as for the millions spent now in cosmetics—well, it all began with rose water and glycerin, cucumber juice (to whiten the skin) and orris root and so on.

Everything, I decided, cutting the shell-pink glads for the trestle table in the family room, everything has a beginning. From lye and ashes came the fragrant pastel soaps we use today. From frozen dried pumpkin pies in winter we have progressed to frozen strawberries and asparagus in January, and whole meals ready at the lift of the freezer top. From open fires to heat the house, we moved on to shutting the fire up in a stove, then in a firebox with pipes to lead the heat around the house. Shortly, there may not even be furnaces, just a push-button to radiate heat stored by the sun. (I have a reservation about this. The sun would have to shine a lot more than it does in our valley to heat anything much.)

Coming in with the reed basket full of flowers, I was grateful for the coolness inside the house. And I was most thankful that somebody invented insulation, for even a very old house may be insulated by blowing the insulation in through small holes in the hand-cut clapboards. We can gauge the outside temperature by the fact that the great hearth-stones turn dark with moisture when it is very hot. But the house itself is cool and, if I remember to pull the blinds, shadowy.

Jill is always unexpected. We were waiting for the charcoal to catch in the grill. The broilers, marinated in barbecue sauce, smelled delicious even raw. But nobody can hurry charcoal. The corn waited to be roasted, and the salad, as usual, was warming up all on its own.

"What are the Seven Wonders of the World?" asked Jill pensively.

"The Taj Mahal," I said instantly. (It is not one of them.)

"Hanging gardens of Babylon?" queried Jill. (She was right.)

"Well, let's make up our own," I said, poking the charcoal and almost putting it out. "I could put a little kerosene on—"

"I don't like chicken flavored with kerosene," she said firmly.

"Well, there are too many wonders," I decided, staying the pangs with a scallion. "But if you have to categorize, I think the flight of a bird for one."

"How about a jet plane?"

"Pooh. The beating wings of a bird are more of a wonder." I ate a leaf of Bibb lettuce. "Think of a wedge of wild geese vibrant against an early morning sky." She thought of it. "And the miracle beat of a hummingbirds wings, faster than you can see. Or the wheeling of a hawk riding the air currents over the meadow."

"Then how about things coming up in the garden," she suggested.

"Yes. That is a wonder, and a miracle. "Growth is always a wonder, when small pellets are planted in the dark earth and the life power in them cracks the earth itself as they push up to grow and bear.

"I am putting the broilers in," said Jill, "and I don't think we should list all our wonders out of Nature. I mean, we need balance."

"Bach," I said instantly. "To make an arrangements of sounds a profound experience to the listener is surely a wonder to be counted. To illuminate the soul without words—"

"He had words in the St. Matthew Passion," said Jill.

"Don't get off the point." (Jill has a way in any discussion of plunging off at a tangent.)

"Well," she said, "that's three."

"You can't leave out poetry," I said, "for poetry is—"

"Yes, I know." She basted the broilers. "If I ever got cast up on a desert island, I wouldn't need any footprint in the sand to know you were already there. There'd be a copy of Keats and the Complete Works of Shakespeare."

I got out the salad bowl and rubbed it with garlic.

"Of course there are wonders and wonders," said Jill, putting the sweet corn in. "Take love, for instance, and friendship, and faith in God—or how about that time when you suddenly know your children do understand what you are saying and sort of feel with you? And I might mention the ecstatic welcome of a dog when you come home after abandoning her for three hours?"

"And it may not fit in," I added, "but memory is surely the sixth wonder of the world. Did you put milk in the corn water?"

Memory is a wonder. By means of memory, we preserve the excitements of first love, the golden moments of maturity. A perfect hour is soon over, but remains in the mind. It is like a fresh-water pearl held in the palm, and time often adds lustre to it so that it is lovelier even than the reality ever was.

For the seventh wonder, it is different for everyone. But it is always the same. It is a home place. It may be a walk-up apartment in the city overlooking a fire escape and well-furnished with soot from neighboring chimneys. Or it may be a mansion (although it does seem to come hard to make a mansion a true home). But it is the place, wherever it be, that men come back to after work, children come back to after school, and women come back to after Red Cross meetings, P.T.A., church committees, shopping or working at a gainful occupation themselves to help the family budget from withering away.

It may be full of tensions and anxieties and it may be shabby. But it is a place where we can be ourselves, without pretense. Where we can confide our fears and worries to the members of the family. Where we can express our dreams, even if they happen to be impossible to fulfill. In this era of rapid divorces and much emotional instability, there are many unhappy marriages and disturbed children, I know this. But a home place is still an anchor. The whole family has a vested interest in the books, the old candlesticks from Grandma, the cross-stitched luncheon set (Mother's Day gift from the tomboy) and dozens of other things.

It may well be a home place is the greatest wonder of all!

In any season, dusk is my special hour. I like the feeling that the day is unwinding. If I have not nearly accomplished all my tasks, I make a list and tuck it on the kitchen counter. It is for tomorrow. I like the light of dusk, and there is always light. In winter dusk shuts into night so fast that there is only a moment when the snow flares with the chilly sunset. But it is a moment of glory. I always say "And the glory of the Lord shone round about them." For it does. The cold slopes of the hills are warmed, the pines look almost black.

In summer, the long leisurely twilight comes so slowly that I cannot say when day is over and dusk is there. Colors quiet down, and the meadow looks shadowy but the sky is still brilliant. The cockers and Irish still dash about the yard tending to their various rabbit-deals and mole affairs. Gradually the air takes on a violet tinge. The birds chirp in a desultory fashion instead of singing madly.

Often, in August, the last of light from the sun meets the first pale gleam of the evening star. It is so still that I could almost hear petals opening on the nicotiana, which loves night.

In spring, in New England, dusk has a moonstone color and the delicate blossoms on the sugar maples seem to give out a light of their own. (What are those yellow and pink trees in the woods? my Viennese friend asked once.)

In autumn, well there is a dusk to remember. Days grow shorter and the sun drops in a hazy ball behind the hills. But the scarlet and gold of the autumn leaves make a twilight full of color. It is as dramatic as a second-act curtain in a play.

Even the garnet of the oaks seems bright after the sun has gone.

But in spring and autumn, there is a sense of urgency about the hour of dusk. In summer, one feels it might go on for years. The only way we are really sure it is night is because the dogs come in. Teddy lies like a frog, back legs flat out, choosing the doorway where there is a stir of air—and where we have to step over him constantly. Holly lugs her eternal bone to the sofa, and the peripatetic Linda settles in the wing chair which has an excellent view of the kitchen. Jonquil wags her way right to the kitchen and sits with a hopeful wag by the refrigerator. Sister retires under my desk, rightly opining that I will be sitting down there shortly.

Now in August, we begin to feel how short summer's lease is, for often it is too cool to eat out in the garden or down by the pond. The pattern of life in our part of the country already begins to change. Blankets blow on the line. Woodsheds begin to fill. Enterprising housewives agitate about cleaning furnaces, whitewashing cellars, painting the picket fence before frost. The men, I notice, are not so easy to stir into activity. They have had it all summer long. Now they prefer to clean up the barnyard, and then go to the store and smoke reflective pipes while discussing the state of the world. It takes a genius to buy snow tires now.

But the country kitchens smell of spices as the last pickles and relishes are put up. Such simmering and stirring go on as the homemaker tries to "save everything."

Now the school children face the inevitable day of wearing shoes and catching the school bus again. They seem intoxicated by their last freedom. They swarm along the roads, towels over brown thin shoulders as they go off to swim. They bicycle madly (and when school begins, they will be too weak to walk a block to get the bus). The parents are trying to get them to the dentist, get their eyes tested, get their school clothes. They are as easy to catch as silverfish. They are just not there. They are off in the woods or down at the river or at the lake. They are too busy living to be bothered. All they ask is a bologna sandwich and a bottle of some pop and they are off, to taste the last freedom of the year.

However, the adults in our valley try not to have cavities in teeth or to break their glasses during August. If we have aches and pains, we sit it out. The Doctor is giving every kind of injection yet invented and if we venture into his office, we feel that we have no right to be there, for the young have taken over. And after all, I reflect, my sinus will rock along, but the squalling small ones must have all the preventive shots for everything if possible. I take my sinus home and give it a few hot towels.

Once school starts, every child with anything contagious gives it to the rest. An epidemic can start easily with just one child whose mother was too busy to bother with this cold in the head. It is too bad knowledge cannot be passed along as simply as a germ.

Everything is geared to Labor Day and the opening of school. I certainly hope I never get a bad appendix or anything when the children are being prepared for the battle of education!

"I suppose you never travel far," said a recent visitor. This was a much-traveled person (indeed, in the Navy one must be) and had made an extra trip to see Stillmeadow.

I thought it over. No, I do not travel far, in a way. I would like to go to far-off islands in the South Seas. I have always wanted to visit Hawaii. I did visit Europe, including Italy, before war had laid a mark on it. I was the most avid sight-seer that could be imagined. I kept on looking at things and walking to see things until my eyes swelled shut and my feet flattened out. But in my memory now I remember most of all going to Keats' house in Hampstead Heath, and in Rome visiting his last dwelling place, and going to the cemetery in Rome where he was buried under the stone with the pitiful words, "Here Lies One Whose Name Was Writ in Water."

On that trip I ate a lot of indigestible fabulous foods in elegant places. I looked at masterpieces. I prayed my own prayers in all the cathedrals. I saw opera in Paris, when the swan broke down in *Lohengrin*. I saw, and did not climb, the Swiss mountains. I heard *Parsifal* in Munich. I did not miss anything, so far as I knew.

But now what remains is the memory of a bare and rather uninteresting house on Hampstead Heath and a grave in Rome. And I had traveled with Keats for a long time in his books.

"No, I do not travel far," I said to the visitor.

But I travel as far as my mind will reach, I thought. Any day, any time.

I was happy to see Keats's house, but I knew him already. I already knew him intimately, from "Beauty is truth, truth beauty, that is all ye know on earth, and all ye need to know," to "Bright star, would I were steadfast as thou art." I had traveled with Keats, and many others, long before I ever walked up the gangplank to the ship taking me abroad.

One does not need to travel far to travel everywhere. Travel is limited only by how far the mind will reach, and anyone can travel to the far horizons from a wheel chair. The only limitation is in ourselves.

Physical traveling can get you around, but only travel in the mind can be satisfying, for I saw many people on my one trip across the ocean who spent their time deploring the absence of bathrooms and hot running water such as they had in Iowa. The galleries were just a lot of paintings and chilly. And room service was sketchy. They had a hard time getting ice for their drinks.

I now confine my travel to a visit to Cape Cod to look at the ocean. It takes over five hours to get there and after the first hour, we begin to worry about home. Did we turn off things and turn on things? Did we leave enough notes for everyone who might come? Did we tell the cocker-sitter to add a teaspoonful of this or that as per the Rx from the veterinarian.

We often stop midway to phone back and be sure everything is all right. But the more miles that we go, the more we worry.

"I forgot to tell the laundryman not to stop," I say in Providence.

"Did you leave a note about watering the house plants?" asks Jill as she heads toward Taunton.

No matter how homebound we are, we all need a small vacation. We go away, as our neighbor says, "to rest our heads," and this is about what we do. We head for Cape Cod and as we drive over the Sagamore bridge, the salty, piny air leaves us breathless. I stop worrying over whether the meter reader will leave the gate open and let the dogs out. I look at the canal, wide and deep, and see a freighter in the distance. Across the bridge we drive between scrub pines and sandy banks. The narrow land lies between the ocean and the bay, and if it is windy, sand blows against our cheeks as we drive. Gulls begin to wheel over, crying and crying.

When we get to our special place, we do not bother to unpack. We go out and look at the ocean, with the waves rolling in and breaking on the bright sand. The crests are silvery and foaming, but the under part of the waves is a black-green. There is nothing so timeless as the breaking of waves on a long beach. I can look at the horizon and know that Spain is the nearest shore. I see a ship moving steadily against the edge of sky.

Suddenly I stop worrying about that coffeemaker at home. If we left it on, let it burn out. It is not vital. What is vital is to watch the breakers, and count to see whether the seventh wave is truly larger, or is it possibly the ninth one?

The beach itself is a lesson in time. I pick up a tiny shell which has been polished and shaped by the waves, but still keeps its original shape. As time goes on, it will become part of the sand. Here and there, a shiny pinky pebble is left when the tide ebbs, and this too is on a course. It will roll and sweep forward with the tide, and retreat with the tide. And always it will be shaped, smoothed, rounded, and lessened until it too is a grain of sand.

As I pick up a cool pebble and hold it in my palm, it seems to me that the tide of life shapes me in much the same way. An edge is polished off in a great storm of grief. A jagged point is smoothed away by dissappointments, disillusionments which have been faced. Gradually life polishes the stone. The surface

of a small pebble is satiny. It feels cool to the palm.

So it is with people, I think. If the core of the stone is sound, the wearing away by the tide results in a smooth oval. If the core is soft, there is no pebble left after a few Northeasters. I have known people buffeted by life mercilessly who still gave me a sense of serenity. The integral core was sound. And I have known people who disintegrated at the first blow as a bit of clay exposed on the great beach dissolves in the first turn of the tide.

But perhaps the great lesson of the sea is that small things do not matter. The horizon is limitless and my own becomes limitless too if I look a long time at the edge of sky and sea. But I am curiously ambivalent. I feel how insignificant all the uses of life are, and at the same time I am filled with energy to make my own life more worth while.

I do not know whether the sea affects everyone as it does me, but I remember driving to the beach to look at the sunset, and seeing a woman in a car parked at the edge of the sand, just sitting.

Her head was bowed in her arms, and her whole attitude that of extreme grief. I wanted to speak to her, but what could I say? She had come to be alone, and I was a stranger. The tide was going out and small pools of pearl were left on the sand. The wading birds lifted delicate legs as they tipped along hunting for small sea creatures left behind as the tide retreated. The sky was apricot and a late trawler was etched against it in charcoal.

Suddenly the last piece of sun sank into the sea and the woman lifted her head and looked at it. Two small leggy boys from some nearby cottage came leaping across the damp sand with a puppy. The three of them played ball, most of the time the puppy won. The sand pools were now mauve. The woman lifted her head and looked at the sea and the sky, and at the small boys tumbling about, and suddenly I could see that she smiled.

And as she started her motor and backed around, she lifted

her hand to wave at me. I waved back. We had, after all, communicated. Without words. We had seen something together, each shut in the shell of our own car. I knew that her grief was eased. She knew that my own problems were lessened. The world was beautiful at sunset with the trawler standing in the distance and the boys and puppy playing on the darkening sand.

After all, words are not so important as shared experience.

I suspect that the main purpose of a vacation or a trip is to make home more inviting. Home seems like a refuge when you unpack and settle in. For one thing, you know where your toothbrush is. It is where it should be, over the back sink, and not on a shelf in a powder room somewhere. You also get back to everything that you cannot do without and forgot to take with you. And then there is your own bed. Nobody has sufficiently praised the value of your own bed. My bed is not as good as the beds in any fancy motel, hotel, or house in which we stay when away from home. The mattress has a way of creeping away from the headboard, so that often I wake up and find half my pillow and half my head hanging down in the crack. It is a very old maple four-poster, which was once a rope bed, and I sometimes think I would be better off with the ropes, for the mattress slides on the springs and the springs do not exactly fit. But it is my own bed and when I climb into it after a trip, I feel that my bones like it. They know where the dips and hollows are. Being an antique, I have to contract a bit when I lie down, but I am used to that. My feet know better than to whack the footboard (so beautiful to look at). A strange bed is just not so cosy although it may be a Hollywood-size affair with inner springs galore. I feel queer when I fall in a bed and there is no answering thwack as everything plunks down on the side rails. It is not natural.

Then of course at home, there is the matter of an Irish fitting in at the footboard and a cocker hanging off the far edge. I read a good deal at night and have my prop pillow there plus a baby pillow for my neck. While I read, the Irish puts her paws over her eyes to shut out the light. The cocker has ears flowing over.

If I reach for a glass of water, the whole bed creaks. I miss this when I am away. Silent beds seem so impersonal, even ominous. So, much as I love to take a small trip, I really like home better. I travel anyway, through books. I have been all through the jungles, up Mount Everest, at the South Pole (at only 50 below zero) and poling through the Okefenokee But I have done it comfortably in my squeaky bed with crackers and Swiss cheese on the bedside table. And if I happen to be reading a mystery, which I seldom do, and feel that dead bodies are all over the house, I can always say cheerily, "Here we go—" and a bevy of dogs will be around, wagging tails and ears flying. Anybody would like a last run in the moonlight, they say. And as I see them dash into the dewy moonlit yard, I do not care how many bodies are lying around in the current mystery. Most of the people who are murdered are not sympathetic characters anyway, I reflect, watching the cockers fly around the yard. Most mystery writers only kill off impossible people. And most innocent victims of crime come out very well and marry the girl in the end.

And by the time the cockers and Irish come in, I am not worried about a stiletto in the back or a hoarse voice warning me that my time is up. I am busy putting everyone to bed in his and her own chair. Then I can go serenely back to bed and see how the Scotland Yard men figure everything out.

Scotland Yard would have a hard time in our valley. We all know everything that goes on. We hear it at the village store and over the party line on the phone, so we have no secrets.

If anyone wrote a mystery about my valley, it would never get to print because everyone would know all about it long before it got set down!

When I am in the kitchen, making a cucumber mousse or eggs in aspic, I often think how cooking has changed. I sometimes wonder how the early families ever got through the meals they had. My friend Sylvia Palmer has a cookbook published in Hartford in 1827 that sold for twelve and a half cents. The muffin recipe calls for one pound of flour, one pint of milk, eight eggs, beat them well (it says), put as much yeast in as you think will raise them and bake them as soon as you can.

Plum cake calls for nine pounds of flour, nine eggs, three pounds of sugar, one pint of yeast, one spoonful of rose water, spice to your taste and as much milk as will wet it.

But my favorite is gingerbread. "Take equal quantities of cream and molasses, a large portion of pearlash dissolved in sharp vinegar (make it hard) and put ginger to your taste." (Pearlash was made by burning corncobs to a white ash in a special part of the hearth.)

Nowadays if you write a cookbook, as I found out while doing mine, you must measure everything to the quarter teaspoon, you give the size and shape of the pan, the exact temperature of the oven, the time of cooking, and just how many people it will serve. None of this using enough and putting in as much of anything as you feel best!

I do wonder how much plum cake would come from nine pounds of flour! And there must have been a surplus of eggs, for most of the recipes call for eight or nine. That's a far cry from one-egg cakes.

They had plenty of food in our valley before the Revolution, for wild game was abundant. Every stream had fish (not stocked by the State, either). There were then few pests to attack crops and the land was fertile. Carrots a foot thick were right for digging, according to a local historian.

And when the Revolution came, the streets of Woodbury were piled high on either side with barrels and hogsheads of pork, beef, lard, flour. Sugar and molasses were scarce, especially "refined loaf sugar." And tea, of course, was in Boston Harbor. Herb teas were popular and dark brown sugar was used. It is interesting to see that the insides of antique sugar-bowls are usually brown from having been filled with brown sugar.

As the war went on, our valley was called on with increasing frequency to supply more food and more clothing. One difficulty in the campaigns was that starving soldiers took to eating fresh meat, raiding farms for plump calves or sheep. Everyone knew fresh meat could cause any number of ailments, but when the supply of salted meat ran out, the men were reckless.

I often think that some of the bravest soldiers might have been those who were fortified by a secret meal of fresh beef thrust on a stick and cooked over the campfire. Meanwhile, at home, women were trying to cultivate the crops, weave more lengths of cloth, store the cabbages and pumpkins and squash in the cellar, cut wood for the hearth fires, and behaving generally the way women do in time of trial.

They picked the apples and sliced them and strung them on cord and hung them out to dry. They did the same with pumpkins. They also cast bullets on Bullet Hill, melting down scrap metal.

And I am sure they gave up using nine pounds of flour for one recipe.

As August draws to a close, evenings are cool. Autumn is already in the air. The signs are small, but a country eye sees them. The grass no longer seems to grow overnight and need mowing. The peppers begin to turn rosy in the vegetable garden, and the tomatoes ripen. The lettuce begins to run out.

The silk on the corn is darker, too, and some of the broccoli shows yellow florets in the heads. But the whole garden still bears luxuriously and the squash is all over everything. Grapes turn purple on the vines at the edge of the garden and the apple trees seem to sag with the fruit.

It is a time to can, to freeze. A time to gather the herbs and tie them in bunches and hang them upside down (poor things) in the woodshed. Mint and sage make the air savory. Herb vinegars stand in neat rows on the fruit cellar shelf. Bay, tarragon, mint, basil and dill are our favorites.

Comes the day when Jill goes out with the fork and just tries one hill of potatoes. No bigger than a pullet's egg, the pinky potatoes tumble out. Scrubbed and cooked with a mint leaf they taste as good as any gourmet dinner. This is a happy moment, yet with a touch of melancholy. The season is changing, goldenrod and chicory mark the way. And some of the birds begin flying in formation instead of singly. They are doing practice flights. They wheel and circle and talk a lot, and a few just cannot seem to fall in line. How do they know that they must fly a far distance before long? Some of them will get as far south as South America, but who tells them this? How do they know they should get ready for the fall migration?

But when they begin to swing over the peaked roof, we know it is a sign. Summer is already walking the path to yesterday.

FALL

Fall

NOW THE FARMERS WORK FROM DAWN TO BLACK NIGHT GET-
ting in the last of the silage and stuffing the barns with last
loads of hay. When I wake in the morning, I hear the sound of
the machines blowing the silage in and it is the sound of summer vanishing. The birds are more organized now. The flurry
of wings and the chattering diminish, they fly with intent. It is
still warm and dreamy, and the leaves are green, but the birds
are as busy as women packing for a long trip.

They still do a good deal of discussing. The mothers are
telling about how hard it was to teach Junior to fly, he just
plopped about. The fathers are fussing over that strange egg
that appeared in their nest while they were baby-sitting and
Mama off for a wing-stretch. It was not their fault. But all the
time they fly and arrange the line of movement. And when they
really fly in a group, Jill casts a wary eye at them and begins
to make a list of fall chores. The birds, she says, are time clocks
of the seasons.

School begins and the children waiting for the school bus look like migratory birds themselves in their bright jackets and with that traveling look. They are traveling on to some sort of education, and this is a journey too, a migration from childhood to a larger world. I always feel a nicking ache that I am no longer filling a pencil case and getting schoolbooks for my child. I don't have to worry over the colds that children pass around all winter. But I suspect all mothers are ambivalent. I wouldn't actually put my daughter back in a pinafore, for I enjoy her so much now as a friend.

It is rich and rewarding to have her sit down and talk about Bach or modern poetry or the newest books, but I still enjoyed the period when she said, "Mama, should I wear the pink dress or the blue one today?" And often, when I see her sitting by the fire, so adult, so assured, I remember the days of her first bunny suit and the small hand reaching out from the cuffs because it was easier to walk with Mama holding one hand.

At that age, when a small trustful pink face looked out from the fringe of rabbit fur on the hood, there were no problems about a helping hand. Obviously that was what Mama was for. But as children grow up and begin to walk by themselves, a helping hand can be frustrating to them. A wise mother must be disciplined and it is difficult to suddenly reverse her role. Mothers who never manage it do not achieve the warm companionship in later years. (Oh, Mom still thinks I am a baby.) Often, in my effort to be wise, I have bitten back the quick advice, the easy instruction. Sometimes I fell badly from my determination, and it never did any good to anybody.

Children have problems too as they move from the shallows of childhood to the deep sea of maturity. I remember overhearing my daughter say to Jill's daughter, "Now just be patient with them. You have to be tactful. After all, they're old." They were about ten at the time, and we did not feel exactly on the shelf.

Now as I see a new bevy of school children waiting for the school bus, I wonder what changes the world will bring to them. But I hope for them that they may have a backlog of family love. A child that is confident that he or she is cherished is armed against almost anything life can bring.

When I was growing up, I loved school. There was nothing odd about this. Everybody else loved it too. I don't know whether it was because in our small town we were blessed with a thoroughly fine principal who had a dedicated teaching staff, or whether it was because overcrowding was unheard of. Or possibly in that pre-war era, we were less accustomed to rebelling against anything and everything.

The only cases of discipline in our High School occurred when the principal gave a talk to someone who had painted "Beat Beloit" or something similar on the sidewalk before a big game. Or when now and then someone copied a theme.

Home life had less tension too. Parents and children did things together. My friend Barbara Shelton had a clipping pinned to her bedroom wall. "Richer than I, you can never be; I had a Mother who read to me." Nowadays few mothers have time to read to the children and if they did, someone would have to turn off television. But there is a special pleasure in being read to or in reading aloud. Long after I could read everything except such words as peripatetic, I pretended I had to be read to every night. And when I was in High School,

Father would take my Latin book and read aloud the magnificent poetry. I was always weak in the grammar but I could recite better than anyone in class, on this account.

Judging by what I read and what I hear, the excitement has chiefly gone from education, and this is a pity. My opinion is that we have too many tired teachers. No matter how gifted a man or woman may be, teaching three times as many pupils as is normal and always trying to do extra jobs to supplement the small salary, drains the enthusiasm.

We seem to be almost manic about teaching science better and re-doing the curriculum in order to train physicists, chemists, and so on. To keep step with Russia, of all things. But I doubt whether we can make scientists out of everyone. And I wouldn't care to live in a world with no time spent on liberal arts.

Although Father was a scientist, he believed that without Greek and Latin and history and literature, no one was educated! It is true he was hampered by the fact that one lifetime is so short. He wanted to know everything himself, and he was very cross with me when I had to limit my courses in college to the number they would allow me to take. With so much to learn, he felt no time should be wasted.

Up to the time he died, at seventy-seven, from climbing a mountain too rapidly, he was still studying. This love of learning seems to be rare now, as far as I can judge. Real scholars have to be careful or they will be thought "queer." In fact, it is often only when an "egghead" wins a hundred thousand dollars answering a lot of obscure and unimportant questions, that knowledge wins respect. If you can name a minor character in an eighteenth-century novel, you have a Cadillac.

My final thoughts on education came when I went to the village to get a shot for a devoted virus infection. The office nurse was not there, and I asked if she was ill. "No, she's at home. The children are having the week off."

In our countryside, the children go to school just about long enough (six weeks) to establish study habits and presumably learn a little, and then they have a week off.

When they go back to school, they have forgotten a good deal. Reviewing is in order. Then they get back in the swing and go to school a few more weeks and then comes another lay-off. The school buildings, meanwhile, have to be heated in winter just the same, the maintenance goes on. It seems to me that when a small community has to invest a million in the plants, pay the teachers, keep the books, it would be well to use the equipment for all it is worth, and if it shortened the school year to have the children go steadily, why not hold an extra session in summer? A good many children could be ready for college in three years, I think, and with expenses what they are in this age, it would be well for them to get to college earlier. They could then, if interested, have time for graduate and special study and still make a living and be able to marry before they are beyond the age at which they should marry.

Subsidized marriages may be all right, but I think self-supporting ones are better. A good many parents stagger under the burden of supporting married sons or daughters and a baby or two when, if education were expedited, the young people would be on their own feet in a reasonable length of time.

In our rural area, not too many can afford college. But the children could get a good deal more education than they do, with a different school program. However, it is unlikely that my opinion will influence the trend. All I can do is hope that today's children may benefit as much as possible from the shining glory of acquired knowledge.

My friend Iris Flanary reminded me the other day of how one feels when a new sidewalk is laid in a city block. She was lamenting not being able to live in the country, but she said it was rewarding to come out to take a bus in the morning and see two names scratched in the wet cement with a heart drawn around them. She saw "Judy and Bobby" scrawled in the damp walk near her house. The cement hardens, the names are fixed in it. But what happens to Judy and Bobby in later years? Do they marry? Or does one go one way and one another? And perchance does only one walk this way again in after years and suddenly remember the sweetness of young love, and wonder, "Where is she now?" Or the other thinks, "How long ago it was—and oh, how lovely." Passers-by will also wonder who Judy and Bobby were, for the names will remain. Iris says she always wishes all love could be as permanent as the names written in the cement.

We have no sidewalks in the country, of course, but we did have to jack up the great hand-hewn fireplace hearth at Stillmeadow and cement the cracks for the years had settled the hearth down almost a foot and a half. The minute the mason finished, my golden cocker dashed in and walked all over the wet cement. I wouldn't take any amount of money now for those paw prints. They are the signature of a most happy cocker and I cherish them.

I am even sorry, now, that an energetic painter painted over the pencil marks we had on one doorjamb marking the height of the children from year to year. I'd like those pencil marks back.

It is all a matter of what you value, I expect. As for me, I am especially fond of the table leg that is gnawed where Honey cut her teeth!

And now zinnias are in their dazzling colors. They seem to be afire. Horticulturists have done a great deal with zinnias. I like the new salmon shades and the greenish-white ones best. I note that the white ones always carry an overtone, or an echo, from the original colors. The second blooming of the Chinese delphinium goes well with zinnias in an antique copper bowl. We keep the house filled with bouquets now, anticipating the frost. And when the leaves begin to turn, Jill brings in branches of rosy red leaves for the stone jug by the hearth. The swamp maples turn first, and their color is incredible. They really burn with color.

I have read diligently as to why leaves turn color in autumn, but I have never understood it. It seems to me the trees feel a prescience of winter in the air. The trees make up their mind, and that is that. To me, the ancient wisdom of Nature is beyond analyzing. I just enjoy the seasons.

Midday is still soft with summer, so warm and dreamy that it seems it must go on forever. Comes the blue dusk, and a cool knife slices the heat of the day. Gardens glow bright with late blooms, wild asters are darkly purple along the old grey stone walls, and goldenrod and chicory establish their pennons on every country road. But there is a feeling in the air, nevertheless. We keep a wary eye on the Farmer's Almanac, and an alert ear to weather broadcasts. For the hurricane season approaches.

I may admit that so far, we have never had adequate warning of a hurricane that arrived. We have had many warnings of those that did not come. But the most severe hurricanes we have had, came without being announced, except by our own country senses.

A hurricane is preceded by a strange stuffy smell in the air. Nobody has ever mentioned this, as far as I know, but it is as if the whole air were shut up in a small space. People sometimes tell me I am silly to say I smell a hurricane, but so I do. Then comes a black sky and a rain shepherded by a dark wind that seems to come from all directions at once. When you cannot tell which way the wind is blowing, it is time to batten down. Often the storm seems to be going over, and then I hear a sound, half wail, half roar, which comes also in all directions at once. At this point, we lock doors and windows, get out the candles and try to make fresh coffee before "the electric" goes off.

We no longer fill the bathtub with water for (a) it takes a lot of water from the well and (b) we never use it.

We spend our energy bringing in wood, for a hurricane, at any time, is cloaked with cold. I haul out extra comforters for the beds. Jill races about with lawn chairs—it is not a good idea to have them flung against the windows. We fill a water pitcher, not for us, but for the dogs. We can drink coffee heated over the fire in the fireplace but the cockers and Irish need fresh water.

My first experience with a genuine hurricane was long ago when I only thought this was a bad nor'easter. I was alone at the time, with the cats (three), a litter of small puppies in the kennel, a houseful of grown cockers. I thought it was a bad storm. It was blowing so hard that water flowed in under the sills. I got sacks of onions and potatoes newly dug, and laid them along the sills. Then I got all the bath towels in the house and stuffed the windows with them. I was tired of the whole business by then, but I looked out in the yard and saw the kennel door had given way under the impact of the wind and all the puppies were skipping and blowing about the yard like windy leaves. Branches crashed from the old apple trees. They were frightened and screaming. I hauled the onion sack from the back door and flew out and spent quite a time scooping up wet puppies. I was hampered by the wind and the rain and by

being able only to carry three at a time. The fourth just fell through. Finally I had them all in the kitchen and got the range going with the leftover wood from a packing crate. I next burned up an old chair. Then I got the fireplace going with the last logs in the woodshed, and made a pot of tea. I lit the oil lamp and fried an egg in the embers at the edge of the hearth. I got out *Wuthering Heights* and read five chapters. I always read that in a crisis, it rests me.

Quite a storm, I reflected, checking on the puppies, who had stopped shivering. Then suddenly the current went on and the phone began to ring.

"Are you all right? Is the house damaged? Are the dogs safe?"

"We are all FINE," I shouted (the connection was fuzzy). "But I had to use undiluted evaporated milk for the formula— they love it."

I had been too busy, fortunately, to notice that the thirteen lovely old apple trees in the back yard had gone down. I just thought the storm was noisy, as I rubbed various puppies with towels. And I hoped the water pouring in wouldn't spoil the potatoes and onions!

Subsequently, during Carol and Hazel and so on, I found that I was always too busy to worry. But I did learn a few things in that first hurricane, which was local but devastating. Now when the sky takes on a greenish tinge and the air gets that funny smell, we mobilize. Fill pails, fill teakettles. Wash lamp chimneys, trim wicks. Lug in enough wood for a siege. Get out all the candles in the house. Make coffee. Stack bath towels for handy mopping when something gives way. Jill fills the vacuum jug with ice for not only do we get terribly thirsty as soon as a hurricane strikes, but those ice cubes can keep something in the freezer from going bad. The freezer itself gets a coating of old blankets, Sunday newspapers, worn grass rugs.

Then we sit it out. We always hope the cables on the two-hundred-year old sugar maples will hold, but when branches crash, we are thankful the roof has survived.

I always think of the unfortunate people who lose their home in such a hurricane. And of those who get flooded out. Stillmeadow, built below the hill and away from the stream, is sound. But how many lose all they have when Nature lets her fury loose! I feel such an identity with all homepeople who lose everything in flood, fire, or hurricane that as I lug in one more sack of onions to brace against my own door, I utter a special prayer for those less fortunate.

Hurricanes can strike us all, one way or another. Even those who are outside the natural hurricane belt may be subject to hurricanes of the spirit, the heart. And there is only one way to meet any kind of hurricane: batten down, ride it out, face it with courage.

As Hugh Walpole said, so wisely, "It isn't life that matters, it's the courage you bring to it."

On a warm September afternoon, I like to go down to the old mill beyond Steve and Olive's house. The mill was once used for grinding flour during the Colonial days. Now it is abandoned, but the water spills over the rocky dam just as always. A cool breath comes from the old mill wheel and from the damp floor of the old millhouse. I often wish someone would operate it again, for water-ground meal is so superior. We have to get our flour from Vermont, but it's worth it for the smell of a loaf of warm bread just out of the oven is utterly satisfying. All of summer seems to be in the warm buttery slices.

Inside our own mill, long given over to spiders, there yet remains a smell of wheat. It is shadowy and quiet, and full of the past. I can almost see the men who used to come here, and the women in their neat gowns. Possibly the miller was too old to go to war and leaned in this dark doorway to watch troops go by. But they had heavy hearts. The miller must have wondered whether there would be any grain at all to grind, come another year. It was hard, too, not to be able to grind any grain for families suspected of being Tories. I suspect the miller, having worked a lifetime with the basic food of life, slipped a little extra flour in a sack and just happened to drop it off at a Tory house on his way home. Nobody would be the wiser.

The water wheel is mossy. Light filters through the roof where the beams have gone. But the stream flows steadily on, just as it always has. The pool below the mill is deep and clear, and small boys fish in it. It is a pity they only think of bread as something squshy in a waxed wrapper. Fishing, however, is not changed. I hope it will never be. A small boy needs a bamboo pole, a hook, a worm.

Autumn is visiting time for us. We especially enjoy driving to Salisbury to see the Borlands. They live about an hour and a half away, as we drive. We go to Litchfield which is a dream village. The houses look as they looked in Colonial days. Leafy shadows fall on the hand-cut clapboards. The gardens are bright with chrysanthemums. The lawns look as if they had been cut to measure and pinned down. Hedges are trimmed.

Litchfield is an elegant village. Most of the houses are mansions and have ballrooms. Our own village was set to a simpler tune except for one or two "great houses." There is never anybody rushing about on the shaded streets in Litchfield, and I sometimes feel the inhabitants might wake up some morning right back in the days when George Washington signed his name on a windowpane with his diamond. I am sure when the moon is full, the gardens echo with laughter as gentlemen with well-powdered wigs and satin small-clothes took the air. The ladies, laced into breathlessness, probably stayed in the ballroom for night air was full of pestilence.

Beyond Litchfield the countryside changes. The first violet peaks of the Berkshires break against the sky. Hidden valleys are tucked under them, still emerald in autumn because they are sheltered. Rocky streams flow through pastures. Occasionally we pass a stand of hemlocks, dark and quiet. Toward Canaan, the valleys are longer. The farms look prosperous.

We take a road that companions the Weatogue River and come to the Borland house which is set snugly on the slope of a small mountain. The river is just across the road, wider here and quieter. Inside the house, we sit by the window wall overlooking the hillside, lovely at any time of the year, and now pricked with red and gold.

When we went this week, there had been great excitement in the household for a herd of albino deer was in the vicinity. Hal and Barbara drove to the best viewing spot, but the deer had moved on. But Barbara said when they got home five regular deer were in their back yard, so they didn't mind too much.

We had lunch in the room overlooking the garden—creamy rich potato soup laced with fresh chives and served in a big beanpot. This was a happy idea for the beanpot kept the soup piping hot. We had popovers and apple honey, a crackling crisp green salad, cheese and fruit and hot coffee. And good conversation about books and writing, gardens and, of course, recipes. When we got home, I dipped into Hal's book, *This Hill, This Valley*, which is always on my table, and re-read his section on autumn.

The earth is so rich in September. Apples and quinces fall from heavy branches. Cabbage, squash, broccoli, peppers, tomatoes ripen in every garden. White and blue grapes hang heavy clusters on the vines. "What is man that thou art mindful of him?" I ask, when I go out to see the harvest. Surely God is in evidence in a garden.

Jill dug potatoes this morning. I am a poor digger, for I always manage to chop the best potatoes in two with the fork. The first potatoes are a delight. But as Jill carried the basket in, she said the air was so still, we could get the black frost at night. It always comes toward the end of September, after an utterly windless day.

As we rush to bring in everything that will be spoiled, I reflect that a parsnip is a pleasant vegetable. It likes to sit in the ground until after the freeze.

The back kitchen overflows with tomatoes, peppers, grapes, the last roses, zinnias and delphinium. Carrots, celery, chard, cabbage can take care of themselves, as can the acorn squash. We bring in the pattypan squash, however. Ripe cucumbers must come in to be baked or made into pickles. There is a great flurry until at last we know nothing more can be fetched in.

Then at dusk on the day of the black frost, I open the door and breathe that sudden, sharp air. "What's out tonight is lost," I say, quoting Miss Millay.

"If we had one more tomato, we'd have to move out," says Jill. And it is true that we can hardly thread our way across the back kitchen floor.

"I don't mind saying," Jill comments, "that I have had enough beans for a while. Let them freeze. Who cares?"

There is—there has to be—a moment the next morning after the killing frost, when the heart is saddened. The zinnia stalks are blackened and oozy, the garden itself has flattened out as leaves wilted. A few clusters of unripe grapes hang amid drooping sorry leaves. This is goodbye to summer, flower and fruit and vegetable.

But there is inevitably a spell of warm weather next. When we walk down the country road, I think, "And straight was a path of gold for him," because the goldenrod does make a path of sheer gold. I learned from Edwin Way Teale's *Autumn Across America* that the English call it "farewell summer." This is what it is. Joe Pye weed frosts the meadows with rosy violet. Swamp maples flicker into flame. The birds are leaving. Farewell summer it truly is.

Recently Jill was given a new camera which prints pictures by itself. So we set out to take pictures. She had the new camera, and also her old favorite (slung around her neck). She also took her color camera, just in case she needed a color shot. She had her light meter around her neck too, and her flash gun in the camera case.

After a few experiments, she went back to the house to get

her stop watch, for neither of us came out even counting sixty seconds while the camera did its work. She tried to photograph the dogs, but they raced around giddily so she decided to use me as a subject. I assumed the stony glare with which I always greet a camera. This confused the Irish and cockers and they raced around me.

"Either stand still or get out," said Jill to Jonquil, "I can't take half a dog!"

The shade on the lawn was spotty, so Jill began circling slowly. Dogs dipped in and out of the scene, barking happily. But finally, just as my eyes began to glaze, she snapped the picture. Then she consulted the book earnestly, set the stop watch. Suspense mounted.

"Now, all you have to do is pull the tab," she said. She pulled, she wrenched, she bent backward and hauled. Half of the tab broke off. Time was passing, but she flew to the house to get a nailfile to pry out the tab. When this didn't help, she dashed in for a pair of pliers.

About once a year, I have an intelligent surmise and now I had the one for this year. "Maybe there's something to push?" I asked doubtfully.

There was. She pushed it. The chewed tab and the picture flew out. Jill mopped her face. We inspected the print. I seemed to be emerging from a foggy sea. A fringe of tails edged the picture.

"It's all a matter of getting used to it," said Jill, getting me back in focus. This time the tab came off smartly, but the picture was perfectly blank.

"Either pulled too soon, or too late," muttered Jill.

She went back in the house to find a damp sponge because

her hands were now sticky from the developer. I leaned against the maple tree. When she came back, the light had changed so she consulted the light meter. Finally, she took a picture that came out, in sixty seconds, clear and definite. Flushed with triumph, we sat down to rest. "It's merely a matter of understanding any new mechanism," Jill explained to me, and tried to close the camera. It would not close. So we read the book again, and worked away. And finally Jill lifted another small tab with a button under it, and the camera snapped its jaws instantly.

After more practice, the new camera justified itself. It is a great help to know at once whether you have what you want in a picture. If not, there is still time to get it. With babies or children, the moment is everything. By the time you send films in and get them developed and printed, the baby has a different look, the young child has moved into a different phase. You can check the lighting, the composition, the focus with the new camera, and if you have snapped Sister and it turns out she seems to have a lilac bush sprouting from her head, you can push her over a few feet and improve the background.

These modern appliances all take a bit of practice before you feel cosy with them. The first time I used the dishwasher, I felt it ought to have more soap. I added more, and we had a deep tide of suds all over the floor, with ripples advancing to the living room.

We also had several cocker puppies paddling around in it. It was excellent soap, it took off the wax on the floor at once. It is a temperamental defect of mine to feel that if a little of anything is good, more must be better. My daughter has urged especial restrictions with regard to garlic. She points out that if it says to rub lightly with a clove of garlic, it means one clove, not the whole bulb. Rub lightly, she says, does not mean to squash it to a pulp and just leave it there in the bowl.

With the clothes washer, I am careful of the detergent, even to measuring it, although measuring is a bother. My battle with the washer was due to my leaving tissues in pockets, pennies and nickels, rubber bands, matches, lead pencils and so on. The plumber explained that it wasn't the fault of the washer, as he took out hairpins and a wad of aluminum foil (I don't know what I was doing with it). The coins were nice and clean and showed no sign of their ordeal spinning madly in the machine.

I am now also careful about color. One entire washing came out a brilliant purple, underwear, slips, blouses, pajamas, socks. Jill said it was our personal mauve decade, as we went around garbed in purple. The curious thing to me was that only one small item dyed everything. A scarf.

Nobody could suggest I am mechanical by nature. I learned to drive Father's automobile quite easily, but I never understood why it ran. On one occasion when he was away looking up an oil well, I was allowed to take the car for a picnic at the lake. Since I forgot to fill the radiator (which had to be done every twenty miles on a hot day) it naturally went dry. The motor began to steam and breathe out smoke.

I decided there must be too much oil inside and with the help of my beau (who knew more about horseback riding than cars) removed the plug and drained the oil from the motor. I didn't plan to drain it all out, but it came out rapidly in a nice gooey tide. By the time we had finished the job, the car had cooled down enough so that the motor started. And so, minus water, minus oil, we drove home.

It cost Father a good deal to get the car fixed. What he said to me was very educational. And I walked for a while after that. But Father himself was high-handed about equipment. I really do not think he ever understood either why a car ran. It was supposed to run. A flat tire was a personal insult to him delivered by the car. A mechanical failure was not to be borne. Sunk in gloom, he would predict that the automobile manufacturers would ruin the economy of the country, putting in spark plugs that gave out, batteries that ran down.

So far as I can remember, Father's care of the car was limited to pouring boiling water over it if it froze or using my bicycle pump to inflate a flat tire. Otherwise, he expected it to run, and run it did. I have often thought that somehow Father's automobiles responded to him. They just held up because he expected them to. They also traveled faster than any car was supposed to in those days. They were faithful when he whipped off into a cornfield or drove down a cowpath looking for specimens. Springs broke, radiators boiled, but the cars went on; the one thing no car of his ever did was allow the buttons to be buttoned on the side and back curtains when it poured. Father would wrestle with them until his suit was a mop, but those buttons just would not button. Mama and I would huddle inside wrapped in an oilskin coverall and Mama kept saying, "Oh Rufus, do get inside."

"Confound these curtains," he would answer, and wrenched until the isinglass gave way.

We do not migrate as the birds do, but I notice there is a change in the rhythm of our life when the season ebbs. Nights are cool, days dreamy with blue haze. There is a quickening in the blood, a restlessness. Suddenly we are full of projects, which may be our own manner of migrating. Now the firewood must be stacked, handy by the back door, the woodshed filled with kindling. That cellar window, broken last spring, must really be mended. The cellar itself is piled high with the debris of summer, as well as broken flower pots, extra mason jars, a mouse trap that does not work, and a few antiques that need to be done over.

When the line storm comes, we know a profound sense that autumn is going to slip away into winter before long. The line storm is as definitive as a backfire on a prairie blaze. Wind whips away all of summer, rain sluices the air. Branches fall. Windows rattle. Smoke backs down the chimney. The dogs get as close to the fire as possible. Especially Me heads for my lap, because storms frighten him.

The soup kettle hangs over the fire and the air is savory with onions and salt pork as Poor Man's Stew simmers. Now we regret the time of roses, and forget the Japanese beetles. Summer, viewed now, seems to have been an idyll. The storm assails the house like a great sea tide. Then it passes, and we open the doors. The air is as sweet as the smell of ripe grapes. The sky is colored infinity. Every grass blade is polished.

Suddenly summer's work is over, and whatever trials there were are done with. My heart is light. No, I cannot lift wings and ride the air currents, and take perilous exciting journeys as the birds do. But I am standing in a new-minted world, summer folded away like a rose pressed in a book. I am a small piece of the universe, but I can step toward the new season knowing that the world begins all over again every morning.

Hello, new world, I say as I let the cockers and Irish out for a last run in the drenched grass.

Now, in October, we have days of gold and blue. Leaves begin to fall, but the trees are a glory and a wonder. The air is crisp as a stalk of celery. It almost snaps when I open the door after breakfast. In the night leaves come down, and the dogs whirl through them. That vast tent of green in which we have lived is now vanishing. Hal Borland says, "October is the fallen leaf, but it is also the wider horizon more clearly seen." I realize how true this is, for I can now see the hill above the meadow, and the steeper hill behind the swamp. I can see our neighbor's lights at suppertime. I can see the postman draw up to the mailbox at the corner and deftly toss packages of mail in the boxes. He never has to get out of the car, and this is a great cross to Jill, for she is never able to drive to the box so as to fish out the mail. Either the door of the box bangs on the car door or won't open at all, since we are too close. If, now and then, the door does swing freely, the mail is too far back in the box to be reached. She always has to back up, get out, and open the box, close it, climb back in.

Yesterday as I watched her banging in and out of the car, I reflected on the subject of skills. Just suppose the postman had to climb out at every one of the boxes on his thirty-five-mile route! Or suppose he had to do what I should have to and paw through every package of mail to find the right one! Most of us have some skills. I do not have many. I am very good at unloading the dishwasher, for dishes and glasses fly through the air almost as if I juggled them. I can sometimes fix an appliance by whacking it. Radios respond to this. Light bulbs often go on again. Occasionally I have been spectacular at stopping a dogfight. But I fear I must be classified as unskilled labor.

I even have trouble with the vacuum cleaner, for it trips me.

Jill, on the other hand, is intimate with fuses, firm with the furnace when it begins to screech and send volumes of gas upstairs. She can put new plugs on light cords and not get electrocuted. She can plane down a screen door or put new hinges on.

My ego is bolstered by the fact that she can never find a recipe she wants out of our own cookbook and accuses me of giving away the custard cups she needs. I never know where my bank book is but I am better than a hound at tracking down a small casserole. The secret is simple. I simply stand and think, if I were a casserole just out of the dishwasher, where would I go?

I also feel proud of being able to smell expertly. This may not be a skill, but nevertheless, I have the gift of scent. I can smell something boiling over before it boils over! So if Jill is cooking (we take turns) and is embroiled (no pun) with a murder mystery, I am able to call from the next room and suggest that something is GOING ON at the range. I can smell an apple giving up in the barrel. Or an unwilling onion in the sack. I also can smell just when the coffee is done. And I have no difficulty in detecting the fact that Holly is coming in the front door with a venerable bone which she buried weeks ago.

I can smell mice in the cellar when they get in via the coal bin. And when I am broiling a steak, I go entirely by nose. When it smells just so, it is done, and never mind the timer.

My sense of smell is useful but seldom important. Now and then I have smelled a fire and dashed out to the kitchen to find a wastebasket ablaze. Once I was quietly pecking away with two fingers at the typewriter and my nose pinched itself. A pan full of fat left in the oven was blazing merrily and covering the kitchen with smoke.

Jill thinks I might qualify as a tracking dog, but I would be useless. I would smell the mint, the thyme, the pine needles, the wintergreen, the crushed leaves. I wouldn't track anything.

However, I have no trouble tracking a plump pork roast, with fresh sage dressing. The smell of drying mint sends me out to poke around in the refrigerator to see if lamb is there. Mint calls for mint sauce and lamb.

October weather makes for good appetites. We seem to be always hungry, from the coddled fresh egg at breakfast right through to the Port Salut cheese and wedges of crisp apple.

I know of no fruit more varied in taste than the apple. Most of the commercial varieties that keep well have not enough flavor. An apple should be spicy and on the sharp side, never sweet and mushy. The prettiest apples generally have no flavor. We are fortunate enough to have a few old apple trees that bear small fruit, crisp and juicy. They were planted long ago and still bear well, even without spraying. True, they do not keep well, but what a treat to put a bowl of them on the cobbler's bench, flank it with hot buttered popcorn, and spend an evening reading and nibbling.

These apples have the cool rich taste of autumn. I often think of Johnny Appleseed as I eat them, and wonder whether he passed our way. I have never discovered what variety of apple he planted, but I always think if we all planted for the future, the world would be a better place.

Our popcorn is out of a can. This is not romantic, but we raised our own several years, and for some reason it did not pop. So we get the can opener and the butter and the seasoned salt and start the electric frying pan, and there we are. Fluffy, buttery popcorn.

Jonquil eats all we dare give her. Popcorn is her favorite food.

Weeds and old raspberry canes must be burned now. Cornstalks should be destroyed with fire, to kill any leftover pests. We wait for a good damp day and get the permit from the fire warden, and then I have a nervous spell, being mortally afraid of fire. This is not due to any peculiarity in my personality. It means that I remember when my father's house burned to ashes in New Mexico, and how it was when the barn went up in flames. And that I clearly recall the day when a brush fire nearly swept away our whole home place. Fire isn't a symbol of anything in my unconscious or subconscious, it is just something I have had experience with. So when Jill gets the permit and begins to burn the garden debris, I shudder.

When the garden is put to bed properly, the bird feeders and suet cages come out. Jill brings home the first twenty-five pounds of wild bird food and chunks of creamy suet. The birds are waiting. Five minutes after the feeders are set up, they flock in. And how they do eat! For seven months now, we wait on the birds. And we worry. I know that wild birds ought to be able to set their own table. If they are silly enough to stick around in blizzards, why is it my responsibility? Nevertheless, I shall be skating across the icy lawn all winter with pans of food.

Sometimes I wake in the night and hear the trees cracking with ice and think of the birds and say crossly, "Why don't you go South?" But in the morning, there they are, eating sunflower seeds. Nobody has successfully explained to me how birds decide on migration. Often a flock will wheel away, think better of it, and come back the next day. There are always hesitant ones, who finally fly far behind the flock trying to catch up. I can just hear them saying, Oh wait for me, wait for me. I'm going along.

The winter residents come in smaller groups, I notice. We can always count them. But when the redwings come back in March the whole air is busy with wings.

Of course Isaiah did not have New England in mind, but he described it: "The mountains and the hills shall break forth... into singing, and all the trees of the field shall clap their hands." Now we store up the majesty to remember in the long white cold. The very air is like a trumpet blowing. Another season moves to the secret byways of infinity.

The thought has sadness in it. When we walk down the road, we see how the trees have grown this season. The lilacs reach the second-story window (how short a time ago we planted them.) The flowering crab almost roofs the quiet garden. The excitement of October has the undercurrent of melancholy which only makes every day more precious.

Wind and rain bring the leaves down in a tide of color. The goldenrod turns rusty and the wild blackberry canes are purple.

Now the summer's work is done, and harvest time ends; there is a pleasant air about the village. It is party time, when neighbors get together for buffet suppers, for nobody has to worry about getting stuck in a blizzard and no one will have to be up at sunrise acquiring the gardener's stoop. We like to serve a simple buffet on a crisp October evening when an applewood fire burns on the hearth.

A casserole of baked kidney beans with ham, laced with burgundy, makes a good basis for an informal dinner. A tossed salad, crusty French or Italian bread, and for dessert a fruit bowl. A tray of assorted cheeses and paprika crackers completes the menu except for steaming hot coffee. We also like baked broilers which have been cooked on a bed of pilaff. With this we serve a mixed garden salad, and the small hot biscuits so easy to make, and for dessert an old-fashioned floating island pudding with the coffee.

Guests fill their trays and carry them to the front living room or the family room. There is always room at the trestle table for some of the men to sit (men just do not like trays). We do not have room in our small house to set up card tables, but we find if the trays are sturdy and BIG enough to hold the main course and the coffee cups, we do very well.

We try to serve dishes which can be prepared the day before, and usually collect the silver, china, napkins and so on the night before. This leaves time for fixing autumn bouquets the next day, dusting, polishing the pewter ash trays.

Conversation is never a problem in our valley. The only difficulty is that with everyone chattering away, it is hard to sort out what is being talked about. I get bits like, "what they ought to do with the international situation is— dip it in egg and milk, then flour lightly— and the Doctor said he should be operated on immediately and so they— ordered a new truck for the fire department last Tuesday."

After the guests drive away down the road, we put the food away and load the dishwasher. Then we let the cockers and Irish back in. They are too cooperative when meals on trays are right at nose level! Then we give them their snacks, have a last cup of coffee ourselves, and decide all over again what wonderful friends and neighbors we have.

And so to bed, while the full moon rides over the apple trees and sugar maples, and a wine-sweet air stirs the ruffled curtains.

Living in the country has some drawbacks. For instance, the problem of trash and garbage is not easy. We do have one local rubbish remover and we tried him at first. All we had to do, said he, was put it outside the picket fence and he would pick it up every Tuesday. Tuesday passed, so did Wednesday, Thursday and a lot of other days. Meanwhile all the dogs for miles around came loping to our trash collection and had a fine time. Phoning pleas to the rubbish man did no good. In the end, Jill drove wrathfully to the dump. Of course, our situation was worse than our neighbors', for at that time we had thirty cocker spaniels. We had dozens of soup bones (rich broth is good for cockers). We had piles of empty mackerel cans (they had fish once a week). We had a canful of eggshells, empty bags and cartons the basic dry food came in, a heap of empty cans (beef came in them). Also, when we were raising a litter, we had half a case of evaporated-milk cans to dispose of, not to mention Pablum boxes and so on.

Our town dump is a hazard. In bad weather you invariably get stuck on what passes for a road. If it is clear, you pick up nails scattered by a previous dumper. In season, a cloud of bees assails you, for there is an ice cream plant in the valley and they use the dump for empty syrup tins. The bees love the syrup but are always ready to swarm around anyone who drives by.

One year we decided to dump everything in a hole back in the swamp. It would then disintegrate naturally. But naturally it didn't and in no time at all we had to hire two men to shovel it up and truck it to the town dump. It was a mean job and they charged nearly a hundred dollars for it.

It is incredible how much trash a family accumulates, even without dogs. For instance, Sunday papers. We tied them in neat bundles and cooperated with the Boy Scouts. Most of the time, the Scouts forgot to come down our isolated dead-end dirt road. Once we lugged a carful and left it in the minister's barn, feeling they would have to turn up there.

Finally we acquired an electric incinerator, which is a godsend, but will not burn cans or bottle tops. And I kept on wrapping steak bones in aluminum foil (to burn later) and parking them on top of the utility cabinet where even an Irish could not get them. Much better than having her take off the cover of the trash container and fish things out.

I felt we were singled out for trouble until we went to a friend's house to a party. The host was a little late welcoming us, and appeared in a deeply pink hue of rage. He had spent all afternoon picking up trash cast along the road by some careless junkman. He had to make a special trip to the dump himself with all he collected.

Our tax rate is always high, but I am puzzled by what happens to the moneys levied. The fire department is voluntary, the ambulance subsidized by the Lions Club. There are no utility services such as town water, sewage disposal, or lighting. It is every man for himself.

I often wonder how much it would cost for the town to hire a man to collect trash weekly. I am not likely to find out, I reflect, as I carry another carton of rubbish to the car. And I wonder what the town officials do with THEIR rubbish? Or possibly they haven't any that can't wait half a week longer by the back door before being picked up.

Theoretically we have the most democratic government, for we operate with Town Meetings. They are much the same as those held during the Revolution, when they also served as newspapers, for the news of the war was read out at a Town Meeting, and also requisitions for more supplies for General Washington. A Town Meeting gives everyone a chance to speak out. But it is not, I think, too democratic, for there are always two or three people who talk all the time, louder and louder. By eleven thirty, it is a question of who can shout loudest. And I am thoroughly confused. In the end, everyone votes on all issues just as they had made their minds up to vote before ever coming to the meeting.

But there is nothing like a New England Town Meeting to rouse people to fury. Afterward people get over the battle and begin to speak to one another again. Those who favor expanding the school (they have six children) and those who think the taxes are already astronomical may be on the same side at next meeting when the problem of zoning comes up.

Often I wonder what a group of Russians would think if they attended just one Town Meeting in Southbury, Connecticut.

Jill has been cleaning and sorting the onions, and storing them in the fruit cellar. She saves out the largest and plumpest for stuffing and baking, and some the right size for glazing for Thanksgiving. Onions are basic to good eating, I think. There really is no substitute for an onion when you need an onion.

It has a long history. The Egyptians spent the equivalent of two million dollars on onions during the years they were building the Great Pyramid. There were countless workers, of course, and the pyramid took twenty years to complete, but this is still quite a budget for onions. I have not found out how they ate them. I would suspect they ate them raw with some kind of black bread.

I do know that the Romans felt onions gave strength (my own opinion too) and they ate them as a breakfast dish with honey. This seems very odd, but then I remember that I make glazed onions with catsup and honey, baking them and basting until they are rich with the sauce. By the sixteenth century, onion juice was dropped in the ear as a remedy for deafness, and in the eyes to clear the vision.

The Spanish exported onions to the new world, but there were native varieties already there. I suspect onion soup must have a originated in France, for its fine bouquet seems so French. And many a peasant soup of the Middle Ages may have been raised to elegance by a judicious adding of onions.

Holding a round, firm onion in my hand, I think how wonderfully it is made. The delicate papery skin is faintly pink or ivory, and the concentric circles inside are a marvel. Nature casually produces this gift to mankind and we take it quite for granted. Of course, everybody has onions.

Happiness is not a thing you can cut off by the yard or measure in chunks. It is a matter of moments when you suddenly know that this moment is special. A few such moments are enough for a long time. The trouble with most of us, it seems to me, is that we chase happiness so hard that when we find it, we have already rushed on looking for more. The truly happy person is one who realizes the happiness of that moment, or that hour.

To be happy, one must be aware. For instance, there is a moment when you catch your breath seeing a pair of cardinals flaming against a dark branch of pine. This is a simple happiness, an awareness of the beauty and mystery of Nature. The happy person says, "I saw the cardinals." The unhappy person says, "Why don't they stay around? Why didn't they come before?"

Translated into other areas, it is the same. The happy person cherishes a golden experience, but the unhappy one wants it to last forever. It doesn't. It is like the marriages that break up, as so many do, because the excitement wears off and there are just two people living together. Glamour flies away, as the cardinals do. But the happiness of marriage can never be exhausted if both partners find new rewards in shared experience, in maturing companionship. No woman ever, I think, forgets the first kiss of her first love. But that comfortable kiss on the cheek after ten years of marriage is even happier. It has in it all the nights sitting up when the baby was sick, the times when there just wasn't any money, the quiet times when nothing at all happened.

I am sure many women would agree that happiness is that peck on the cheek at suppertime and the earnest inquiry, "Is everything all right?"

Maybe he doesn't notice the new hairdo or the new dress. But he wants to know if everything is all right. So this is a special moment, it is happiness.

Children nowadays are raised very differently from the days when I raised mine. Sometimes I wonder, when Connie and I are having such fun together, if I did everything wrong. I never knew anything about the aggressive age, the dependent age, the age for turning to Father and all the rest of it. We just rocked along, and it all came out splendidly. She is the nicest child a parent could dream up. But all I operated on was love and the advice on feeding from the local Doctor. I never knew whether she was advanced in one area or not.

But the young parents we know have at their finger tips just when Johnny does so and so and when the psychological urges change. A child can now do anything up to murder if it is the period of assertion. If it is the time they should scream, they scream. When they wish to break things, you just let them do so, but try to get ahead of them and grab up the choicest glass.

I think it makes an easy time for parents. They do not have to worry. Everything is in the book. But I cannot go all the way on this new deal. It seems to me when a child grows up, a basic sense of manners can be quite important, and it is much easier to learn when you are very young. No matter what period she was in, my daughter never felt free to maul anybody. Mama said NO. She knew she should not screech when the room was full of adults trying to talk. I do not think it damaged her. It may have resulted in her having a soft and pleasant speaking voice. But it did not give her a trauma to be told to speak quietly when company was there, or not to interrupt.

Times change. But I do like the result of the upbringing that Connie had, because it is rather nice to be considerate rather than to be busy expressing oneself.

I remember the autumn day when we took a picnic lunch up the hill to the old orchard. There is an outcropping ledge there, and we spread our sandwiches and eggs on it. There is something peaceful about an old orchard. You can feel the past. The ancient apple trees were planted by some early owner of Stillmeadow; probably a father and his sons went up to clear the slope, dig the holes, set the saplings straight. The trees grew and bore russets, greenings and snow apples. From the orchard came many pies, jellies, apples to bake, to roast over the coals, and to turn into flaky dumplings. Sweet cider was made, too, and apple vinegar. Small boys carried apples in their pockets as they hung around the iron kettle bubbling with apple butter, dark and spicy.

Apples were sliced and strung on cords to dry in the sun. The orchard was vastly important to family living. Now the old trees still bear some fruit, and we fill the picnic basket with it. The windfalls feed the little people of the woods, squirrels like the seeds and pheasants peck happily at them. Occasionally a deer comes along. And after the autumn storms, we have applewood for burning, a final gift of beauty. I thank the man who planted our orchard.

I like to remember going to Provincetown to watch the *Mayflower* come in. It was a bitter, foggy day with gusts of rain. Provincetown itself looked like a lost land, for the silvery grey veiled the town. We went into a restaurant at the water's edge, and waited, along with a crowd of other people. Waitresses dashed about giving the wrong orders to everyone and often carrying loaded trays to the windows and staring out at the sea. The guests were chiefly honeymoon couples, most of them looking, on that grim day, as if they feared they had made a dreadful mistake. The brides were fretful, the grooms melancholy. But one very young couple ordered one bowl of clam chowder for HER (so expensive). When the chowder came, he just dipped his spoon in and ate with her.

"He will be president of his company one day," said Jill.

Two older couples could afford lobster and sat eating it in gloomy silence. But suddenly someone cried, "There she comes!" The whole assembly rushed to the windows. We had binoculars, so we passed them around. Half an hour later, a pretty Portuguese waitress said, "Who owns these?"

"I do," I said mildly, and got a look myself. It is unfortunate that I have to shut my left eye when using binoculars, but I managed to see her foggily.

She came on, then, a tall ship with a squarish front. The sea was wild, the fog heavy. We made out flags flying and the dim shapes of the cutters escorting her. They looked like whippets. I wondered just what the Pilgrims felt when they first saw the bleak lonely land. What dreams and hopes rode with them on the deck of the tall ship we cannot know. But there was the new land, and there they would bide.

As we drove back through spitting rain, I was glad we had seen this landfall. I didn't care about the costumes, speeches, bands playing and fanfare to come in Plymouth. I never like trappings for my imagination. All I wanted was to see the shape of the Mayflower, as she came with difficulty around the point and finally dropped anchor. This was worth remembering.

The night Shirley Booth came to dinner, I had to pinch myself to believe it was real. After all, you meet many people as you go along, but it is seldom you meet the one in the entire world that you most wish to know. I would be pleased, of course, to have tea with Queen Elizabeth (especially if Philip were there) but it would not raise my blood pressure. But Shirley Booth—well, that is a different matter.

Most of the theatrical folk I have met seem to be in a world apart, and often, no matter where they are, it is still a stage. But Shirley Booth walks in casually and you feel you have known her all your life.

"How is Little Sister?" she asked at once, "and how is Holly?"

Then she curled up comfortably in an armchair and we talked about cockers and cats (Siamese) and cooking. At dinner, I tried to analyze the charm of her voice which is completely individual. It is a little flat, very honest, and has a sudden rise in tone when she is moved. It sounds young, sometimes innocent as a child's, but by a mere quiver in a vowel, Miss Booth can evoke tears.

I asked her how she worked out the line "Come back, Little Sheba," so the four simple words told a whole tragic story.

"Very simple," she said. "I saw a shabby old woman walking a shabby old dog one night on the street. I thought of her, and it just came out that way."

The curious quality which we call genius is difficult to define. Talent is a gift, and if accompanied by enough hard work, often seems to rise to the genius stature. But there is always something mysterious about a great artist.

It is better not to worry about it, I decided, as we had our coffee. Why is Shirley Booth a great actress? Simply because when she sets foot on the stage, the air suddenly becomes incandescent.

On another evening we went to dinner at Helen Beals' with Shirley. Lilac Farm is a gracious eighteenth-century house and the antiques which furnish it look as if they belonged there. We talked about books, and gardens and people and the best way to make strawberry shortcake. But finally Helen said, "How does it feel to win an Oscar?"

Shirley Booth said the main thing was that she had a very full, elegant gown, and she told the designer she just knew she could never walk in it.

"Do not worry, madame," he said, "it will just float around you."

"It didn't float," she said drily. "I put my foot through it on the first step and fell right down on my knees." So she had to be scooped up and finally made it to receive her Oscar in a rather different manner from what is customary.

The air begins to smell of windfalls that have been frosted. As the leaves drift down, some of the branches are bare. We see more sky. Night shuts down early. I miss the long summer twilights when day seems to linger indefinitely. But the mornings have a sparkle, and I love to see the shadow of the house silver with frost when sun has melted the rest of the crystals on the lawn.

Next week, I think, we might take the screens off.

Being troubled recently with what a young friend calls "imsomnia," I got up to watch the autumn dawn. It seemed silly just to wear the bed out by lashing around. I went to the kitchen and heated milk, popped in a dollop of butter, added plenty of freshly ground pepper. As I filled the glass, I wondered why it is that night always makes any worry or trouble worse. Daytimes we face things with equanimity, but once we are in bed, how things do pop up to cause anxiety! Even a small thing such as realizing that I have made appointments simultaneously at the dentist (Woodbury, seven miles in one direction) and the beauty parlor (nine miles in the other direction) can worry me. It is at night I wonder whether I really burned up the missing check or just put it away in a safe place where nobody would find it.

I took my steaming glass to my room and sipped it at the window. The sky was quite dark, almost charcoal when I got up, but now it began to have a silvery look, and then the horizon looked as if it had been dipped in pearl. Before I could realize it, color came in a tide of apricot and broke in flame as the sun came up. How small my worries seemed. How unimportant my anxieties. Everything would solve itself. The new day began in beauty. I finished my milk, went back to bed, and slept long past breakfast time. When I got up, I could not remember all the things which had troubled me in the night!

I believe for most people grief, worry, trouble, problems, do seem to balloon at night. I wonder whether it is a heritage from the primitive age when man could see the enemies by the light but at night those creatures who hunted by dark might fall on him as he slept. Also he could run better in daylight, but at night he was one of the less well-equipped creatures, having no decent night vision. It seems likely.

Or I suppose part of it might be because in the daytime even the grief-stricken must be involved with the routine of living which splits the attention from the sorrow.

Then when day is done, the routine ends, the activity of the body is over. All of the scientists seem to say the pulse is slower, the heart beats quietly. So possibly our defenses against the stresses of life also lessen. Or again, I reflected, turning the bacon for my brunch, light may have something to do with it. For a grey dark autumn rain depresses me, but if the sun breaks out, I begin to feel brisk and capable.

In spite of all man-made illumination, I think we live chiefly by natural light. We are no longer sun-worshipers as the pagans were, but the sun measures our days just the same. We plan what to do before the sun goes down, or before it gets too bright in summer. As we have less daylight in autumn, we shorten our activities accordingly. Modern lighting is a miracle, for any house or apartment can be bright with the new well-planned lamps and concealed lighting. Nevertheless, when the sun sets and the night closes down, most of us settle for quiet chores such as sewing on those peripatetic buttons or answering those letters. We put off scraping a chest of drawers, or sorting the washing, or brushing the cockers because "it will be better in the morning."

There have been times, it is true, when Jill and I have been stirring catsup around midnight or slicing cabbage for sauerkraut or making grape jelly. But usually we put the kitchen to bed after supper and do a few small jobs such as trimming candles, straightening the bookshelves. Then we read or listen to music and I spend a little time on my crossword puzzle trying to figure out who a Theban poet in 500 B.C. might be.

Crossword puzzles interest me as a game of words but also because I think I can guess what kind of person has made them up. A crossword puzzle-maker could never conceal his identity if he or she tried to disappear. There are more clues than you can count as to the personality.

"This man," I tell Jill, "is mad about ancient Greece and

about mythology. Likes ancient Egypt too. Is a real scholar, because few people bother about who was a neighbor of Colchis. Or what a trireme was."

I am better off with him than with the one who asks who sang in what opera and who wrote *Lakme*, or the one who goes in for strange animals with semi-hooves, fur-bearing creatures with prehensile tails. I do poorly with hepcats and former athletes or boxing terms but I am restored when I meet, via the puzzle, someone who wants to know the names of characters in Thomas Hardy, Emily Brontë, Spenser and what the last part of a sonnet is called.

But the main fun in a crossword puzzle is that you read the dictionary. The dictionary is incredible. You look up one word and find yourself traipsing around the African bush, looking at queer plants, and finding out at last that a golden buck is not fur-bearing, but is simply Welsh rabbit topped by a poached egg.

A few crossword creators I would not wish to meet on a dark corner. They cheat. They, in short, forge meanings for words. They are capable of fixing a whole block so that not one word can be discovered to set a key for the rest. I suspect they beat their wives, or if female, meet strange men for lunch and tell their husbands they were getting their hair done.

But on a chilly autumn evening, I settle down with the latest one while Jill pops the corn. "What physicist first called Eureka," I ask.

"Must have been a Greek," she says, "that is a Greek word."

November is a quiet month in New England. Colors are muted, haze stands over the hills, shadows fall long on the lawn. The air is dreamy. It is a curious time, an intermission between the excitement of October and the coming of the snows. By now almost everyone is ready for winter. When we drive along the winding country roads, I note neat stacks of firewood by back doors, tractors covered by the barns, and around many of the old farmhouses, banks of evergreen packed against the foundations.

The oldest houses have to be shored up against the cold to come. Evergreen branches are best, for they do not wither. Incidentally, they give a pleasant look to a house. Storm windows go on, screens are cleaned and painted on a sunny day and stacked in barns or cellars. Since most of us now have furnaces, the coal truck labors down the roads or the oil truck goes by. But some still fire the furnaces by wood, and their woodpiles are impressive, and their cellars are full of good seasoned wood. It takes skill to heat a house evenly with wood, but tended with skill, a wood furnace gives a good heat.

Indian summer brings such warm days that nobody wants to believe in winter. It is a time of enchantment, when the air is blue with the smoke of burning cornstalks from gardens and the intrepid roses put forth an occasional extra bloom. The last leaves are raked from the lawns. When we first moved to the country, these leaves were burned in a lovely sweet-smelling bonfire, but times have changed. Leaves are hoarded for mulch. A few careless souls still just burn them up, but most lay them carefully between rows of this and that. Oak leaves make an acid mulch for such plants as rhododendron and azalea. Maple leaves are fine for covering the border. Layers of leaves, potato parings, cabbage leaves, and so on, with lime between the layers, go in the compost pile to make good soil.

Country living has changed a great deal in a short time. The addition of freezers has changed the pattern of canning. Formerly everything had to be canned or pickled or made into relishes and preserves. Only the stout root vegetables would survive storage in a root cellar or a cool fruit closet. Now most homemakers look to the winter ahead with well-stocked freezers so they may have asparagus on New Year's Day or raspberry shortcake in February. And if they get short, the local market provides melon balls in December and frozen broccoli in April.

Now, instead of canning everything, we can confine our efforts to those family recipes for tomato mustard, thirteen-day pickles, and spiced herb tomato juice. Or wild elderberry jelly, spiced cherry preserve, wild strawberry jam.

Another change has both good and bad features, as so many things do in this world. The old iron range was a comfortable friend. In winter it heated the whole kitchen while the turkey roasted. Beans could simmer all night on the back, right by the stovepipe. In summer, a quick fire would cook meals on the top of the range without causing too much heat. Now the old iron ranges are vanishing. We see them sometimes painted pink and sitting in the windows of antique shops with philodendron or ivy growing from the tops. This is the age of the push-button. The good features are many. No kindling, no ashes, no lugging in an extra load for the firebasket. No polishing and getting that black stove polish all over your hands. On the adverse side, the old range had more personality. There was nothing streamlined about it, it had, indeed, fancy scrolls all around the edge and on the oven door. And it cooked ham, turkey, a rack of lamb or a pork roast to any Queen's taste. As for baked beans—rich with molasses and salt pork—well, nothing could be better.

And then the shelf over the back was always sweet with mint and tarragon just warmed enough to dry.

I think the reason the old range cooked so well was that it had absolutely uncontrolled temperature. Once you got used to it, you were safe. On our modern range, we set the knob and know the temperature will stay just there. It neither advances nor slows. But the secret of those perfect baked beans was that during the night, the fire died down and the temperature diminished. In the morning, when you tossed in the kindling, they got a browning all of a sudden. I think I would like a modern stove that would lower its heat gradually, tapering off to just being barely warm. Our modern oven, once set, will stay at 350 for years. It will cut itself off entirely, if you can work the timer, but it has no personal feeling about when to die down!

And as for soups and stews, I used to know to an inch how far back to push the pot and when to move it forward a shade.

I would certainly not give up my modern electric range with the lovely double ovens, the buttons to flick, the lights that flash on in the panel, and the electric clock-timer. But I felt sad when we had to retire the old iron range from the back kitchen and put in a radiator. The radiator is more reliable about not letting all the pipes freeze and burst, but the old stove was a center of living. Children's mittens were pinned on a line over the reservoir, boots steamed away under the bottom of the oven. A rack at one side cosily dried snowsuits. (There is a point for no insulation! With our current wonder, you can set trays of ice cubes on the top and they won't melt for some time.)

I suspect that my viewpoint stems from a belief that in every area of living, the past has some value, as well as the present. Although we move beyond it at a satellite rate, I think we should be grateful to the best gifts of yesterday. I have known women who tossed out all the pine and maple, burned up the hand-made quilts, scrapped the hooked rugs, put the old oil lamps in the rubbish. Nothing old was fashionable. Some time later they were paying fancy prices to buy old pine chests, maple drop-leaf tables, hooked rugs, and were hunting for oil lamps to electrify. They also, I regret to say, made spinning wheels into planters, and old hitching posts into lamp bases.

Possibly because our country is relatively young, we feel we have to always change. Whatever is the fashion must be better than what we have. This has always been true, for I have seen many very old houses in which the dignified early Colonial mantels were ripped out and varnished Victorian curlycues put in. Picket fences were burned up and metal grills used as fencing. Often now, as we drive around, I notice these are passing and split-rail cedar is going in. This type of fence is so much like an early stockade that I wonder whether we are going back now to pioneer days!

As for clothes, some of those in our attic would be fine on Fifth Avenue, if we could lace ourselves in enough, but one thing is obvious, the modern woman's frame, thin or fat, has more to it and is less pliable than it was in the early days. I remember hearing about my grandmother hanging on to a bedpost while being laced in, but no amount of hanging on anything would ever get a modern woman laced into a waist like a hummingbird's.

Currently, as I write, women dress to look like carnival tents, but this, too, must pass.

Walking down the country road this morning, I noticed the swamp in late fall has lovely colors. The chalky purple of the wild blackberry canes, the cinnabar of frosted weeds, and the garnet of oak seedlings seem like music. Farther on, the cut-over fields have variations on the theme of brown, from tawny to copper. Squirrels go a-marketing under the hazel bushes, for under the burs the satiny brown nuts begin to show. A fawn-colored rabbit hops ahead along the grey stone wall, and a pheasant leads three females toward the thicket.

As I pass the neighbor's old red barn the smell of dried hay is sweet as honey. Pumpkins and cabbages and smoky Hubbard squash lie in the garden. Blue smoke rises from a pile of burning cornstalks. "Season of mists and mellow fruitfulness," Keats called it, and also "Think not of spring, thou hast thy beauty too."

It is a quiet beauty, and the rhythm of November is a quiet one. Nature and man seem to me to be gathering strength for the long cold. In the village women are putting harvest decorations on the front doors, a sheaf of corn, gourds, evergreen branches. This custom surely goes back to the days of ancient Greece when the harvest festivals were held. We no longer wear garlands and wreaths but we wreath our doors. Many front stoops have also pumpkins and squash on each side of the door, a symbol of a bountiful season. We learned to keep an eye on the pumpkins, for once a severe freeze came unexpectedly and the next morning when we opened the door, the pumpkins exploded.

The dogs are enchanted. Holly races around and around the house, her flying Irish paws skim over the leaves, barely stirring them. Her face has a rapt look, her tail is a windy flag.

Teddy manfully pounds after her, golden cocker ears gathering bits of leaves. They play a definite game, with rules. When she gets too far ahead of him, she reverses the field and dives toward him. He scuttles around the house. When she catches him, she nips up one of his ears and tugs him along. The older cockers look on this as childish and silly. If the game comes too near, a sudden snap of jaws or a growl warns the players to mind their own business and not disturb people.

After Teddy gives up and just sits down, tongue out, Holly makes a final whirl and then sits with him. They always sit facing the same way and Teddy tries to sit like an Irish, which is straight as a die, when naturally he would sit with one hip sidewise, as most cockers do. The tall elegant Irish and the compact golden cocker look beautiful to me, especially when the wind ruffles Teddy's ears and drifts the leaves around Holly's plume of a tail. (Since this is the only tail on the place, we have to remember not to shut a door too quickly and nip it.)

Generally dogs "settle down" when they are fully mature and give up flinging themselves about unless there is something important that needs chasing, but the Irish has the heart of a child always. I once asked a friend when Holly would settle down, and he said his Irish showed faint signs of it at the age of eight, but very faint.

Cats seldom give up playing games at any age. The staidest cat will make up pouncing games, go on imaginary mouse-hunts, leap into paper sacks and bounce around.

One of my favorites is the grocery store cat. She isn't exactly

pedigreed, unless all cats are pedigreed, as I often suspect. She
has a good thick practical grey coat and a dignified face. She
chooses her friends carefully, has been known to hiss at unlikely
persons. This makes everyone she does like feel smug. I am
one of the most flattered, for she will purr and rub against me.
How wonderful to be liked by the grocery cat!

"She don't take to everybody," says the grocer.

During the busy hours, she makes herself comfortable in a
small carton, not any special carton, but one that happens to
be empty. She fits herself in neatly, rests her chin on the edge
and keeps a sleepy eye on the customers. There is probably no
animal that can fold up as completely as a cat, unless her wild
relatives can. When she thinks best, she has a family, and customers order a kitten with their meat, vegetables and canned
goods. It works out very well for everyone. A friend of mine
once phoned and said, "I need a roast today, rib, a head of
lettuce, a pound of butter, and send along a kitten."

My Siamese cat, Esmé, had an enormous vocabulary. Most
cats think a lot but say little. They growl low in the throat at
danger, hiss with rage, or mew piteously when they want some
of that chicken you are frying. But Esmé talked incessantly. If
nothing at all was happening, she simply conversed, comment-
ing obviously on the weather, the fact that one chair was out of
place or that she was frankly tired of balanced meals. The voice
of a Siamese is sharp and raucous, many people do not like it,
but once you fall under the spell of it, you are charmed. For
weeks after Esmé died, the house seemed hollow as a drum.
And when I had to go away, homecoming was not the same,
for even the welcoming, forgiving barks of all the cockers and
Irish did not replace the fluent vituperation with which Esmé

addressed me. Shameless one, she began, never again shall I knead your lap with these paws. No more shall I leap on your chest and wash your face.

Never again shall I speak to you, she said, speaking loudly. You are faithless, go your way. Then, after a time, when the exuberant dogs subsided, she would stalk in, stuffed with dignity, and graciously put out one long brown velvet glove and tap me. But never do this again, she indicated.

Recently I went to the city to visit on the air with one of the nicest broadcasters, who also cooks, gardens, and takes care of her children, as well as run a daily hour on radio. I am no feminist but I think it remarkable that women so often can juggle a full-time important job and a family. I think possibly men have to channel their lives but women have always had to do "a number of things," as Stevenson would say. On this day, Mrs. D. had been up part of the night with one of the children who had a temperature. But she was on time, and brisk. We fell to talking about animals because her daughter keeps a full quota of all kinds. Currently she has a raccoon. I asked if it was a house raccoon.

"No," she said, "but he has a split-level house of his own. His father built it for him."

Instantly I could see Papa raccoon busily sawing away and pawing at nails for that split-level house. It was a charming picture, with the prospective inhabitant watching. By the time I realized she meant her husband had built it, I was just seeing Papa 'coon lifting the ridgepole. I did not think he could paint this split-level house, because fur does not accommodate at all to paint.

November means Thanksgiving. This is our particularly national feast day. It is more solemn than it was when I was a child and the world had never heard of missiles and bombs. In those days, it was just a family gathering when everyone ate too much and was grateful that the family could be together again, and there was always the idea that Thanksgivings would go on forever. There have been times since when it seemed doubtful.

A good many men have died trying to preserve America. The wars have ended Thanksgiving for a good many boys. I think of them, as Stephen Spender says:

"Born of the sun
They travelled a short while
Toward the sun
Leaving the vivid air
Signed with their honour."

It is for us to justify some way, somehow, the fact that they traveled a short while. It makes Thanksgiving, for me, more sober. There is a grave responsibility for us who are left, to defend what they died for. Thanksgiving should be a time of prayer, of feeling humble, and of reaffirming our faith in God. When the grandchildren are propped up on the dictionary and encyclopaedia and reach for a turkey wing, I look at them, and pray quietly that they may live in a world at peace.

But when I was growing up, the feast itself was more important. We never tasted turkey except at Thanksgiving, that was what turkey was meant for. We dreamed of it, rich, brown, savory with chestnut stuffing. The quivering cranberry sauce was only for Thanksgiving, too, and oh, the giblet gravy and the glazed onions and fluffy mashed turnips! Turkey for Thanksgiving was as special as the orange in the toe of the stocking at Christmas.

The onions and mashed potatoes, the pumpkin and mince pies were traditional. The turnips were beaten to a fluff, dressed with melted butter, salt and pepper. I do not know whether the Thanksgiving menu was what it was because of trying to copy the Pilgrims' first one, or whether we just had what was available. But how good it all was.

Now the younger members of my family simply loathe turnips, and squash, so one year I substituted their favorite peas with mushrooms. "Oh, Mama," cried my daughter in anguish, "it has to be turnips for Thanksgiving!" They were all outraged. They said I couldn't go around changing Thanksgiving, for goodness sake. So I went back to the big bowl of turnips which they do not eat. They were satisfied emotionally anyway.

I myself dislike change. So I understood their feeling. We only had oyster dressing once, because oysters were for stew in the little town where I grew up. Chestnuts were for dressing and many a blister have I acquired while perched on a stool beside Mama, helping get the shells off those intractable nuts. Often Mama made a simple stuffing with onion, celery, toasted or dried breadcrumbs, melted butter, sage, seasonings. After all, a properly roasted turkey imparts its own flavor to the dressing. And the dressing should be delicately moist, not dry, but not gluey as so many stuffings are. It should never lump up in a ball on the plate, but fork easily.

Cranberry sauce, of course. We now use it year round, enjoying the dark tangy flavor with roast lamb or baked chicken or grilled chops. I do not think it fits with roast beef or steak, but I have no idea why. But even though we use it constantly, it still seems special on the Thanksgiving table.

After grace is said, there is always a moment of silence at our table. What grave thoughts go through the minds of the younger folk I shall never know, but they have a quiet look. I think of all the Thanksgivings past, and of all the hopes for the future. Then the carving knife makes the first slice, and yes, the turkey is exactly done, tender, moist, rich. And pass the giblet gravy at once.

Later on, the table cleared and the dishwasher blessedly running, we can add an apple log to the fire and sit toasting our toes against the November chill, while the bowl of apples and nuts goes around and one of the family brings out the old cornpopper. And I am always amazed at the fact that no matter how big the dinner is, around dark the younger members of the family get that hungry look again. Maybe a cold turkey sandwich, they suggest. I have a feeling that the table has just been cleared. So I say they can help themselves and before I know it, trays appear with salad, turkey sandwiches, cranberry sauce, hot coffee. And wedges of Wisconsin cheese on the side.

"Are you sure you can't eat anything?" asks Connie.

"Well, just a bite of turkey," I say weakly. So we all overeat quite happily. Someone says, "Perhaps cold is better than hot."

Day ends as the trays go out to the kitchen. The cockers and Irish have had their share of the end pieces and the fat. They doze comfortably by the fire. They may dream of having their share of the lovely turkey soup which I make the next day, who knows?

For our family no turkey is big enough to be a problem as to leftovers. I love turkey timbales, creamed turkey and mushrooms, turkey soup. I am lucky if I have enough to put in the

big iron pot and simmer with a lot of other things added.
When the house quiets down, I have a glass of hot milk.
Then I say my prayers and give my thanks to God who still
makes Thanksgiving possible. On Thanksgiving night I pray a
long while for everyone all over the world who may not have
a Thanksgiving.

I have noticed that all of the famous people who are pic-
tured in magazines are always relaxing. Barbara and Dick relaxing by their swimming pool. Elaine relaxing at a night club
with her escort, the famous polo player. (How do they relax
at a night club?) Mrs. Gainsborough relaxes on the front porch
of "Woodmere" (country touch). Scott Marlow 3rd relaxes
with his family by the barbecue (with twenty steaks on the
grill). Even the great political figures relax with their four or
more grandchildren. And this, I may say, is a good trick. We
cannot relax with just two grandchildren, far from it. We find
them charming, lovely, intelligent and a good many other things
but never relaxing.

It occurs to me that these people relaxing must some time or
other DO something. Otherwise would they be worth photographing at all? Now and then obviously they are active. But
you would never know it from the pictures.

"Holly Relaxes by the Wisteria Well," would be a suitable
caption for the photographer. She relaxes by the old well with
her collection of choice old tin cans, a tired galosh, a bath
towel and a pink rabbit (snitched from a summer visitor). She
keeps a paw on her bone to warn the cockers away. When she
decides to come in to see what I am cooking, she chooses a treasure to bring in and offer me proudly. And the way I feel about

Holly, I prefer that old tin can with her love to a diamond bracelet any day.

Now, toward the end of November, rain falls steadily and it is a chilling rain. The bare branches look black and the browns in the meadows are deepened. The pond's level rises and we can hear the water pouring over the dam and on into George's brook. Th small-paned windows of the house are a wash of silver. The lamps go on early in the day.

When we go out to do the chores, the air smells of wet fallen leaves. It is a curious musty smell, but pleasant. Jill brings in an apple log from the woodpile and the fire burns brightly. The cockers and the Irish doze on the warm hearth. It's a good time to have Brunswick stew, that delectable combination of chicken, tomatoes, lima beans and corn simmered with seasonings in the old iron soup kettle.

When the rain finally ends, usually at dusk, the whole world looks polished. The horizon has a rosy glow. The air is like vintage wine, properly cooled. When we open the door, the dogs rush out and dash around the house. Rain's over, rain's over, they say, barking happily. Inside, with the rose-colored light coming in the windows, the house takes on new life. The milk glass gleams, the brass and copper shine. And the soup kettle is ready to be lifted from the crane, the popovers are hot.

"Next thing we know," says Jill, dishing up the stew, "it will be snowing."

WINTER

Winter

THE EARLY SNOWSTORMS DON'T AMOUNT TO MUCH. THE
flakes drift down idly, almost seeming suspended in the air.
They melt as soon as the sun comes out. They are utterly dis-
arming. We may have days no colder than October afterward
and everyone in the village says cheerfully, "Guess it won't be
much of a winter."

Then the temperature drops sharply and winter is in business.
During a real snowstorm, the flakes seem not to come down
from the sky, but to drive in horizontally. I wonder whether this
effect is due to the wind or to the stormclouds hanging so low.
If you walk out, you feel almost blinded. I suppose all snowflakes must be equally cold, but the early snow seems cool and
pleasant, while the later snow feels arctic.

Faith Baldwin usually comes to visit in the lull between
storms. She lives about an hour and a quarter away, in an old
house (though younger than ours). It is no longer farming
country there, but she has meadows and woods and a shallow

pond big enough for ducks. A friend drives her up, for getting from her house to ours by train would puzzle the president of the railroad. Besides, she brings baskets of things, too many to lug on a train if there were a train. She comes in well wrapped, mittened, and with fur boots, and a basket on each arm. More baskets follow. She unpacks the treasures. Four cans of boneless sardines for Holly. A pound of freshly ground hamburger for Little Sister, a special favorite. Another package of hamburger for the rest of the cockers. Smoked shrimp for me and a jar of special jelly or English marmalade for Jill. Usually a tiny mug for Connie to have when she comes, for she knows how Connie loves little things.

The last mug she gave her is about right for a fairy to quaff dew from. Sometimes she brings a wedge of cheese or fruitcake which are part of presents to her. The second basket is books. It was Faith, of course, who had a bookfinder find the out-of-print *Asey Mayo Trio* and two other very rare Phoebe Atwood Taylor mysteries. For me, she located the book by Elswyth Thane about her Finch, Chee-Wee, one of the most charming books I have. Elswyth herself couldn't find a copy for me. And she always adds a few books such as Henry Beston's *Outermost House*, or Katherine Dos Passos' delightful book about Cape Cod.

The third basket (by now we are dizzy) has a mug for my own collection (the current one is French and intricately patterned with deep blue and edged with gold). For Jill, a pencil that writes in three colors or a self-charging flashlight. Faith is a giving person. Her chief happiness, I know, is in giving. We have made a small joke about it. When we pack up our Christmas or birthday gifts for her, we put in a note saying,

"Just take a look at these before you give them away!" For if she thinks it is something someone needs, there it goes.

But the giving of things is not as important as the giving of herself. She may only weigh eighty-six pounds but I think her heart must account for most of it. No one in trouble ever turns to her without receiving spiritual as well as material help. She is known to countless people not as the writer of seventy popular books but as the friend who comforted and sustained them when they felt they could not go on any longer.

In her own life, she has had heavy burdens to bear, with serious illnesses of her four children, a long tragic illness of her mother, the death of her husband, as well as the loss of a favorite nephew in the last war. She has borne other burdens too, more than most of us can acquire in a lifetime. But I have never known her to ask for sympathy under any circumstances. She has a devastating wit, and I, for one, would never risk saying I sympathize with her for anything. She would bring me to my senses with the fact that all that worries her is that a suit of armor chased her around the Metropolitan Museum the last time she went there. "And I haven't had a sense of balance since I was twelve," she added drily, "and you can imagine how much sense of balance a suit of armor has! We really lurched around the museum."

After the baskets are unpacked, she gets into comfortable slacks and sweater and we sit by the fire. She once wrote a severe article about women who slopped around in slacks but that was before she knew me. It may be starting to snow again outside, but we don't notice. We talk about writers and writing and people, and when we disagree, we both hold our own. Jill never has a chance to open her lips. "You and Faith," she says, "talk both at once and constantly, and I can't even think."

We also talk about what we believe in and what is the meaning of suffering and other rather insoluble things. Faith summed it up in *Face Toward the Spring*, I think. "We shall be judged," she said, "by the love we have offered, given, and shared: the personal love of family, friend and neighbor; the impersonal love that is service; the love we cannot quite put into words, not even in prayer, that is the love of God."

And the snow falls outside, and we do not notice it.

In a queer sort of way, we New Englanders are proud of winter. We have had many hard winters, some easy ones, some almost arctic ones. But I have never heard anyone complain about the weather. "Quite a storm," the postman may say, "but we have to expect it."

"Pretty cold last night," says the grocer. "Went down to ten below on my thermometer. This time of year we generally have some cold."

Even when it took our neighbor, Joe, four hours to shovel us out after one storm last winter, he only said, "Lot of snow fell this time."

Cars stall, motors freeze, wires go down sometimes. Roads drift deep with powdery snow. Branches crack and crash down. But neighbors get out to help one another and there is a good deal of joshing as to whose thermometer falls to the lowest mark. Winter, I think, is a common denominator, as well as a challenge to Yankee staying power.

When I was growing up, I found winter exciting. In Wisconsin, where we lived, it was often thirty below. Winter also came to stay, it began early and ended late. But it meant skating on the solidly frozen lake, tobogganing with my beau (I invariably fell off). It also meant sleigh-ride parties when Gracie (who pulled the town hearse also) plodded along at her usual slow pace but with very lively freight.

We rode in a flat wagon which had runners replacing the wheels of summer. The wagon box was filled with clean hay. Gracie clumped along at a decent pace, no galloping for her. We were young and innocent and if mittened hand held mittened hand, that was excitement enough. We sang "Juanita" and "By Thy Rivers Gently Flowing"—and then we came to my house, for Mama was always willing to fix oyster stew for any number. Snow was tracked in, wraps melted on her best Chippendale chairs, boys skidded on the best rugs, knocked things over. Girls giggled. But Mama had the oyster stew in the big tureen, gobs of butter melting on top, a dusting of paprika. Plenty of toasty buttery crackers to go with it. Hot cocoa was our drink then and there was a big pitcher of that. A bowl of whipped cream accompanied the cocoa. Actually Mama's hot cocoa was a fine brew, for she had been in Mexico with Father and learned the Mexican chocolate way. She had a wooden beater to froth it, and she added a touch of coffee.

And after some of the gang had gone home, Mama never cared if my beau happened to note an apple pie lonely in the icebox and ate half of it. Father was fretful about these invasions but Mama was fine at managing. She usually had him over at his best friend's, the family Doctor, planning a camping trip.

As we have such a problem these days with juvenile delinquents, I often think there is only one recipe for juveniles, and unfortunately you cannot get it by any amount of legislation or law or consultants. What juveniles need, in any level of society, and at all times, is a home. The gallons of oyster stew and the gallons of hot cocoa kept me and my companions satisfied not to go to any "joint." Better food and more fun at home.

But it wasn't just the food. It was Mama not minding when some awkward boy broke a cherished piece of china. "My goodness, these things *will* break," she would say. And if things got too noisy, she would remark, "The neighbors hear everything."

It seemed quite natural to me that anyone in trouble just came over to talk to Mama, but I now realize it was quite unusual. Not only young boys and girls found it easy to talk to her, but the college students did too, and also older people with heavy burdens. She never, so far as I know, told them what mistakes they had made, or how wrong they were. She listened, and poured hot tea, and made a suggestion so gently that they always felt they had thought of it themselves.

And as the season turned toward Christmas, Mama was busy making gifts for everyone who needed them. She had a fierce dedication to Christmas. It was, for her, a giving time. She felt it implied thought for the one you gave a gift to, not just buying something and wrapping it because it was the thing to do.

She was a noticing woman and she could spend all year noticing what some friend did not have and needed. Whenever I feel sad about the over-commercialization of Christmas, which has become such a big business, I think of Mama, happily wrapping the jars of quince preserve that one friend so loved. For the non-cooks, she made the most elegant of fruitcakes. For prospective mothers, she made practical layettes, things she called "tubbable." But for me, she spent her saved pennies for a special book of poetry.

For my mother, Christmas was a time to express love and friendship.

Almost everyone has a love of tradition. I notice that those friends of mine who were raised without benefit of a traditional Christmas are the most dedicated when they have their own homes.

"This angel is ALWAYS going on the top of the tree," said one to me. "It is going to be traditional."

I think it is a fine idea for young people to begin traditions. When they marry and may live in a city too far to go home for Christmas, they can still hang the mistletoe on the chandelier, light the bayberry candles, trim a table tree with gold and blue balls. Emotionally, I think most of us have a Currier and Ives feeling about Christmas, complete with sleighs, fur robes, prancing horses, and Grandfather cutting the tree in his own woodlot. There should be plum pudding steaming on the old iron range. Grandmother is basting the turkey. This is, in a way, an inherited Christmas memory.

But of course Christmas is primarily a thing of the spirit and can be observed anywhere, in any manner, if the spirit is there. Here in the country, we fortunately have no Santa Clauses on every corner. For one thing, we have no corners. I really think there should be a law prohibiting the flood-tide of Santas that bedevil the cities and towns. It makes a mockery of the good St. Nicholas. He should not be seen, even once, he should be the one who comes down the chimney at night, mysterious and wonderful. The hooves of his reindeer paw the snowy roof. His pack just does squeeze down the chimney.

What child is ever going to enjoy the delight of this when he has seen ten Santas in shabby costumes in all the stores all day long? Santa does not have to ride in from the North Pole at all, he can step out of the supermarket and go right down Elm Street and there he is.

In our valley, so far, we have not made a mockery of Santa Claus. We have a giant evergreen in the center of the village, and this is decorated. Since we have no street lights, we are spared the festoons of colored bulbs, we have the stars and the tree. The village store hangs wreaths in the windows, and the farmhouses have candles and wreathed doorways. Not far away is a town that has a competition for Christmas decorations, and this I deplore. It brings out cardboard Santas riding on the roofs, elaborate effects in the yards, some beautiful, some not. But I wish we could keep Christmas simply and with reverence as a spiritual time. Gay and festive it should be, but not a commercial enterprise, or a carnival.

At Stillmeadow, we use hemlock boughs from the upper woodlot to decorate the old narrow mantels. They are not sprayed with gold or silver. They are just green boughs, for it is the green of evergreen boughs that symbolizes immortality. For the tree, we use the old ornaments, including the lamb that some puppy once ate a portion of. I set the fat Christmas candles in the windows, but ever since the barn burned down I set them in saucers for safety. And we no longer have the bayberry candles burning away in the midst of a nice decoration of tinder-quick evergreens. Every year there are disastrous fires from tinsel and tissue paper, candles and pine needles, and it is strange that people never learn about fire hazards except by experience.

We are now nine for Christmas dinner, although Jill's grandson is still eating out of jars. In another year he will be reaching for his turkey with everyone else. The modern baby foods in jars are a wonder for they include meats, vegetables, fruits all ready to warm up and spoon out.

One thing I am always glad of, and that is the end of the wrapping of gifts. I have absolutely no manual dexterity, and my struggle with tissue paper that parts at the corners of packages, ribbons that wind up in balls, colored tapes that cling to my own thumbs instead of the packages, is really something rather epic in a gloomy way. I use cellulose tape in large amounts to hide imperfections and to keep things from bursting out. I invariably break into a cold sweat when I am wrapping things with peculiar shapes because no matter how I try, the objects keep gliding out of one end of the box or snatching the paper away from me. Although I buy matching tags and stickers, they never turn out to match anything.

How I admire the gifts that come to me with rosettes of ribbon, with crisscross ties, with neatly tucked in ends. I hate to open them for I like to see how pretty they look. My one and only successful year of wrapping was the one when I stuck silver stars on everything until a neighbor's child was so enchanted by the stars that I gave her the whole box that was left, and went back to my pedestrian efforts.

I always begin to wrap early because I seem to wrap with my neck and back muscles and I ache. Half an hour at a time of unwinding those ribbons and folding the paper and picking everything up from the floor, and I give up. I can cook a big dinner for six or eight people more easily. There is one problem about early wrapping, however. I never remember what is in those curiously shaped packages. Indeed I label them with small bits of paper, but these fall off. I suspect them of climbing out of the tapes deliberately. Consequently if I am very anxious to give a certain something to Connie, she may get two of them.

Jill and I are the only members of the family who can be said to be non-wrappers. Jill's idea is to stick a tag right on a box. Why bother to tie it all up in glazed papers and fuss with ribbons when it gets opened right away and you have all that extra muss to clean up. But my daughter Connie and Jill's daughter and daughter-in-law spend a lot of time making productions, and I think it gives an air to the holiday.

It is, however, absolute folly to try to gift-wrap an electric frying pan. Or a special long-handled window cleaner. Or even a pair of antique candlesticks.

I notice of late years that the children eye the things in cartons and are anxious to open them first. There could be a good iron in one of those unwrapped cartons or the portable beater so needed. Although I think Christmas should be for gifts that are things you normally never buy for yourself, I find that practical gifts for the young marrieds rate very high. Electrical equipment makes life easier and is more gratefully received than a luxury item. A good blanket drew more exclamations than any amount of gold lipsticks or fancy bootees from our family. Most young marrieds live on a rigid budget and manage very well. But a really nice fluffy blanket is quite outside the budget and is very welcome.

Which brings me to think that Christmas gifts should be carefully planned to meet some special need. Sometimes even a good double boiler is a fine gift. Putting one pan in another always means the water in the lower pan boils up and over. And a good waterproof bag for diapers can be very important.

It isn't the gift that matters but the thought that goes into it.

We always think of Christmas as a time of snow and icicles hanging from the old well and snow over the valley. But I had a friend who was newly married and went to live in the tropics. She felt sorry for herself as Christmas drew near. She wept. And then her husband brought in some tropical flowers, to decorate the house, he said. And it came to her suddenly that Christmas was not a place, nor was it weather, it was a state of mind. After all, she thought, Christ was not born in the North, he was born in a stable in Bethlehem. And so she got a small palm tree and put flowers on the flat leaves, and was gay and merry. It was, she said, one of the best Christmases ever, although they afterward moved back to New England where the snow fell and the pine trees were silvered.

It is certainly true that Christmas is only seasonal in the heart. The snow may be clean and deep outside, or you may be in a dingy city apartment or you may be in a steaming tropical country. But it is still Christmas. Whether you serve the plump crispy turkey, or something exotic wrapped in pandanus leaves, the feeling of Christmas is there. It is in the mind and in the heart. The faith we have in the good rises like a tide and wherever we are, we feel it. Christmas graces any board and gives a new lift to our life, and as we hear once more the familiar carols, we thank God for the birth of His son. "O little town of Bethlehem, how still we see thee lie— Above thy dark and dreamless streets the silent stars go by."

As always when the old house creaks into quiet, I snuff the

Christmas candles, and check to be sure nobody has left a turkey bone where the Irish could get it. The colored ribbons and tissues are swept up, the fire has died down, and I let the cockers and Irish out for a last run in the new-fallen snow. They take nips of it, roll in it.

And now, as always, I have a special reunion with my Honey, a golden cocker who died a time ago. I hear her paws softly padding beside me as I put the house to bed. I can see her golden feather of tail wagging happily. Some might say this is foolish for she was, after all, only a dog, and she is dead. But the fourteen years of love and loyalty she gave me are very much alive as I say "Good night, Honey."

The house talks, as old houses do. A beam settles. A chair rocks. A floor creaks with unseen footsteps. I like this, for it reminds me of all the lives that have been lived under this roof, and I feel their friendly presence as I poke the embers. Christmas is over. It is time to burn the wrappings, write the thank-you notes, return the calls, set the house in order for the New Year. It is also time to consider where our lives are bound, what purpose steadies our course. How much have we helped our fellow men this year, and what good have we accomplished? Has the world been better because we were in it? If Christmas means anything, it means good will to all. I doubt many of us truly live up to that, but we can try again.

As I let the dogs back in, I smell the snow. The walk is silver, the picket fence wears pointed caps. Night herself is luminous with the falling snow. A flurry comes in with the dogs and melts on the wide floor boards. No two snowflakes, I am told, are exactly alike and this is a mystery. Now the intricate shapes are gone, and only a spot of water remains. It is not very practi-

cal to stand in the open door at midnight and let the snow blow in. But it has been my habit for years to close Christmas Day just so, sending my blessing out to all the people in the world, those I know well and love greatly, and those I shall never see. And as I close the door, I repeat again my Christmas blessing. "God rest you merry, gentlemen."

The winter sun burns like white fire on the snow. Ice glitters on the cold side of the branches of the sugar maples, melts on the warm side and falls with a soft sound. I do not know why white seems more pure as a color than green or blue, but so it is, and the countryside in winter has a purity we never see in any other season. Under the shell ice at the pond's edge, the water is like polished onyx. When I walk there, I follow rabbit tracks. The prints of small folk make delightful patterns everywhere in the snow, shortly overlaid by the prints of galloping cockers. Holly goes in great leaps and then rolls in the snow, reminding me of the angel-wings we used to make when I was a child.

Now the pine needles are nearly all swept up, except those that linger in the cracks of the wide floors. The Christmas ornaments are back in the attic packed safely in cartons. An old house doesn't have much closet space, so the attic is stuffed with everything from old picture frames to the broken spinning wheel (to be fixed one day). In earlier days, children used to play there and crack butternuts and eat apples. Occasionally we can hear their voices, sweet with laughter.

About now, Jill decides to clean the linen closet. This is simply a long, low space under the eaves which you have to crawl on your hands and knees to get into. You have to back out when you are through. At the far end, there is a hidden opening into a still smaller secret closet. Presumably a man could hide there, but it would have been very uncomfortable. When the British were burning Danbury, a good many families were thankful to have a secret place, although the British never came up the valley. They were turned back in the battle at Ridgefield chiefly because of Benedict Arnold, who was an intrepid soldier and still, at that time, a faithful one.

Later there was great excitement when General Washington spurred his horse across the ford at Sandy Hook. The old residents still point out where the ford was. How the children stared when the tall General rode by. He was the hope of what seemed more and more a hopeless cause. Most of the time the Continental army appeared to be on the run. And most of the time the post riders brought only orders for more salt pork and barrels of beef, more ammunition, more men.

Rochambeau's arrival at Newport in July, 1780, added 6,000 French troops and the sight of them raised men's hearts. But on September 23, Benedict Arnold's treason was discovered— the same brave man that spurred his white horse from New Haven to Ridgefield and saved that battle. This was a grievous blow to our valley, for General Arnold was our own.

When the news came that Cornwallis had surrendered on October 19, 1781, with 7,000 men, it was almost impossible to believe. Church bells tolled in Woodbury, Southbury and all over the state. Prayers of Thanksgiving were said. The town then counted up its losses. The cemeteries were full, and many men had died and been buried on strange battlefields. Food was scarce, money was worthless, farms had run down, many were ill from the scanty rations during the last part of the war. It would be a long time before things were all right again. The people were sober. Had it been worth while? Independence had a fine ringing sound, but oh for the days when a body could buy the fine brown sugar and the good India tea and when a woman could have a bonnet from France.

"Praise God from whom all blessings flow," they sang.

"And his peace be upon you," prayed the minister.

Houses have their own personalities, I think. Some houses seem happy. The minute you step through the front door, you feel it. Some houses are unhappy, you feel a shadow as you go in. It may be that houses absorb something from the people

who have lived in them. But often an elegant house may have
a sad air, and a simple one may glow with happiness.

In the country, we perhaps become more intimate with our
houses because each house is so separate, surrounded by its own
land. And then when winter draws in, we spend much more
time in them than city people do. When we are snowed in, the
house is our world, we are a part of its very being. Toward
the end of autumn, we take special care of the house. Storm
windows and storm doors snug it down. The woodshed is
thrifty with seasoned logs and kindling and baskets of pine
cones. Jill lugs in the window boxes and sets them on bricks on
top of the radiators. We cut ivy for the grey stoneware jugs,
and fill a dough tray with branches of pine to keep summer's
green with us a little longer. Comforters and quilts, smelling
faintly of moth balls, get a good sunning.

The emergency shelves are stocked with staples, the freezer
is full, the fruit closet has its jams and jellies and relishes. So
when the furnace begins to purr, we are settled in. Books laid
aside for winter appear on the cobbler's bench. I favor books
like Edwin Way Teale's *North with the Spring* for January
days. Mr. Teale evokes spring perfectly and his poetic strong
prose is a joy. And although Mr. Teale is a naturalist, he never
talks down to a lay reader. He teaches a great deal, but in a
casual easy way.

Autumn Across America, a companion volume, is another
favorite. This is the time too for books such as Bruce Catton's
A Stillness at Appomattox, or James Gould Cozzens' *By Love
Possessed.* There are few interruptions on a snowy day so you
can give yourself over to a long book and not be jumping up
every few minutes when someone comes to the door. This win-

ter, I plan to re-read Shakespeare, taking time to savor the majestic sweep and eternal beauty of the lines. I often wonder what it would be like to come suddenly on Shakespeare after growing up. What an experience that would be.

I also like to re-read Peter Fleming's *Brazilian Adventure*, one of the most delightful books I know of and not widely known, unfortunately. *Wuthering Heights* is a February kind of book and fits a stormy February day. Every third winter, I pick up *The Forsyte Saga* and it never disappoints me. Jill, of course, reads Dorothy Sayers' *The Nine Tailors* again, although she almost knows it by heart now. She also reads parts of Cothren's *Ancient History of Woodbury*, but this has to be in small doses for the print is so fine and the pages so yellow that a headache is inevitable.

Katherine Mansfield fits any season but the Letters and Journal are particularly fine now, for her translucent prose brightens any day. Books that take to reading aloud are scarce. There is Thurber. And there is Thurber. Otherwise we find an occasional gem such as *The 101 Dalmatians*. I had trouble reading that however, as I laughed so hard I cried and then I could not see the words.

A good book, a cup of very hot tea, a fire burning well, cockers and Irish dreaming of rabbits, and let the wind blow!

A pre-Revolutionary house has great charm but also drawbacks. I thought of this when we had a sudden January thaw this week, for suddenly in the night the house seemed boiling hot. I got up and turned the thermostat down, but the furnace paid no attention. I hardly expected it would, since that thermostat has been leading its own life all winter, no matter what the service men did. So I decided to open a window and get a breath of air, and partly open one door. Connie was home for the weekend, and I remembered how the heat rises in our house and felt she must be suffering. I did not worry about Jill, for her room never is really warm, something to do with the eccentricity of the pipes.

The door was quite easy. I opened the inner door to the back kitchen, and propped the storm door open with a piece of kindling. All the dogs, of course, rushed out. After they came in again, I put the kindling back and shooed them into the family room. I shushed them as best I could, for Connie is supersensitive to noise. Then I crept quietly again to the back kitchen, found the toolbox, got out the hammer, went to the woodshed for a block of wood and returned to my bedroom. I put the block of wood against the edge of the sash, laid some tissues over it, and gave a soft tap with the hammer. The theory is that the window goes up and you hastily insert the Old World atlas (out of date now). Then you reach out and force the storm window to swing enough so the metal pieces unlock. It is really quite simple. But this time, the dampness had affected the window. I tapped harder. By now an inquisitive Irish nose got in the way. I shushed her. I banged. Finally I raised the hammer and leaned back and really let the window have it.

Suddenly Connie and Jill materialized, wild-eyed and screaming, "What's wrong? What is it?"

"Everything is fine," I said quietly. "I am merely opening a window."

As I got back to bed, I reflected that modern windows must be incredible. Just imagine opening a window by hand! I was, of course, too wide awake to sleep but the smell of the air coming in was worth it. Melting snow, the curious winter scent of the swamp and a small whiff of applewood smoke from the fireplace made a heavenly blend. I lay sniffing happily. Then there was a buttermilk sky around four in the morning as a thin moon rode down the horizon. At the same time, the temperature dropped, a cold wind swung in, and the house was colder than a mackerel. (I wonder why a mackerel is so cold?)

"Oh, never mind," I said crossly to Holly, and I stuffed a bath towel in the open window. I could hammer it shut again in the morning. I could not, I felt, face Connie and Jill again.

I did turn the thermostat up again, but by now the furnace had stopped breathing, so that was that. The furnace is directly under my bedroom and I can hear it very plainly. And I used to be able to tell if we had left the cellar light on by peering down the crack by my bedside table, but subsequently Jill filled the cracks with some kind of plastic substance. (This keeps coming up and the dogs love to poke small chunks out and play with them.)

By the time we had breakfast, the furnace suddenly mobilized, all on its own. It was 75 inside and 2 below outside, so we were back to normal again.

There have been so many drastic changes in our time, the invasion of the air, for instance, and of the underseas; technical advances, wars, hot and cold, a world of terrible and awesome content. There is an almost complete change in our way of life. There have also been unimaginable changes in architecture, art, music, literature. What a far cry from Corot's misty romantic paintings to the savage assembling of triangles, squares and circles that make up a modern work of art. In music, the sentimental melodies give way to rock 'n' roll. In literature, elegance has generally been superseded by writing as hard as a beaten biscuit. Poetry has possibly changed as radically as anything.

Before this period, it was expected that a poet would set down his interpretation of life or his emotions so they could be understood. Now it doesn't matter. Much of modern poetry does not sing either. It jerks along in a curious disconnected fashion. It is all very well, for it is a swinging away from the gentle Victorian rhythms and is a sign of growth. But I suspect one reason so little poetry is read today is because the poet does not bother to communicate except with himself. He does not, I often think, undergo the discipline of making himself clear.

The one modern poet that seems to me most to rise above fashion in verse is Dylan Thomas. He wrote poetry. It is true the richness of imagery can be confusing, and it is also true that he is difficult to understand quite often, at least for me (and I took two years of poetry in college).

But if you keep Dylan Thomas on the bedside table, and read in thoughtful quiet hours, instead of gulping, you will find the excitement and glory which should be associated with poetry. I do not think he will ever go out of the world of poetry in time to come. It is a pity that his troubled life has been exposed, dramatized, that he has been fought over and flung about by misguided people. But this will be forgotten, and people will still read, "Do Not Go Gentle into that Good Night."

The voice of the wind is strange and wonderful. In summer, it is soft as a bank of violets. In autumn, around the hurricane season, there comes a heavy roar with an overtone of shrillness as if some Scotch bagpiper were tuning up. It blows in all directions at once before settling down to its real business of flattening everything that can be flattened. Now, in January, it has a wild and lonely sound suggestive of the frozen wastelands where it comes from. By March, it will thunder in, exultant, sweeping the ice from the pond. The voice of the March wind is happy. It blows away the doldrums of winter. Later, the soft breezes of April and May are no more than ripples in the sea of air.

The winter wind makes me feel, as I beat my way to the kennel, that I should be rubbing sticks together to make a fire in some snowy cave, and facing the wolves with a proud smile. "Mush on," I say to Jonquil, who has no idea of mushing at all. As the wind stings my eyelids, I almost expect to raise a mittened hand and look for caribou drifting like smoke along the ice. But this adventurous spirit lasts only briefly, and I am glad to scuttle back to the fire and the smell of pork chops and cabbage baking.

I have been told that blubber is delicious once you get used to it, but although I can eat almost anything except caraway seeds, I somehow do not think I would enjoy a diet of blubber. The pork chops, browned with onion, well salted and peppered, and bedded down on sliced cabbage in a casserole with milk to cover, well that is about my idea of a winter meal. Plus a fluffy baked potato to spoon the resultant gravy over.

When I was growing up, I planned to spend my life traveling. For one thing, I was hull-down with John Masefield and doing India with Kipling. And then the desert islands with creaming surf and coral reefs, and emerald birds singing . . . But now I wonder who would fill a cavity in that tooth on a desert island? And what would happen as I trimmed the sails on some weedy bark bent for the farthest seas if my bifocals fell overboard? My current bifocals have a way of slipping casually down my nose so that I see things three ways at once sometimes, but this is better than not seeing anything unless it is half a mile away. No, on the whole, I prefer to be within striking distance of those neat blond young men who fit glasses and put on new bows.

After all, we have plenty of adventures in our own back yard, and if we even sprain an ankle, the Doctor lives just one hill away. So I am glad to do my whaling with Moby Dick right at home and round Cape Horn without even leaving the warmth of the open fire.

If I am late filling the feeders or Jill is slow cutting the suet, we hear from the chickadees. They twitter from every icy twig, scolding in a nice way. They are my favorite winter birds, for their dee-dee-dee has a bright sound and they wing so bravely through falling snow, cocking their black-capped heads toward us. They are small, compact birds, grey with the satin-black markings but when they come close, there is a soft, almost apricot color on their breasts. They can crack sunflower seeds with the best of the bigger birds, and they can sit right down on their stomachs to eat the suet in the window feeder. They tuck the delicate legs under, put their tailfeathers flat behind as a balance and sit at table in a most amazing manner.

The nuthatches, that have that silly way of running head-down on a tree trunk, are less sociable, but one or two are now tame enough to come to the window feeder and look curiously at me as I type. They are a streamlined bird with long slender bills and small bright eyes. The grey is more bluish than that of the dees. In the early mornings, the woodpeckers and blue-jays come in, as noisy as a suburban train. The jays remind me of women who always scream when there is a crowd. The downies and red-capped woodpeckers hammer the trees as if they were riveters. Evening grosbeaks come, and towhees, later mourning doves and fox sparrows. We have endless varieties of sparrows but they are as confusing to me as those "confusing fall warblers" the books tell about.

The pheasants feed early and again toward dusk, and it takes some skill to maintain a bevy of hunting dogs with six or seven pheasants. We watch the clock and when mealtime comes around for the pheasants, we get the dogs in, and herd them away from the windows. In the swamp are ruffed grouse, but they do not face the hazards of a yard, so Jill takes grain down for them.

Once, in June, we were driving down a dirt country road when we came upon a mother pheasant steering a brood of minute babies across. We stopped the car. The babies looked too small to walk but they twinkled along after Mama, who cast an agonized eye on us. They reached the opposite side of the road, and the bank was too high for the babies to get up. The least one, scurrying, did not even get a foothold. And now, instead of dashing into the safety of the woods, the mother pheasant turned around, and made a desperate decision. She herded her babies right back across the road, helping the least one along with fluttering wings, and special advice. They vanished in the thicket, but we sat quietly for some time. Yes, she was only a wild bird, but she would not save herself at the expense of her babies. She also had the quick intelligence to perceive they could not make the bank and she must get them back across that fatal road.

Naturally she had no way of knowing that we would simply wait for her. Any careless driver speeding along would have killed all thirteen. They were so very little. We were thankful that we were the ones who had met the family and let them live a little longer in a world difficult for birds. We have spoken about them often since and especially hope the least one grew up. And that the valiant little mother survived to care for another brood.

The cock pheasants we have at feeding time always lead the way and also have the best of the food, I notice. But they keep a wary eye out for danger, and the females depend on them. In case of danger, they all lumber into the air, for a pheasant flies heavily, and it seems to me, as a lay observer, that they do not ride the air currents as some birds do. They barely clear the fence and then fly in awkward swoops toward the saftey of the swamp.

The flight of birds would make a lifetime study. I notice the jays plummet down as if they were bolting from some upper-air gun. The mourning doves seem to have trouble getting under way and then take a scooping flight. The hummingbird is nothing but a quiver of wingbeats. But the hawk seems hardly to make a wingbeat as he planes in, sending the lesser folk to cover.

And when we go to the seashore, I can spend hours watching the air-borne gulls. They are big, heavy-bodied birds, but they can catch an air wave and ride as far as I can see them. Then with a slight tilt of wing, they ride all the way back. Their flying seems absolutely effortless.

Sometimes, during the worst of our blizzards, the smaller birds have a hard time flying at all. The wind, snow, and cold send them in weak spirals to the shelter of the feeders and the pine trees. But it is amazing how a good dinner in the shelter of a feeder restores their strength. And it makes me wonder how many birds die because of no friendly dinner-service when we have a bad winter.

And I also wonder why the juncoes wait until it is unbearably cold before coming at all, and then leave the minute the weather is decent. When they come, we know the bitter cold is coming, and when they leave, we know we can think of spring. I wonder why they are so dedicated to winter? As I sweep the snow away and set flat pans of extra feed out, I often tell them they could just go farther south and be comfortable. But they are birds that feed right in the blizzard, their pearl-pink beaks twinkling, and their tiny wings fluttering.

Well, I tell myself, shaking the snow from my boots, I can't expect to regulate the life habits of the juncoes!

Although January ushers in the New Year, I think this is a mistake. What it really ushers in is February, which is more of the same. The New Year should begin with the first warm air of spring, and the misting of green on the trees. January is a waiting time, not a beginning time, as far as I am concerned. The sap is quiet in the sugar maples. The lilacs keep their shellacked buds tight under the snow. Even the pale Christmas rose is drifted with white.

However, the New Year begins according to the calendar, and the usual celebration of it is frightening. It is almost as if a strange fear possessed the celebrants so they must carouse, pop balloons, wear paper caps, and get too much food and too much to drink. One cannot shout down the fact that another year has gone. And no amount of night-club hopping can strengthen anyone for another year. In fact, the morning after, a good many people wish they were dead. What worries me is not the annual letting-go but that it seems to symbolize a kind of panic we have. The mobs massing in Times Square in New York are not individuals, they are an enormous and troubled herd. If we make enough noise, we won't have to worry, the roar seems to say.

Our New Year's Eve is quite different in the country. There are plenty of parties for the young-marrieds and enough all-night affairs, but what with baby-sitters and distances to drive, and for most of the men work to do in the morning, whether milking the cows or commuting back to the city, the valley does not exactly blare into New Year's Day. In our area you commute back January 1st as the January 2nd trains do not get you in on time, being late, as well as jammed and getting later as they go on toward New York.

We favor roast pork with spicy apples tucked around it for New Year's Eve dinner, and a savory dressing with the pork. Frozen asparagus from the freezer helps level the calories, and it is pleasant to have the asparagus picked in May served at the year's end.

And what do we do after dinner? We sit around the open fire and talk about what has happened in the past year and what we hope for the coming year. We listen to some music, choosing the records with care. Around eleven we have our binge, which is popcorn popped fluffy, liberally doused with butter, well seasoned, and accompanied by mugs of hot coffee. An apple is at hand, and a slice of Port Salut cheese from Wisconsin, and a plate of crisp crackers.

By this time it is getting latish, so the cockers and Irish have a last race in the snow and we lend an ear to the weather report as to snow or clearing tomorrow. And then we simply go to bed! We have seen the old year out comfortably and serenely, with time to think, and we are ready to look toward the new one.

My New Year's resolutions are simple. I resolve to be more patient, less selfish, cherish my friends, and in my small way help whoever needs help. I cannot conceivably influence the world's destiny, but I can make my own life more worthwhile. I can give some help to some people; that is not vital to all the world's problems and yet I think if everyone did just that, we might see quite a world in our time!

Now the New Year comes in with nights like a block of crystal. Joe comes to shovel us out when the drifts get above the picket fence.

Erma, his wife, phones as soon as the snow stops falling to say not to worry, Joe will dig us out as soon as they are dug out. On one occasion, she phoned every hour for four hours to say that Joe was still digging but not to worry he was almost down to the road. He would be over.

When we were dug out, there was a wall of snow almost as high as the car and narrow runways led to the kennels and bird feeders. The rest of the land was a sea of snow, glittering, beautiful and rather deadly. Two of the smaller cockers got off the path and were embedded to the ears, and had to be hauled out. They felt it was a very exciting and wagging experience.

We consult the Old Farmer's Almanac as a check on the weather reports. In case of doubt, we stick with the Almanac, which is more often right than wrong. I note that now our favorite weather broadcaster also gives the Almanac forecast along with the weather bureau's.

The oldest almanac we know of in English was found in a chest in Edinburgh and was dated 1495. The first American almanac was printed 144 years later, and was "calculated" by a Captain Pierce, who was the Captain of the *Charity*, the *Ann*, the *Lion,* the *Desire.* My own ancestor, Cotton Mather, edited the Boston Almanac in 1683, and I suppose he did not think witches influenced the weather. Weather comes from God, who is all-powerful. Witches cast spells on human beings, who are fallible, on animals who are more so. Gifted witches can wither crops to some small degree, because crops are of the earth and not part of Heaven. Only God directs the lightning. Benjamin Franklin's Poor Richard's Almanack is still a prized item. Now in the 165th year of the familiar Old Farmer's Almanac, Robb Sagendorph carries on the tradition from Dublin, New Hampshire. Fortunately, he keeps the traditional format, even to the name of Robert B. Thomas on the pale yellow cover as publisher.

The Old Farmer's Almanac is well worth reading. It is a choice collection of bits and pieces from the almanacs of the years past, wise and witty, and even includes recipes. It has advice on planting, "Aspects, Holidays, Heights of High Water, as well as astronomical calculations for those who are not frightened of numbers." How the almanac so often forecasts the weather more accurately than the weather bureau, is a mystery. The present editor, when asked, says the founder handed on his secret formula to subsequent editors.

Weather forecasting is a chancy business, it seems. An expected hurricane veers off just as everyone is battened down. Some of the worst have come on the heels of a predicton for clear, warm, fair. It is almost as if weather did not wish to be regimented. The long-range reports from our farm bureau give a fair over-all picture, but whether it will snow on Tuesday is a different proposition. Local valley people have a sixth sense, however, which is helpful. They sniff the air, look at the sky and say, "Good now, but wait until tonight." Since living in the country, I can myself usually sense a change in weather, but I do not know why. Possibly the birds fly differently, or the sky has a pale look even though the sun is shining. Or there is a stillness in the air. Or I may have a premonitory twinge as of a sinus headache coming, which means damp, chilly weather.

"Look and see what the almanac says," I call to Jill.

"Says rainy, damp, chilly," she reports.

So there we are.

I go into this New Year without the companionship of Little Sister, the small black and white cocker. She was never any trouble and she died with as little trouble as possible, her tired heart just beating into silence. She was a funny little person, shy and retiring, unlike the rest of the cockers who are leap-into-lap-at-once people. When strangers came, she retired under the sofa and just poked a small black rubber nose out. If they were very quiet, non-jingling people, she would eventually emerge and casually enter the social group. If they made advances too soon, she got under the radiator and squeezed flat.

She sat under my desk whenever I typed, with her head on one of my feet. Whenever I looked down, one bright dark eye was looking up at me. When I went in the yard, she heeled beside my left foot, steady as my own shadow. She did not bark at the laundry man. She was neat and tidy and drank her water without spilling it all over the floor as some did. She ate as if she were dining out on Spode china. Her son, Tiki, always spreads half of his meal on the floor and skates around in it.

She had little sense of humor, whereas some of the others felt they had a career as comics. She worked soberly at being a Utility Dog in Obedience but even when she won her loving cup as top dog, she had no feeling of superiority, whereas the Irish is a born trouper. The only time she moved fast was when I started to go away without her. Then no door, no gate shut quickly enough. She was mule-stubborn about ever being away from me, even when I went to the dentist. Many a time I had to lug her small plump form back from the car and plop her in the yard, and no matter how I explained, she looked betrayed. Then she would take up a vigil on the terrace and just look down the road. In her later years, I got so upset over this that I would have some member of the family take her to the back kitchen and offer her a piece of chicken while I stole out the front door. It never worked. She knew.

Perhaps her outstanding quality was the ability to put up with strange dogs coming in, and I felt this was outstanding when she was so dedicated. Once we had a visiting dachshund and Sister was the only one who even tolerated him. Once we had five Irish setters and in the pandemonium, only Sister accepted the deal. She got quietly under the bed and said nothing. She did not even snap when two very large Irish males opened the back kitchen door and came in to suggest they would be pleased to take up part of my bed. She bore with cats. If the Siamese was in a prima-donna mood, Sister would turn her head and stare in the other direction.

She was beautiful only to me, for she was a small old-fashioned cocker, nicely put together but no glamour girl. Visitors who came exclaimed over the rest of the cockers, but only the discerning noticed her peering thoughtfully from under the couch. Non-dog-lovers who came never knew there was a dog in the house, for we simply put the rest in the kennel

and let Sister alone. She minded her own business even if
broiled chicken was going around. For one thing, she knew I
always saved her a really adequate helping of whatever I had.
After everyone had gone, however, if I did not set her plate
down at once, she nudged me. Her small muzzle would bang
against me indicating she had waited long enough.

Possibly I could sum it up by saying Sister was a gentle-
woman. But who can ever sum up one small cocker who in-
habits one's heart? I can only be grateful that I was privileged
to have her for her lifetime, and quite sure she is no farther
away than the floor under my desk as I write this.

Walking to the mailbox in the snow, I reflected that one
has to know the change of the seasons to believe in spring
when it is January. This also, I thought, is true of the heart.
The heart can endure its own winter, provided there is faith
in spring. All of us have times when trouble seems to be more
important than anything else. Sickness and death make us
wonder why we keep on. Almost everyone, I think, has had moments of wondering whether it is worth it. Economic hardships
can wear courage down too, especially when there are young
children to take care of.

But life has its rhythms as the seasons do, and the most bitter
times may be followed by an easing. It is very important, in
winter, to remember that spring is coming along. The new
tulips will blossom in dark splendor, the lilacs will pour forth
a headier fragrance. In the spring of the heart too, we have
gardening to do, planting seeds of good will, helpfulness, and
faith.

And so, as I take the seed catalogues from the mailbox and

go back down the snowy road, I think of the spring coming and as I open the picket gate, I brush the snow from my mittens.

Happy New Year to everyone.

The bluejays are harbor blue as they flash to the feeders with their wings spread dramatically. They drop through the air like meteors and they gobble and squawk incessantly. They try to tear chunks of suet off and wing away with it, and often get such large pieces that they stagger as they fly. The chickadees and juncoes are more modest, they eat daintily, and utter grateful chirps between seeds. The grosbeaks are quarrelsome, and when four or five of them try to get in the window feeder, I notice they spend so much time shoving one another about that a lot of seed goes down into the snow and nobody gets a bite. Very much as some humans behave, I reflect.

If it is possible to have one favorite bird, mine is the rosy purple finch. This is a small, graceful bird with a rich raspberry color. He has a retiring nature but in summer, when he comes, bringing his Quaker-garbed wife, he flashes like a jewel. We have one who has come for two summers and now will sit on the feeder and when I talk to him, cock his head and stay quietly, establishing the fact that we are friends. He is more brilliant in color than the rest, and a shade larger, and he is braver, for he will stay with his dinner even when the larger birds wheel in. I call him "My Little Man." And I am quite sure he knows his name when I speak to him. His wife has no patience with this carrying on, and never even looks at me, but then she has a lot of thinking to do being a very busy person.

As winter wears away, the birds eat more and more, for it is food that provides fuel for them as well as nourishment. We buy chickfeed in twenty-five pound lots and serve panfuls along with the birdfood, sunflower seeds, suet, breadcrumbs (our birds have been known to eat two loaves of bread in one day!).

It is a lot of work, Jill says often, but what would we do without the birds in winter?

Along in February we feel we can hardly wait for our own garden lettuce. How limp and uninteresting the store lettuce is, with its pale color and bitter taste. The rule for a tossed green salad begins with selecting the finest, freshest greens, absolutely fresh. I often wonder how many miles that small knob of winter lettuce has traveled before it gets to our village store. A good green salad calls for two or more varieties of greens, plus such items as chicory, water cress, mustard greens. Well, we buy our lettuce in plastic covers, and a sorry sight it is when we get home with it in February.

We do render first aid. We rinse the lettuce under cold running water, then soak it in ice water, cutting around the heart with a sharp knife just enough to let the ice water percolate. Then overnight in an enamel refrigerator pan. (Lettuce will take up flavor from other pans.) Most restaurants chill their greens twenty-four hours. We break the lettuce in pieces two or three hours before serving time and put them in a chilled bowl. A half hour before dinner, we add the dressing and chill again, covering the bowl with aluminum foil. When serving time comes, we add Parmesan cheese, grated, or herbs, or crisp croutons. I like a green salad with a light dressing, oil and vinegar or lemon juice, with just the bowl rubbed with garlic. But a salad adapts to any taste from robust men's salads with slivers of tongue or chicken and cheese to a non-calorie bowl with cottage cheese and fruit juice.

Many experts deplore adding tomatoes to a tossed salad, because the juice tends to dilute the dressing and the tomatoes themselves overpower the flavor of the greens. As far as I am concerned, I toss in almost anything we have on hand from Italian small bitter olives to crisp bits of bacon.

But chiefly for a good salad you do need fresh garden lettuces, and in winter you just dream.

On a snowbound day, I wash the milk glass. This might seem to be a chore, for it must be washed by hand, in mild suds, rinsed carefully in not-too-hot water, and put back in the old pine cupboard. But a collection is not just a number of objects. It holds the memory of past adventures, happy days of exploring, triumphs. Every piece of our milk glass has a personal meaning. The swan compote recalls a hot day when we poked about in junk shops with a dear friend and I was tired and thought we should just go home and rest. And then there it was, the swan compote, dusty and half-hidden by old rags. Poking the cobwebs aside, we took it out, and dusted it off with a handkerchief and the swans seemed to be sailing.

The blackberry egg cups bring back a day of loafing along autumn roads with a burnished landscape rolling on either side. In a small shed, we found the egg cups, very rare. But more rare was the friendship we made with the gentle ladies who had the small shop. Some of my most cherished pieces were gifts from friends, given because I was collecting, and carefully wrapped and mailed. The cornucopia blue milk glass vase, and the ring and hand, and the miniature log cabin with windows pressed into it, belong in this category.

I do not think it matters what we collect. The things themselves have only a relative value. What is important is collecting memories. I happen to like milk glass because of the pearly
glow it gives forth, and the quaint patterns. It reflects an earlier,
more innocent age. But I have a friend who is very happy with
her collection of match book folders, and I think that is a fine
collection too!

Connie collects mugs, and just by starting with one mug
which I gave her, now has a comfortable collection. Mugs are
fascinating, and also useful for serving hot bouillon or hot
chocolate. I like those that say, in gilt, "Love the giver," or
"Remember me." The alphabet mugs are very choice and wonderfully colored. I like "G is for Gander, Goose and for Gift."

When I come upon a Benjamin Franklin mug, I am particularly pleased. But there is a great deal of charm about a simple
ironstone mug labeled, "Johnny." Mugs were common in the
nineteenth century, and earlier in England. They are colorful,
and I myself have one miniature mug which must have been
made for a small child, in which violas or pansies or tiny rose-
buds make a fine bouquet.

As I finish washing the milk glass and set it all back, I reflect that we all collect, all the time, in one way or another.
We cannot go through life without collecting. We collect experiences, happy hours, sad days, memories. We collect the day
the red fox drifted across the pasture and stopped short to look
at us. We collect the trip up the hill for butternuts when
autumn was afire over the countryside. We collect hours when
friends sit around the fire and the talk is warm and gay.

Some people, alas, collect grudges, hatreds, misfortunes. I
am sorry for them. Jealousy is an easy collection too, for there

is always someone who has more, or gets farther. But who would really like to fill the shelves of their lives with nothing worth the wear of winning? I know a few people who bring out and polish family feuds, and keep bright the memory of old injuries done them. I doubt if such collections are worth while.

Since we collect, how much better to collect something that will increase in beauty as time goes by. It is better to take anything not of value to the town dump, as Jill says. And dust the shelves and find something happy to put on them. How much it costs has little to do with it. For money never buys memories. One of my favorite pieces is a small pill bottle which cost a quarter but was bought for me and given to me with friendship.

As the woodshed has less wood and the kindling pile diminishes, comes the day when Erma, our neighbor who helps take care of Stillmeadow, gets a certain look in her eye.

"Mrs. T., we have to clean out the woodshed."

I am never brave enough to face it until Erma delivers the ultimatum. But I know better than to argue. I advance nobly, open the door and the picnic grill hits me on the head. When I recover, I take stock. The woodshed is small. It is off the back kitchen and it holds everything that there is no place for. I see the summer bathing suits, the bathing shoes, the fertilizer which was not used up last fall. Also the corn popper, the plant sprayer, several boxes of moth balls, and a leftover storm window (we never come out even).

Last fall's red corncobs spatter a few seeds on me. A can of frozen paint tips from the shelf where my flower containers are.

A small wheelbarrow left over from a grandchild impedes passage. I close the door and weakly advise Erma that I have to type and just to call me when everything is out. I will come later. By mid-morning the back kitchen overflows, and Erma calls me. Jill comes in with the snow shovel (which she planned to put in the woodshed) and utters a few remarks as she snakes through to her own room. I can hear her saying to the cockers, "No organization around here."

"Now you just tell me where you want things," says Erma with courage worthy of a great cause. "You sit down and just say."

I look dimly at the backwash of a year's living. "Well," I finally say, "just keep the grill and toss everything else."

"You aren't thinking of taking the bathing suits to the dump?" Erma is firm.

Bathing is far from my mind. "Well," I say, "after all—"

"They can be mended."

I suddenly remember that I must start a roast. I wave vaguely at the mountain and say, "Erma, you just sort it out."

Then I feel inferior all day. But Jill pokes about and adds a few flower pots in which she plans to repot my African violets, plus the dog's tracking flags and stakes, plus a couple of pieces of old marble she is going to DO SOMETHING with. Meanwhile Erma tries to cope. The rusty ice skates go in the attic, the mice-nibbled auto robe goes in the pile for the dump. She puts a hood on the oil lamp for hurricane days. And when it is all over, I am just tired out. But Erma hums in with more wood for the woodshed, and extra kindling. She then asks me nicely if I want three galoshes or should she leave a pair?

Naturally I never bought a solitary galosh. And I do not

know where one fur mitten came from. We do not wear fur mittens.

I am always willing to admit that I am not well organized. I might as *well* admit what is so obvious. But I still think the woodshed has a gremlin personality. Certainly I am not responsible for that piece of masonite that lurks by the door for I am no carpenter. Nevertheless when the woodshed was being "done" and my daughter, Connie, was out for the weekend, she said thoughtfully, "Mama, I don't know how I ever got to be in this family. Can't you ever FILE anything?"

"Well, if I file anything, I don't know where I filed it," I said miserably, "so it does no good."

I didn't add that filing ice skates and bathing suits and wheelbarrows and old nails and paint cans was kind of a problem. I knew I was no filer. Then she gave me a sweet smile and said, "Never mind, Mama, even if you never know where anything is, you get along."

I felt much better.

There is no twilight now. We finish the chores early and around four thirty it is getting dark. But still the days grow longer. Actually the first sign of spring is in the light, not the weather. Jill comes in stamping the snow from her boots and says, "Days longer now." Her mittens melt as she pins them over the radiator. But there is a change in light and that means the end of winter is approaching. Often now there is a slow sound at noon as a fall of snow loosens somewhere in the woods, and a pencil of dark water edges the pond.

Comes the February thaw and we invariably think spring has come, although we know better. We shall have weeks more of winter, but this deceiving softness makes me want to go over the seed catalogues again. Surely we can plant early this year. Jill notes that the freezer level is lower. The lost barbecued spare ribs emerge, and the last package of edible-podded peas is right at hand without too much fishing about in the arctic depths. They smell of spring as they cook. We feel the secret softening of winter as the deep freeze gets nearly empty.

The best logs in the woodshed are gone. Now we begin to burn the crooked ones, and soon we shall knock up crates for extra kindling.

On a cold starless night, the neighbors come in for a buffet supper. Everyone is very gay, as if the end of winter is really intoxicating. The casserole of ham and baked red beans with burgundy vanishes like magic. The lime-cheese salad mould vanishes as fast. The little hot biscuits are gone. Everyone has an air—yes, an air—of relaxation.

"Guess winter's about over," says one.

"We really had a stiff one this year," says another, having more ginger mold.

When they go home, they drive down the road without having to shovel. Now this is a big improvement. The lights diminsh over the hill, and Jill says, "Spring is coming. Nobody's motor wouldn't start."

"I think your grammar is incorrect," I say.

"I'm too tired for grammar," she says. "We have the kitchen to clean up."

"You mean everybody's motor did start," I say, emptying plates. Nothing on them but crumbs.

"You know what I meant. Bring the platter before Holly eats the scraps. She has had all she should have today."

Cleaning up after a party is not much fun. We usually put on a good stirring record. While the music plays, we stack and rinse in time to the beat. This is usually quite fine but now and then we get everything packed in our precious dishwasher and it won't work because someone has stuck a plastic fork in and that does it. So then we take everything out and wash dishes.

Dishwashers have their own protocol, and it must be observed. However, by the time we have discussed whether dinner was all right and everyone was happy and how nice so-and-so was, the dishes are done anyway, and the cockers and Irish feel it was successful as they had plenty of tidbits all along the line from this one and that one.

"I thought we would have leftovers for tomorrow," says Jill, "but maybe we better have a cheese soufflé."

"May as well," I agree, seeing the two bites left.

And so we turn the thermostat hopefully down, and go to bed. And Holly gives a big sigh as she settles down. I do not like late hours, she seems to say. I need my rest.

Life, like a coin, always has two sides. If I turn the February coin over, I find that we have had time for many pleasant things while the weather was bad. Trying out a new recipe which is one of the fancy, time-consuming ones, for example. Or rereading a favorite book which we already practically know by heart. Or writing leisurely letters to friends. Letter-writing is a fine way to share oneself with one's dear but faraway friends. It is, alas, a luxury most of the time, and I always regret dashing off brief notes saying we are all right. Now I can really visit without feeling the pressure of everything I ought to be doing. I have a few very special friends that I could almost write a book to and at least now I can write a chatty letter instead of a quick postcard.

Also the shut-in days give me time to think.

"What are you doing?" calls Jill.

"Sitting and thinking," I say.

Life seems to come like breakers on the great beach on Cape Cod. Every day we are experiencing so much. It is good to take time to reflect, to relive the experiences we have had in the past year. For the richness of living is not only of the moment but can be best appreciated as we think it over.

I like to just sit and remember the pale yellow rose that bloomed after the black frost, and the wedge of wild geese going over, and the first time a friend sang "The Ash Grove" for me. Or the woman in the roadside stand who brought a clean bowl of water for the two cockers in the back seat, and asked if they would like hamburgers. Or another day, when the man at a very dingy gas station offered to take the Irish setter for a run. "She might feel restless," he said.

Everyone's life has many such small moments, and they are worth cherishing.

I think there was much to be said for his point of view. An un-birthday gift is a surprise and very nice. It has nothing at all to do with convention or dates. Father was a lot of trouble at Christmas because he thought it was a silly thing to go around giving presents just because it was Christmas. But often when he went away to locate a gold mine or an oil well or to make a speech he came home looking like a bemused Santa Claus and his suitcase would be full of extravagant gifts he could not afford. This was his personal holiday.

But Mama liked the regular holidays. Once I gave her a

bouquet of violets bought by saving my allowance for weeks ahead, and although it faded overnight, there was a look in her eyes as I gave it to her, and I felt proud. The next day Father said, "Pshaw, you see what happens." The violets were completely and rather terribly dead.

Mama said, "How lovely to have them on Valentine's Day."

My own most cherished valentine came from my daughter, done in crayon on a piece of brown paper. It said simply, "Bee my valentine." The crayon was smeared, the edges of the paper uneven, but to me it was lovely.

Valentine's Day is a time to think with love of those dearest and best, and all the commercialism which now surrounds it cannot really spoil it. It is a time to think of young love, gaiety, and also, quite seriously, of those who are dearest to our hearts.

It is a happy holiday, and if it be true it is very romantic, who doesn't need a little romance from the first box of candy done up in satin to the potted plant that says, I love you.

Valentine's Day is a charming holiday. It is a time of the heart, it is like a Viennese waltz, gay and untroubled. Like most holidays, it has become too commercial, and along with its being commercial, the greeting card people have lost their senses and try to make it funny. Humor has its place, and we could not live without it, but jokes do not belong on valentines.

This is a holiday to be sentimental about. It belongs with romance, with pink cakes and candy hearts and bunches of violets (so expensive in my youth). It belongs with lace-paper-edged missives rhyming love and dove. It belongs with a special present presented shyly to the one you love, if you are very young. In my days of growing up, it was more personal than Christmas, for it was a time when one really declared one's heart. Be My Valentine meant just that.

But Valentine's Day is not exclusively for the very young. It should be an assurance to older people that being young in heart is more important than being young in years. The husband who brings a small bottle of expensive perfume home to his wife, who has just finished getting three children fed, bathed, and in bed, this husband is a Valentine's Day man. He can't afford the perfume, but never mind, he still feels she is his glamour girl, even if she hasn't had time for a beauty parlor in some time. She walks lightly for days. She is cherished.

And take the husband who comes home after a hideous day at the office when all the deals fell through. He has had it. Then he finds his valentines. "I luv you, Daddy." "Bee mi valentin." "Roses is red, vilets blu. Sugar is sweet, so are you." He finds his favorite dinner on the table, candles lighted, and his wife dressed in her Sunday frock. Comes the cake for dessert with "I Love You," written in pink sugar. This is the best of all Valentine's Days.

A visitor asked me yesterday whether we could distinguish between the dogs by their barks. I looked at her with surprise, for it had never occurred to me that there should be a doubt about it. When you live with a bevy of dogs, you know that every one has a special way of phrasing things as well as a different tone of voice. We can even tell when an argument begins over a cherished bone whether we should drop everthing and run, whether it is a diplomatic protest (and whoever takes those seriously?).

Holly, the Irish, has the widest range. A high, rusty squeak means, "Come quick, let me out [or let me in]." A deep contralto woof indicates that something strange is around, and what is it? This has a questioning lift at the end of it. Woof? A low bass rumble means that no paw should step near her bone or her dish. A long, pealing sound affirms the world is just too exciting, a person can hardly stand it. And finally there is a soft gentle murmuring in the throat which is purely conversational. This sound is inflected and rises and falls gently as long as I am willing to visit with her.

The cockers have their own vocabulary too, from the excited feminine tones of Jonquil to the sober measured bark of Especially Me when he sees a strange dog outside the fence. Get along now, get along, he says with meaning, this is private property. Linda, the small black one, has a special bark for the laundry man, whom she dislikes with fervor. Even before the sound of his truck is heard, we know the laundry man is coming, for Linda begins to express herself. She never uses this particular bark on any other occasion.

In the night, if strange creatures seem to be around, Jonquil leads the whole chorus. She begins with a sharp, nervous bark which gradually rises into what I can only describe as a high soprano howl. It reminds me very much of some singers I have heard as they labor into those silly coloratura passages. There is something magical about this, for at once every other dog begins to howl too, accompanying her in baritone, bass, and Irish contralto. Once begun, the whole passage must go on to a definite end. As I turn on the light and wait for them to quiver into the last note, I wonder what dim racial memory rises in them? It is a ritual which must have developed far back in time, possibly when they communicated from wild hill to wilder valley. I do know this, Little Sister was always embarrassed by this performance, and held out as long as she could. Then she would give me an apologetic look and very softly join in. And when it was over, her dark muzzle would be laid on my lap and her eyes looked anxious. Silly performance, she indicated.

But Jonquil always looks smug. She has, she feels, taken care of a situation, although by now she has not, of course, the slightest notion of what started all this racket.

Just how long a dog remembers is a point of disagreement between me and the psychologists. Dogs remember better than most human beings. We had a small particolored cocker once who was a dedicated mother. One of her puppies went to a new home at eight weeks of age. Years later, the owners brought her back. As she came in the gate, Clover began screaming and jumping up and down, rushed over and began to wash her offspring's face. She was ecstatic the whole afternoon, wagging and skipping about. Now a four- or five-year-old dog cannot resemble an eight weeks' puppy, and Clover had had subsequent litters. Other visiting cockers left her indifferent, they were not her own. Her daughter remembered too that a bowl of warm milk should be in the back kitchen, and went directly there to check.

After a good many other instances of dogs' remembering, I often wish my own memory were as reliable!

The familiar question we countrydwellers always face from our city friends is, "But what do you do in winter? How do you stand it?"

We answer vaguely, for there is no use trying to explain. Actually we need winter, even February, which can be the worst month of all in New England, with March running a close second. We need to tighten our belts and shovel the paths, thaw the pipes in the back kitchen, pile the logs on the fire. Subconsciously, I think, we need the discipline of the long dark cold. And then too we have an awareness of spring to come, and summer, and autumn. We are at home in the changing seasons, they are an integral part of us.

Some of the experts say the weather is changing. They do not agree, naturally. Some of them say New England may eventually be tropical, which has something to do with the Gulf Stream, I think. So I wonder as I slosh to the mailbox what it would be like to have palm trees instead of sugar maples lining the road, and bougainvillaea instead of rambler roses. Some experts, on the other hand, say we are approaching another ice age and may expect harder winters and longer ones from now on. Then I wonder how the swamp would look with the long finger of a glacier reaching over it.

As I look back, I remember that when we first came to Stillmeadow, we expected to be snowed in off and on all winter. We expected frozen motors and temperatures of fifteen below not infrequently. Of late years we are surprised if we have many deep snows. Often the winters are open, with a good deal of rain. Then we have a winter such as '57-'58 when snow tops the picket fence and we cannot even open the house doors until we are dug out.

We have had summers with scarcely a drop of rain, when the ground bakes and brook beds are dry. But then we may have a summer of such heavy rainfall that it breaks all weather records. Shoes mildew in the closets. Sheets feel damp. The pond overflows into the vegetable garden where pale tomatoes rot on the vines.

So, on the whole, I cannot decide between the opposing experts. One seems right one year and the other the next. And possibly we shall have blown the Earth to bits before either side wins the argument.

But now, toward the end of February, although we still shovel snow and thaw the water bucket, the yeast of spring is in the air. The ditches along the old grey stone walls begin to

run with melting snow. In the meadows, the frosty purple black-berry canes rise above the lessening drifts. The ice on the pond is lacy, with black water showing beneath. Icicles break off from the old wellhouse and tinkle to the flagstones.

At sunset, the sky is a warm primrose, and twilight lengthens blessedly. In the mornings, people linger in the village store to discuss a new hybrid corn or blight-resistant tomatoes. The first run of maple syrup was exceptionally fine, they agree. The shiny pails still hang on the sugar maples along the road, but the last gathering will make the darker syrup which is the only kind city people ever get. The pale translucent syrup is usually reserved for the family table, where it enhances lacy butter-milk pancakes or crisp golden waffles.

Yes, we are turning toward spring, no doubt about it. And now we agree that the winter was not bad. Pretty fair on the whole.

There is no guessing about March. I wake in the night and hear the black stallions of the wind pounding along the sky. Their hooves beat over the slanted roof of the little farmhouse, and the rain blows back like flying manes. Where are they bound, I wonder, to what ethereal wild pasture in the sky? And who, when the horses of the wind lower their foam-flecked heads, will stable them?

The wind drives the water down the brooks, crashes branches on the lawn, sweeps the drifts away, and uncovers the frozen secrets of winter. Now all the lost toys emerge, the cold bones, the soggy pink plush rabbit, the torn bath towel, a bathing shoe. As soon as there is a break in the weather, the dogs rush out and retrieve all the delightful things they mislaid during the first snowfall. Holly and Teddy have a good tug-of-war with an old sweater of mine. Jonquil snips up the rabbit (which is Holly's) while Holly has her back turned. When they all pile in again, they bring the treasures plus as much thawing mud as can be accommodated.

This is the time of the year when the house looks shabby anyway, and between mop-up jobs, we notice the wear and tear of winter. This year, we decided to get fresh pull-curtains for the family room, a soft apple green with an antique brown pattern over it.

"But that is all we shall do," said Jill, firmly. "We've got those insurance bills coming in. Just the curtains."

"You are absolutely right."

The curtains looked lovely. But after they were hung, the walls of the room looked worse. The open fires all winter long, plus the coal gas which our furnace affects had ruined them. So we repainted the walls to match the green in the curtains. It really looked beautiful but the woodwork was a sight. We had to do over the woodwork, which led, inevitably, to new slip covers for the chairs and sofa.

"Certainly dangerous to put up new curtains," said Jill.

"Well, it's all done now," I said, and added, "except we really have to paint the insides of the corner cupboards. That cherry red looks awful. We need a darker tone of the green."

"And wouldn't you like the floor sanded and redone too?"

"Well, not until the mud season is over," I said meekly.

I didn't mention the kennels, but they needed repainting too. Jill decided to do it herself. There was a little difficulty about the color, as the shade I chose was, of course, out of stock. I settled for the next shade to it, and the tiny cardboard sample looked very well. But it's a far cry from a color card to a paint can. When the paint was on, and dry, it turned out to be a flamingo. The inside of the kennels resembled one of the more lurid night clubs, and I expected to see Linda and Tiki doing a tango any minute.

"It's cheerful all right," commented Jill, cleaning the brushes. "And I daresay it is unique. I'll bet there isn't another flamingo kennel in the country."

"It will fade," I said.

"Maybe in five years it will be shocking pink," she said.

Two or three cockers at once poked their noses in to investigate and came out dotted with flamingo. If there is any way of painting anything without the dogs' help, we have not found it. When we paint the picket fence, they appear striped with white.

When we paint the trim dark green, Holly has a green tip to her mahogany tail. We don't mind touching spots up for a few days, but the problem of getting the paint from the dogs' coats is a difficult one. You cannot use the normal solvents, for dogs are allergic to them. Shampoos have no effect. We try to comb out as much as we can, and oil the fur and brush it.

As Jill says, it is just something to keep us from being idle!

March is not the beginning of spring in New England, it is a postlude to winter. Some of our worst blizzards belong to March, along with heavy flooding rains. Then we may have a few days of pure gold with the air like sherry. Although we know better, we all begin to predict an early spring. We celebrate with a buffet supper for the neighbors, and everyone is merry. The talk is of spring projects, of crocuses poking up in sheltered corners, and of a robin that hopped around looking for an invisible worm.

Any day now, we say, we'll be out pruning the lilacs and tending to the rose bushes. We do not get so giddy as to serve a spring buffet. We stick to a rib roast, scalloped potatoes, coleslaw with sour cream dressing and pineapple upside-down cake. The moon is out when the guests drive off, and the world looks as scrubbed and fresh as if it had just been created.

But the next day, black rain and violent winds are right back, galoshes come out, mittens are found, storm jackets are in order.

It was on such a day last week that Jill had to go to the city. A near-hurricane gale was blowing and the road ran with water. Since she had to catch the train in the town ten miles away, I was anxious. But just then the phone rang, and there came Phil Thomson's voice saying he would drop by and take her to the train. He'd be there at 7:45, plenty of time to get to the 8:12. Not a bit of bother, he said, in his pleasant, somehow British-sounding voice. And he came on the minute, splashed across the lawn to carry her bag, waved a dripping glove at me as they drove off.

There is nothing better than good neighbors, I thought, as I mopped up the water that blew in. At 8:20, there was a slight lull, so I hurried to the village store. George was just opening up, the other two boys were whistling as they unpacked cartons.

"How about some hot coffee?" asked George, "and a fresh cinnamon doughnut?"

He ran to the back of the store and brought me a mug of steaming coffee. Warming my hands blissfully on the mug, I sipped away, reflecting on the blessings of a country store. We visited about town meeting, the new highway that might go through (we hoped not) and the latest weather reports (bad).

The village store is a special institution. The boys who run ours act as an informal bank, a news service. They help find lost dogs, deliver groceries personally when someone is sick. They always have room for a cake sale for the church, although this certainly lessens the sale of their own cakes and cookies. At Halloween, they have a competition for school children, awarding prizes to the lurid, chalky pictures done on the clean store windows.

Yes, I thought, as I set down my mug, I am thankful for my small corner of the world. It gives me faith in the larger world as well.

I never can wait to get the storm windows off, and on the first mild day I suggest it. I like to look at the world without that extra layer of glass between it and me. Erma says firmly it is too early. Jill says it is too early. Erma's husband says it is too early.

But I am a stubborn woman about storm windows and after a few more mild days, Erma is washing windows, and the storm sash is in the storage shed. And inevitably it snows the next day.

"You see," says Erma. But she is already washing the ruffled curtains.

"Too early," I say, "with the furnace still on."

"I can't stand them another minute," she says.

The smell of wax invades the house. An unwary neighbor drops in and skids wildly, flailing arms in the air. The rug wraps around his legs. Saved, he sinks thankfully onto the unwaxed sofa.

The truth is, I do not think a satisfactory floor finish has yet been invented, although I have heard of a non-skid wax just out. A waxed floor, especially if it be a very old floor pegged with square hand-made nails, is the most beautiful to look at. Also the wax preserves the wood. Varnishes and lacquers have their points, but also some disadvantages. If you are not addicted to shining floors, you may use wall-to-wall carpeting. Of course if someone drops a burning cigarette on it, you cannot simply sand down the one spot and re-wax. No, you are in trouble. Also carpets naturally react to being tramped on and very soon you can see crisscross trails where the traffic goes.

The problem of cleaning them floors me (no pun). So we settle for wax and meet people at the door saying "Watch your STEP."

Whatever doesn't get waxed at Stillmeadow, gets scoured. The sharp tang of ammonia blends with the smell of the wax. Erma is dedicated to ammonia for everything from china to mosquito bites. (No, the dishes will NOT taste of it, she assures me.) There is practically nothing that a dash of ammonia doesn't improve, with the exception of food. And we have to admit curtains are snowier, milk glass gleams, sheets brighten.

By the time spring arrives, spring cleaning is over with. But, as Erma says, it's better to be ahead than behind with things. And it is a happy feeling when the house glows and we look toward spring with outdoor living beginning again. Because who wants to dust books when the violets are in bloom?

Fishing deep in the freezer for the last of the zucchini, I am glad the asparagus will come along before too long, and the rhubarb. And when Jill brings up the last peas, she says the freezer can be defrosted any time. Our freezer is an old-fashioned farm freezer and occupies half a wall in the cellar. To defrost it, you first stand on your head and excavate the remaining packages. Then you sit down while the blood gradually resumes its normal course. Then you scrape ice sheets from the sides. Then you sit down. Then you start a bucket brigade to lug the slush up the ladder-steep stairs. Then you lug the vacuum cleaner down and turn it to blow air in the depths. This melts the ice faster, and leaves a good deal of water to scoop out, sponge up. But it means you can re-establish the orphan packages before they also have begun to defrost.

Then you lug more pails upstairs. Finally you sink down and wait until things get in focus again.

"I wonder if it's worth it," remarks Jill.

What we need, now the children are away so much is a small modern compact freezer UPSTAIRS. But we would have to give up the washing machine as that is the only place it could possibly go. I have heard of some people who kept the freezer in the front parlor, but I hardly like the idea of a freezer beside the record player.

But at least we don't have to defrost the freezer very often, and that is a comfort. And what a joy to have casseroles, roasts, pies, cakes, vegetables and fruits ready to use. And also, since we live in the country, it is a help to have extra butter, bread, rolls at hand, not to mention oysters, shrimp and lobsters.

The frozen dinners are good for emergencies too, although so far, I think there is room for improvement. The servings are pretty small, for one thing. But almost every time we shop, we find new combinations, and they are constantly improving in flavor, texture, and in quality.

When we freeze our own complete dinners, we double the portions, and add extra sauces or gravies and come out very well, even if we are feeding unexpected teen-age guests with healthy appetites. We add a tossed salad, and ice cream (from the freezer) and cookies. We never have any objections.

What a long way we have come, I reflect, as I set the table, from the days of salt meat, dried corn and beans and lentils and dried apple slices and root vegetables as a winter diet. Maybe we should have oysters Rockefeller tomorrow!

I have some friends who like to bound out early in the morning. Ed and Barbara Shenton have even been known to take a brisk hike around six before breakfast. Faith Baldwin faces the day with the same bright spirit which her wonderful *Face Toward the Spring* evidences. When visiting us, she used to get up with Daphne, the Irish we had, and just play with her from six on. Around seven thirty she and Daphne would wake me up, Faith bringing a cup of coffee and Daphne a ball. Hal and Barbara Borland are briskly at their typewriters or in the garden long before I would consider creeping about.

The truth is, I think, that sleeping and waking times are individual, just as blue or brown eyes, blond or dark hair. And my waking time has seldom coincided with the break of day. Occasionally I do get up and look at the sunrise, for it is so beautiful, but then I go back to my snug bed. I purely hate to get up early and be brisk. Taking guests to the milk train in the next town is a horror. It keeps me awake at night when I know it is inevitable. Or when I have had to take the miserable thing myself, I look at the clock every hour all night in case I should oversleep and miss it. This is not a recommended preparation for a day in the city, I may add.

When I do wake up, I am not bounding. I like to think. When

the house is quiet and nobody is banging around, I can stay tucked in comfortably and let my thoughts wander. I think first, properly, of what I must do when I finally get up. I lay out the hours in neat chunks so that I have a PLAN. Not that the plan has ever worked out, but I have made it.

When visitors ask me what my writing hours are, I have to admit they are whenever something else doesn't interfere, such as the washing machine flooding the kitchen or a puppy finding a fish hook or some caller does not close the gate and we spend an hour retrieving a bevy of hunting dogs from the swamp, the old orchard, the neighbors' barns. Or a neighbor phones that a visiting great Dane is missing, so everyone goes out to comb the area.

This may be one reason I write a good deal at night when presumably nothing much will happen. Of course it often does. In winter or March, winter's stepchild, the current may go off, and candlelight is romantic to eat by but hard to type by. It wavers. Or I let the Irish out and then, the unmistakable smell of skunk drifts in my window and I rush out, calling Jill. For even canned tomatoes, rubbed in well, followed by two shampoos, do not quite eliminate the odor of a skunk. It has to wear off.

Then there is our furnace. One night I was quietly working away when I heard a cow bellowing in the cellar. Distinctly. I flew to the door, scattering sorted papers in my flight.

"Jill, there's a cow down cellar!"

"Nonsense," she said crossly, for she had just dozed off.

Moo moo moo—it went on. "Does sound like one," said Jill, and started down the stairs. Came back looking grim.

"Furnace busted again," she said. "Start a fire in the fireplace."

Our furnace man comes from miles away, so the house congealed while we waited, but he came, stamping the snow from his boots, and had a session.

"Well," he said, "the circulator is frozen, as we say. Bad news."

"Is there ever any good news about the furnace?" asked Jill bitterly.

"I'll have to get her rewound," he said.

We apologized for routing him out at such an hour. "It's my business," he said. "I'll hurry on this. Good night."

I have noticed over the years that if any appliance has anything go wrong it is either on Sunday afternoon, late at night, or when we have company coming. There may be a reason for this, but it is true as truth. It so happens, as the farmers say.

But in the early morning hours, I make my plan for the day hopefully. Then I think about what I have been reading and analyze why it is good or not good or could be better. This is a pleasant game. Then I spend some time worrying about the world. We have not gotten used to the atom bomb and here we are in the supersonic age all banging away at destroying the earth and the inhabitants thereof. I met the little Japanese minister who was a hero at Hiroshima and sat with him at dinner once. And I shall not forget his gentle, sorrowful face as long as I live, or his quiet un-resentful conversation.

Our young minister often uses as a text "Love thy neighbor as thyself," and I think following this would save the world. But how can troubled nations find the way? Many, many mornings, I did my thinking about Hungary, and although I felt many nations compromised with honor in that situation, what would have happened if they had started a new war to destroy the world? I always come back to What can a simple country-woman do? All of us have responsibility but few have power.

We can all pray. Peter Marshall, that great minister, believed in the positive power of prayer, and I do feel constant, earnest prayer may negate some of the evil that covers the earth with radioactive fallout. I have been reading *Mr. Jones, Meet the Master*, and *A Man Called Peter*, and find a renewed faith in good overcoming evil. These books should be required reading for all leaders in the world and for all troubled adults.

I spent a bleak pre-day time thinking that the experts now caution about being so careful of radiation from X-rays, and at the same time other experts are sending bigger and better bombs up to rain down insupportable amounts. It does not make sense to a countrywoman.

What does mankind need? A chance to work, to love, to have children, to make some friends. To enjoy an uncluttered sky with only sun, moon, and stars and clouds in it. It would not seem too much to ask that the peoples of the world should live out their appointed time without being bomb bait. And it is difficult for me to understand why countries with surplus foods cannot share with countries where children die of starvation. It is all to do with economics, which I never studied. But in our small community, those in need get helped by those who have what is needed. And despite transportation problems, I would feel this might extend into larger areas, and to other countries.

Love thy neighbor as thyself covers a lot. For love involves sharing. And as Madame Chaillot said in *The Madwoman of*

Chaillot, "There is nothing wrong with the world that a sensible woman could not settle in an afternoon."

When I get up in the morning, I let the dogs out, and Jill has coffee made. In March there is no question about carrying trays to the Quiet Garden, but we can carry them to the family room and eat by the open fire. Or, if my arthritis is twinging away, I go back to bed with my tray and enjoy my boiled egg and toast and coffee along with a chapter of a favorite book. It gives me a feeling of luxury, as indeed it is. I shall put in a good twelve hours of work one way or another before I go to bed, but the feeling of not hurrying is one of the blessings of living in the country. Everything can wait. The only time clock that has to be punched is the time clock of Nature, which means you must prune, you must clean up the yard, you must fertilize, you must mow, you must do the chores, you must clean the kennels—but not at nine a.m.

This reminds me of one time when we were on Cape Cod during a wild and bitter March. Two clammers stood hip-deep all day in the icy water gathering Quahaugs. Jill went out and said to one, "Isn't this a hard way to work?"

"I'm my own boss," he said, in the flattish Cape voice, "nobody tells me what I have to do when. Suits me."

This is the feeling farmers have. They may work longer and harder than if they did a nine-to-five stint, for often we have seen our neighbor getting in hay at nine at night by the light of a few lanterns. But it is their own decision, and they feel they are their own masters. Often at ten at night, I have wandered over to Willie's to say he should stop tinkering. "Still and all,"

he always says, "nobody tells me I got to work overtime!"

I fully realize that in the city nobody could run any business on the basis of some people wanting to work until midnight (it would upset the charwomen and the elevator staff, for one thing). Or if someone felt like turning up at seven thirty in the morning, well, nothing would be opened up. When you work in groups you simply have to be more or less regimented, and regimentation is the one thing farmers and countrydwellers will not support. I myself, since becoming one, pay no attention to hours. If I wish to work until one in the morning, I so do. If I feel like spending a whole day puttering, I so do.

But on the whole, I think regular working hours have much to be said for them. During the years I taught at Columbia, I often came home on the six o'clock with the regular commuters. The men were finished for the day. They were not going to get up and stay up all night with a cow who was ailing, or who was having difficulty calving. They carried their briefcases with some homework, but they were really on their own. Farmers, who deal with the seasons, the weather, and with livestock, have no way of locking the door and having the evening off. But like the clammer, they are independent. They make their own rules.

I am sorry to see the small farms go. Most of our friends who have had to go into factories and give up the cows and the crops are not happy. They preferred to work harder but to decide for themselves whether to go field chopping one morning or the next.

When we moved to the country, we worked more than twelve hours a day for the first years, in fact, I never knew how hard a person could work before. But it was always our choice. As we eased our aching muscles into bed at night, we felt a kind of pride.

"I'm going to put the lettuce in tomorrow," said Jill, "no matter what the books say."

And I think it is fine that she can plant no matter what the authorities say! May be impractical, but it is fun.

It is strange to think how our dreams change. When I was growing up, I cut out pictures of yachts and planned to live on one of the most elegant. It took growing up to make me realize I could get seasick even at a movie which showed a boat rocking. I dreamed of being a Red Cross nurse, too, without knowing that I suffer so over a bruised paw that I would never have been worth my salt. In emergencies, I am fairly good, but as a nurse, I would have worried the patients to death. I would always have had every ailment known to medicine, and my temperature would have risen with that of anyone whose temperature I was taking.

When my daughter was born, I dreamed that she would fulfill all my dreams, up to and including being an actress as great as Shirley Booth has become.

Now my dreams are more fitted to an adult life. I dream of travel, but do not wish to leave home. I would wish to get back in time to feed the dogs and look at the moon rising over the swamp. For the truth is I get homesick if I even go away overnight, so what would I do in Calcutta? I would worry over whether the roses had aphids and whether Holly was brooding. I think it was Scott Fitzgerald who first said that one gets vulnerable as life goes on. The more you love a person, the more vulnerable you are.

And so as you have children, you begin dreaming of a golden future for them. A good many children, I think, suffer from trying to fit in to parents' dreams which are not at all their own. It is better to let the children have their own dreams, and follow them.

But in any case, people without dreams are unfortunate. We all follow some star, and without a star, the sky can be very dark!

It is interesting to note how much like the seasons people are. I know some who are summer people, and I am happy to be with them. They are gay and easy and full of pleasant talk. But they would never do for an emergency. Then they are too busy or they are going away. There are people like spring, too, volatile and blowing one way one minute and another way the next. They are charming. Autumnal people are sober and grave, I find, but with bursts of sudden color.

But winter people are the best and there are few of them. They are the friends who are deep and true, once you penetrate to the secret warmth. The surface may not be as gay and charming but under the austere surface runs the living sap of loving-kindness. These are the friends to call when there is an emergency, big or small. They are the ones who never expect gratitude for favors done, it is a matter of course to help out, think nothing of it.

But it is wrong to expect summer people and spring people and even autumn people to be different than they are by nature. We cannot all be alike, and indeed it would be a sad world if we were. How much better to enjoy the gift of personality which everyone has and not expect a summer person to sit up all night with you while you watch a sick puppy. Ask that of a winter person, but enjoy the summer people for what they do give and for what you give them.

One of the wisest remarks anyone ever made to me was long ago when I was sad because a very dear friend had failed me in a very real way. Faith Baldwin said to me then, "Love people for what they do have, never for what they do not." And she added, "Love them for what they have meant to you no matter what they may mean to you now."

In other words, she meant to take the present as it is but never let any failure in relationships sully the happiness in the past. I think of this when I get letters from people who have suffered a grievous disillusionment with husband, father, mother, children, friends or lovers. Often they simply go over and over the wrong done them. They never remember a moment of good. And reliving the wrongs is a kind of poison.

Since I seldom argue, and am very mild, unless a spark of my father explodes at an injustice to a child, a dog, or a cat or anything helpless, I have had little trouble in my life with resentments, squabbling, recriminations. Like Little Sister, my tendency is to get under the sofa and stay quiet. But when one very dear friend became alienated through circumstance beyond my control, I decided to remember only the very happy times we had had, which were many over a long period. Why should I give up these treasures in order to indulge myself in being angry at a small piece of time? It is much more rewarding to store the memory with a golden day by a trout stream, being merry over cold fried chicken and iced coffee. That day was precious and there is no need to give it up just because of a subsequent unhappy event.

On the other hand, I would hope never to be guilty of betraying a friendship myself. If my feelings do get hurt, as everyone's do at times, I think hard before I hazard something as precious as friendship in order to salve my pride. Not worth it, I think. I always feel sad when someone says, "I shall never speak to her/him again."

No matter how justified, it is lonely to be on the right side all by yourself!

Yesterday we had a long-distance phone call to announce that Stillmeadow Hollyberry Red C.D. was now a champion.

"You have yourself a champion," said Art Baines, his voice muffled by the sounds of the dog show. I dropped the receiver and sat down and cried. Jill finished the call.

"So what are you crying about now?" she asked. And took off her glasses and cried quarts.

We didn't give a fig for Holly getting her championship in the beginning. We liked her right at home, and we knew she was perfect. But since she was a descendant of champions and her father was an international champion and obedience dog to boot and her mother a champion and a field dog too, the breeder begged us to put her through as a tribute to her sire, Rusty, who had died.

For regular accustomed dog people, it is quite simple. You just pick the best of the litter, get a handler, and pay no more attention. But we sat up all night wondering whether we could part with Holly for one weekend. We couldn't show her ourselves for you have to run like a race horse in the ring, and kneel, and stand on your head, and travel from show to show, none of which we could do.

Finally we took Holly to one show and sat with her all day so nobody could pat her and give her a germ. Then Art Baines came over to meet her. He is a small, quiet man, brown and smiling. He sat down by her and said, "Hello, Holly," and she got in his lap. "You look like your mother," he said.

Holly kissed him, and he kissed her back.

This got us in for a lot of trouble. For one thing, it got us into commuting late at night to the parkway to pick her up or deliver her, so she did not have to be away from home much.

It also led to a late phone call when Art's light comfortable voice would say cheerily, "Meet me at Route 128 Station near

Boston at eight tomorrow morning. Do you girls good to get up early once."

This led, of course, to our getting off at four in the morning, running out of gas in a town forty miles from Route 128, finally getting refueled, only to get started on the throughway in the wrong direction. My tearful voice and Jill's explanation changed the whole course of traffic as the tollmen flew about taking down barriers and putting up barriers, and the traffic piled up for half a mile. In the end, we went backward the wrong way and got Holly delivered, tail wagging.

We also commuted to East Longmeadow quite frequently, where Art and Audrey live. This is only a half day's work. And after all we went through, I said resentfully, I should think Holly wouldn't carry on so when Art says, "Well, sweetheart, you look good, come to Daddy."

The truth is, she loved him. He was an Irishman and just her kind of man anyway. And he said Holly was born to show, she just went in every time to win.

In the end, with two points to go, he took her to Virginia and we moped around, deciding we would simply give this up. We would write him tactfully and say we just didn't feel, etc., etc.

Then came the phone call, and back came Holly (we only had to go to Mahopac, New York, to get her this time). Holly was glad to be home, but had a regal air. Naturally winning a four-point show and her championship could not register with her. But she felt she had made Art happy, and somehow had done what she was supposed to do. Her whole being radiated with success.

It made me wonder whether it is imperative for everyone, human or canine, to fulfill the destiny one was born for. Holly's main interest in the rosettes is to snatch them and race around and play tag with them with Especially Me. But there is something, nevertheless, that she acquired. For one thing the constant admiration of so many people gave her a sense of being even more important than all the spoiling we have done. Her very walk indicates a sense of royalty.

I guess it was worth it, although when we look at the mass of ribbons and rosettes, I sometimes say that I think we won them, too. I would not wish again to go through with such a schedule or have my Irish away from me, even briefly.

But the championship certificate hangs right over the picture of Holly and her royal parents and I like to see it there. "Irish setter Stillmeadow Hollyberry Red, C D," it says and goes on, "has been officially recorded a CHAMPION. By the American Kennel Club."

Now she races around, untrimmed, and getting burs in her long feathers. No longer does she get rubbed nightly with vitamin-A oil from a famous beauty salon. She can stay out in a downpour and just get dried with her towel when she comes in, and who worries about how much damage it has done to her coat? She may look like a country dog, dusty and bewhiskered, but the certificate is framed and even if she gets in the briars and loses part of her petticoats, who cares? Her life is very busy, what with pointing quail and pheasants, chasing rabbits, helping the service men by removing their tools whenever they lay them down, and so on. I wonder whether she ever thinks back to the days when, brushed and satiny and with no feather blowing back, she pranced in the ring? Perhaps not, but I know that when we go to visit Art, she will climb in his lap and melt as only an Irish can melt.

She really liked living up to her parents, I think.

Country auctions are fun. They begin early in the season, with the auctioneer selling odd lots of glasses, thumbprint but cracked, and umbrella stands, rickety. As the season progresses, the choice items come to the auction block. But those of us who live in the valley often get a flowing blue bowl for fifty cents before the season really gets under way. The antique dealers keep a wary eye out and if anything fine comes up in or out of season, they are there. In midsummer, we go to the auctions just to sit and visit and eat sandwiches and drink coffee. We know we cannot afford the expensive secretaries and sets of cup plates and so on. But now and then a small mug is within reason and once I bought a chest of drawers with eight coats of paint on it which turned out to be a very rare piece after we spent two weeks taking it down to its original pine.

Once I bought a box of odds and ends and came up with some very fine pressed-glass knobs which fitted a chest we had and which needed some. Usually we come home with a stoneware jug and an old tin lantern and feel quite pleased.

But it is always a good thing that Jill is along when we go to auctions, for bidding just seems to go to my head. We certainly do not need that chandelier for we have no place for it. But I get excited, I can't help bidding. Then, just before the chandelier is knocked down to us, Jill gives me a firm armsqueeze and hisses, "No more." Afterward as we drive home with the jugs and the box of odds and ends and a soapstone

pancake griddle, I admit that we have no place for a chandelier, no matter how beautiful.

"You just seem to go out of your head," remarks Jill.

"But such a bargain," I say.

"Nothing is a bargain you can't use," says she definitely.

And that settles that.

There are people who really like days of rain. We have one
friend who likes nothing better than to don slicker, boots, oilskin hat, and tramp through the woods in a downpour. I do not
mind a thunderstorm or even one whole day of rain, but beyond that, I do not enjoy it. I feel depressed when we have to
have the lights on all day long. I love light. Possibly I was a
sun-worshipper in some former reincarnation. The only time I
like rain is when it is stopping.

But the sun coming out after a spell of March rain is like
being born again. The countryside glistens and the sound of
the brooks running between ferny banks is music. And now the
garden earth looks rich and dark, and the lawn emerges from
the lace of snow. And also, the dogs begin to dig. So the moles
must be busy. Walking to the kennel is an obstacle race, for
there are a dozen holes to dodge. And until the ground dries
out in April, there is no use filling them up, tamping them
down, and seeding them. There is a particular spot by the front
gate that is deep as a small mine. It is Jill's opinion there must
be truffles there although we have never heard of truffle cockers
or truffle Irish.

Especially Me digs so hard that he is practically up-ended
and when he comes in the house he looks like a mud pie. We

tell ourselves he must have some fun, after all. If a dog cannot even dig up his own yard, it is really too bad.

While he digs at a hole, the rest sit around in a circle and wait for their turn. When he feels he cannot work another minute, the nearest one takes over. Now the hole is so deep that Linda, who is small, is almost hidden when she has her turn. Strangers who come to Stillmeadow always look at the hole with surprise. We pretend not to notice.

It is all a part of March.

Now when I hear again the cool sweet song of the peepers in the swamp, I feel the excitement of a new cycle beginning. It is really for us countrydwellers the start of a new year. From now on, the chorus will deepen in tone and later on, the bullfrogs will chunk away by the pond, adding their steady bass notes. The robins come back, and there is a great to-do about who sees the robins first. They look chilly as they hop about the lawn hunting for frozen worms, but nevertheless, they are back. It is a great moment.

There are signs everywhere. The swamp takes on a rosy glow as sap rises in the thickets at the edge. Lilac buds seem shinier. Once more the skunk cabbage spirals a leaf up down by the brook. The grass changes from rusty brown to green, except where the debris of winter covers it. And when the redwings come back and rock the branches of the sugar maples, we know it must be spring indeed. They have always announced it, year in and year out, and so they do now.

Everyone moves out of doors to clean up, rake, burn trash. Small kittens pounce on imaginary enemies in barnyards. Children put away their ice skates and get out their bicycles and

ride whooping down the roads. Cows are turned out in chilly
pastures where there is nothing to eat as yet, but they are free
of the barn again.

The clean sharp sound of chopping comes from the hill
where a neighbor is cutting up a fallen tree. The air smells of
the last melting snow and of thawing earth.

Emily Dickinson called spring "This whole experiment in
green."

I think of this as I walk to the mailbox up the hill. There is
a haze of green in the swamp as the bravest leaves begin to
unfurl. There is also a delicate pink for many of the swamp
bushes bear rosy buds. The old grey stone wall is dark with
moisture, but the chipmunks skip over it happily, so the stones,
I take it, are warmer than the chilly earth.

In the mailbox, beside four wasps, are the packets of special
seeds Jill ordered in February. Soon it will be time to plough,
and plant again. "Plant when the maples are in leaf," says the
wise farmer. Also some things should be planted in the full of
the moon, and some in the dark of the moon. Who is to say
whether the moon which pulls the great tides of the oceans has
not also some effect on the earth itself?

Coming back to Stillmeadow, I see Jill is raking the yard
with the help of six cockers and one eager Irish setter. The
house itself looks very white in the spring sun. The crocuses
are in bloom by the worn stone steps.

"No single thing abides, but all things flow," said Lucretius,
writing fifty or sixty years before Christ was born. "Nothing
abides."

But as I move into another year of country living, I find this
only partly true. Seasons flow one into the other, today moves

inexorably toward tomorrow and we cannot keep even the most enchanted hour. World events shape different unknown destinies for mankind. Nevertheless these abide: love, friendship, faith in God. These armor us against the transitory aspects of life on this planet.

And so, as I look toward summer, my heart is thankful. And may God bless my neighbors all over the world, I pray, as I open the picket gate.